The State of Developmental Education

EDUCATION POLICY
Series Editors

Lance Fusarelli, North Carolina State University
Frederick M. Hess, American Enterprise Institute
Martin West, Harvard University

This series addresses a variety of topics in the area of education policy. Volumes are solicited primarily from social scientists with expertise on education, in addition to policymakers or practitioners with hands-on experience in the field. Topics of particular focus include state and national policy, teacher recruitment, retention, and compensation, urban school reform, test-based accountability, choice-based reform, school finance, higher education costs and access, the quality instruction in higher education, leadership and administration in K–12 and higher education, teacher colleges, the role of the courts in education policymaking, and the relationship between education research and practice. The series serves as a venue for presenting stimulating new research findings, serious contributions to ongoing policy debates, and accessible volumes that illuminate important questions or synthesize existing research.

Series Editors

LANCE FUSARELLI is a professor and director of graduate programs in the Department of Leadership, Policy and Adult and Higher Education at North Carolina State University. He is the coauthor of *Better Policies, Better Schools* and the coeditor of the *Handbook of Education Politics and Policy*.

FREDERICK M. HESS is a resident scholar and director of Education Policy Studies at the American Enterprise Institute. An author, teacher, and political scientist, his books include *The Same Thing Over and Over: How School Reformers Get Stuck in Yesterday's Ideas* and *Common Sense School Reform*.

MARTIN WEST is an assistant professor of Education in the Graduate School of Education at Harvard University. He is an executive editor of *Education Next* and a deputy director of Harvard's Program on Education Policy and Governance.

Ohio's Education Reform Challenges: Lessons from the Frontlines
   Chester E. Finn, Jr., Terry Ryan, and Michael B. Lafferty

Accountability in American Higher Education
   Edited by Kevin Carey and Mark Schneider

Freedom and School Choice in American Education
   Edited by Greg Forster and C. Bradley Thompson

Gentrification and Schools: The Process of Integration When Whites Reverse Flight
   Jennifer Burns Stillman

Intersections of Children's Health, Education, and Welfare
   Bruce S. Cooper and Janet D. Mulvey

President Obama and Education Reform: The Personal and the Political
   Robert Maranto and Michael Q. McShane

Educational Policy in an International Context: Political Culture and its Effects
   Edited by Karen Seashore Louis and Boudewijn van Velzen

The Politics of Parent Choice in Public Education: The Choice Movement in North Carolina and the United States
   Wayne D. Lewis

The State of Developmental Education: Higher Education and Public Policy Priorities
   Tara L. Parker, Michelle Sterk Barrett, and Leticia Tomas Bustillos

The State of Developmental Education

Higher Education and Public Policy Priorities

*Tara L. Parker,
Michelle Sterk Barrett, and
Leticia Tomas Bustillos*

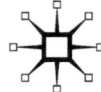

THE STATE OF DEVELOPMENTAL EDUCATION
Copyright © Tara L. Parker, Michelle Sterk Barrett, and Leticia Tomas Bustillos, 2014.

All rights reserved.

First published in 2014 by
PALGRAVE MACMILLAN®
in the United States—a division of St. Martin's Press LLC,
175 Fifth Avenue, New York, NY 10010.

Where this book is distributed in the UK, Europe and the rest of the world, this is by Palgrave Macmillan, a division of Macmillan Publishers Limited, registered in England, company number 785998, of Houndmills, Basingstoke, Hampshire RG21 6XS.

Palgrave Macmillan is the global academic imprint of the above companies and has companies and representatives throughout the world.

Palgrave® and Macmillan® are registered trademarks in the United States, the United Kingdom, Europe and other countries.

ISBN: 978–1–137–38288–7

Library of Congress Cataloging-in-Publication Data is available from the Library of Congress.

A catalogue record of the book is available from the British Library.

Design by Newgen Knowledge Works (P) Ltd., Chennai, India.

First edition: December 2014

10 9 8 7 6 5 4 3 2 1

Transferred to Digital Printing in 2015

For Nikki, who helps me to remember what is most important in life.
—Tara L. Parker

To Tim, whose unconditional support and love consistently inspire me to be a better person.
—Michelle Sterk Barrett

To all my family and friends who cheered along the sidelines during this incredible journey.

—Leticia Tomas Bustillos

Contents

List of Figure and Tables		ix
Acknowledgments		xi
1	Introduction—The State of Developmental Education	1
2	A History of Developmental Education	17
3	Developmental Education as a Strategy Toward State and Institutional Goals	33
4	South Carolina	41
5	Oklahoma	65
6	Colorado	87
7	North Carolina	111
8	Kentucky	133
9	Rethinking Developmental Education Policy and Practice	153
Notes		165
Bibliography		183
Index		193

Figure and Tables

Figure

3.1 State developmental education policy and institutional
behaviors   34

Tables

4.1 Six-year graduation rates for full-time, degree-seeking
freshmen entering four-year universities in fall 2005   43
4.2 Three-year graduation rates for associate, certificate,
diploma-seeking students entering two-year colleges in
fall 2008   44
8.1 Graduation rates of 2003 cohort by college-readiness   134
8.2 Six-year graduation rate for full-time, degree-seeking
freshmen entering four-year universities in fall 2002   135

Acknowledgments

This book is the product of a larger collaboration between the Education Commission of the States (ECS), the University of Massachusetts Boston, and Knowledge in the Public Interest. We were fortunate to be a part of the team for Getting Past Go (GPG), a national initiative designed to improve developmental education by working with higher education state and system leaders. The research presented in the book was, therefore, supported in part by an ECS grant funded by the Lumina Foundation of Education. We are especially indebted to Tina Gridiron who served as a supportive program officer for the project and to Bruce Vandal who directed the project and provided support and critique throughout the research.

Part of our responsibilities as part of the GPG team was to conduct case study research of five states, a task that required more than three individuals. We are especially grateful to the researchers who helped us with data collection, data analysis, and/or the production of this book, all but one of whom were graduate students. The contributions of the following must not go unnoticed: Laurie Bartell Behringer, Loni Bordoloi, Liya Escalera, Randi Korn, Ellise LaMotte, Lyssa Palu-ay, Kimberly Russell, Diann Simmons, and Tammy Vargas Warner.

Together, we conducted more than 100 interviews in five states in a relatively short period of time. This research would not have been possible if people were not willing to share their time and experiences with us. We therefore acknowledge all of those unnamed policymakers, system and institutional leaders who offered their time, wisdom, and insights to us during the interviews. Their tireless dedication to serving students within their states and institutions despite limited resources was evident and commendable.

On a more personal note, we are especially thankful to our many friends, families, and spouses, who helped to motivate, care, and support us throughout the research and writing process, in particular, Tim Barrett, Elizabeth Barrett, Joan and Bob Barrett, Dara Concagh, Heather Parker, Joseph and Mary Parker, Nikki Parker-Reese, Hope Reed, Kimberly Rogers, Maureen and Bill Sterk, and Jamara Wakefield.

1

Introduction—The State of Developmental Education

Developmental education, as a course of study, has been a presence on US campuses of higher education since the opening of Harvard, and in the years that followed, many college and university administrators witnessed large proportions of students entering their institutions underprepared for college-level work—at times, unexpectedly. Today, developmental education is most often viewed as a function exclusive to two-year or community colleges; yet, as we have seen at some of the country's most elite four-year colleges and universities, developmental education permeates all institutional types and has done so throughout the 400-year history of American higher education.

Questions concerning the appropriateness of developmental education in college campuses and its impact on higher education excellence have been asked repeatedly throughout its history, eliciting a tension-filled debate about what is and is not the purpose of higher education. In the past two decades, this debate has intensified, yielding policies that have curtailed and outrightly eliminated developmental education from some postsecondary settings. Indeed, increased attention to college completion, as opposed to college access, has led many states to reconsider serving students with developmental academic profiles at all.

Although the issues surrounding developmental education have been contentious, there remains some confusion as to what developmental education really means. Therefore, it is important that we take a moment to have a brief discussion on terminology and language. Although we recognize developmental education as a field of practice and research,[1] we use the term to refer to specific courses, regardless of whether they are credit-bearing courses. Once commonly known as remedial education, our use of developmental education refers to those courses designed to support college-readiness and academic preparedness. The term "remedial education," however, is no longer used by developmental education practitioners and scholars because remedial tends to refer to academic deficits and "academic content taught previously in middle or secondary school."[2] Developmental education, however, focuses on building skills and knowledge required for a college curriculum. These distinctions, while clear to those who study or work in developmental education, are much less clear for state policymakers and the general public. In states where developmental education courses are under attack, for example, policymakers tend to use the term remedial education. We choose to use the term developmental education throughout this book to help further public understanding about the need for these courses and their relevance to academic success. Because this book is focused on public policy, we do use the terms remedial education and developmental education interchangeably in the state chapters (chapters 4 through 8) in accordance with the language used by the policymakers and institutional actors who participated in this study. Indeed, the tendency of some policymakers to prefer the term remedial education may be indicative of its unpopularity in some states.[3]

A recent report by the Southern Education Foundation found that in 2012, 14 states had formal policies limiting developmental education to two-year colleges or that limited or reduced public funding for developmental courses at four-year colleges.[4] The state of Louisiana, for example, prohibited public universities from admitting students who need developmental education coursework; Connecticut has passed a law embedding developmental skills in college bearing courses arising concerns that students with varying academic skill levels may be at greater risk of not successfully completing coursework. Ohio recently ended funding for developmental courses in the state's four-year institutions causing concerns that students of color and low income students will be the most affected by the state policy. Perhaps the most unique is Florida's decision to consider any student "college-ready" if they entered the ninth grade in a public Florida high school (as of 2003) and graduated. Therefore, in Florida, high school graduates are no longer required to enroll in developmental education courses or even take a placement exam.

In states where formal, written policies do not exist, legislative debates such as those that have taken place in North Carolina have discouraged four-year institutions from offering developmental education courses. In addition to state policies, some university systems such as the City University of New York (CUNY) and the California State University have enacted system-wide policies that prohibit or discourage four-year colleges and universities from offering developmental education. In states where limits have been placed, policymakers often argue that developmental education reduces educational quality and baccalaureate degree completion and is best located at community colleges. Some community colleges, however, seem to disagree. Arizona's Pima Community College, for example, no longer permits students who test at the lowest developmental education levels to take classes at the college. Instead, these students are redirected to adult basic education programs where their chances for transitioning to college or earning a degree are further reduced simply because it is an additional barrier required to reach their degree goals. Similar strategies were implemented in the state of South Carolina and Baltimore City Community College.

Despite these policy shifts, renewed public attention on student success has led a few states to rethink their approaches to serving students who are considered underprepared. In light of President Obama's goals to increase college degree completion, several states, like Kentucky, and university systems, like the Tennessee Board of Regents, have begun to consider developmental education as playing a role in increasing educational attainment and improving workforce development. The fact that developmental education impacts students from all walks of life, regardless of socioeconomic status, race/ethnicity, and residence (urban/suburban/rural), suggests that no state can afford to ignore developmental education.[5] Further, while national attention on college completion is often front and center at the educational policy stage, college access remains a growing concern of the American public, particularly for students who are African American, Latino, and/or low-income.[6]

To be sure, developmental education in college is a question of access and equity as low-income students, first-generation college students, and students of color are most likely to enroll in these courses.[7] Complete College America found that among students at two-year colleges, 67.7 percent of African Americans, 58.3 percent of Hispanics, 46.8 percent of whites took developmental education courses.[8] Among students at four-year colleges, 39.1 percent of African Americans, 20.6 percent of Latinos, and 13.6 percent of whites enrolled in at least one developmental course. Furthermore, 64.7 percent of low-income students at two-year colleges and 37.9 percent of low-income students at four-year colleges require some developmental education. The significance of developmental education to people of color, however, is not limited to enrollment. In fact, 50 percent of black baccalaureate degree holders and 34 percent of Latinos who earned a bachelor's degree took at least one developmental education course during college.[9] In other words, one-half of blacks who completed a baccalaureate degree and more than one-third of Latinos who did the same, had some developmental education while in college. If developmental courses were not available in four-year institutions, it is highly likely that these students, if admitted, may never have persisted to graduation. Perhaps worse, they may never have had the opportunity to enroll in college at all. Given the high need evident among matriculating college students, serving students who are considered underprepared through developmental education is not just an academic necessity; it is a social and economic imperative. Because to limit students, who are more likely to be students of color or low income, to begin their college careers in one sector of postsecondary education (community colleges) while white and high-income students have greater freedom to choose any college sector raises important questions of equity. As Arendale argued, "The risk is de facto resegregation of postsecondary education in the United States and all the disastrous results for individuals and society that would occur."[10]

Despite the increased attention that policymakers have given developmental education, there is very little in the literature that examines the role that policy plays in the implementation and execution of developmental education on campuses, particularly at four-year institutions. We therefore know little about the ways state policies influence institutional behaviors (i.e., policies, practices, instruction), and we know even less about the role of four-year colleges in developmental education reforms. We hope to fill this gap with this book. While research on developmental education effectiveness is increasing and states and institutions are experimenting with various educational reforms, we are still unable to conclusively explain why these courses and/or programs are or are not effective. A detailed analysis of how state policies influence institutional behaviors, however, could help inform the discussion on developmental education effectiveness as well as its value in meeting states' college access and equity goals.

Developmental Education as a Critical Policy Issue

In debating educational reform, state policymakers deliberate over Common Core State Standards, college readiness and alignment, and the need to improve educational outcomes to maintain economic competitiveness. Because developmental education is intertwined with all of these issues and these issues have not yet been conclusively resolved, developmental education remains important to the success of students and higher education systems. Yet, as we struggle to resolve these long-term dilemmas, critical policy questions emerge, including: How do we pay for developmental courses and academic support services? In what type of institutions should developmental education be offered? How can we measure its effectiveness?[11] What compromises are we willing to make in terms of college access and success? In other words, are we continuing to engage in a futile debate about access and quality? The ways in which higher education systems respond to these policy questions today are likely to help determine whether we will reach President Obama's goal to have the most educated citizenry in the world by 2020.

The Cost of Developmental Education

Policy debates in the past 20 to 30 years have questioned whether developmental education is a drain on resources or a "best buy" in higher education. National estimates on the cost of these programs range from US$1 billion to nearly US$3 billion.[12] Existing research on this issue has inadequately responded to this debate, due in part to studies that primarily focus on developmental education in individual states, disagreements about how to measure cost, and data that are no longer current.[13] Although scholars such as Breneman and Haarlow conducted a survey of the states, and Strong American Schools analyzed institutional data originally collected from the Integrated Postsecondary Education Data Survey (IPEDS) to assess costs associated with developmental programming, the data gathered are unreliable as states and institutions measure costs differently. In the Breneman and Haarlow study, for example, some states only included funding allocated for developmental instruction, but failed to include actual expenditures. Further, some states included the "true" costs of offering developmental services (including overhead) while others only included the cost of instruction.[14]

The Strong American Schools analysis used higher education expenditures reported in IPEDS to determine the cost per student in public two- and four-year institutions.[15] They estimated that two-year colleges spent between US$1,600 and US$2,000 and four-year institutions spent between US$2,000 and US$2,500 per student on developmental education. Cost estimates included direct and indirect instructional costs. Assuming students took at least two developmental courses, the report concluded that US$2.89 billion were spent in total educational costs for developmental courses.

The Alliance for Excellent Education took a somewhat different approach in estimating the cost of developmental education by focusing on savings, rather than expenses. The analysis was based on combined estimates of direct and indirect costs for developmental instruction and additional earnings that would be realized if such instruction was reduced.[16] The analysis suggests that the United States would save more than US$1.4 billion a year if fewer students enrolled in developmental education courses. Additionally, it was estimated that the nation would benefit from increased revenue of approximately US$2.3 billion annually, earned from wages of college graduates whose contributions would otherwise be delayed by taking developmental courses specifically in reading. The alliance thus found that reducing developmental education in public community colleges alone could save more than US$3.7 billion a year.

Dowd and Ventimiglia, however, argued that aggregated cost estimates are problematic because they do not account for the number of courses or course sequences of required developmental education.[17] Their study focused on one program specifically that was designed to improve students' chances of passing a required proficiency exam. This institutional study estimated the cost of a community college developmental education program and related it to student success as a measure of cost-effectiveness. The researchers found that the cost to successfully provide services to students with the most academic needs (in this case those who repeatedly failed the placement exam) is over two-and-a-half times as expensive as nondevelopmental community college courses and approximately the same as the cost of four-year college courses. The real contribution of this study, however, extends beyond cost estimates as it highlights the importance of disaggregating data to understand costs associated with different types and levels of developmental education.

Phipps argued that costs for developmental education may indeed be more than US$2 billion, but this is a "modest" price to pay when the option is between educating students or simply allowing them to drop out (or never enroll).[18] In his case study of the state of Arkansas, he found that the cost was "comparable to or lower than many other academic programs."[19] Merisotis and Phipps thus suggested that policymakers should consider the financial gains that institutions may obtain when students successfully complete developmental programs and continue their education.[20] They argued that such successes are "beneficial for the institutional bottom line since it enhances revenue that can partially offset costs associated with providing remediation."[21] Few studies, however, make this connection, leaving policymakers with little to reflect upon when making decisions around cost-effectiveness.

Despite the lack of conclusive data on costs, many policymakers and higher education leaders nonetheless contend that because of the perceived high cost of developmental education, students would be well served to take developmental courses at two-year institutions. In addition to lower tuition costs to the student, educational costs of public community colleges are lower than public and private four-year colleges. In 2010–11, for example, educational expenditures were approximately US$7,700 per full-time equivalent student at public two-year colleges, compared to more than US$11,500 at public four-year colleges.[22] A simple comparison of tuition prices and instructional costs, however, does not tell the whole story. Selecting a college because of its perceived lower cost may not be the most effective strategy in terms of student success.[23] Moreover, beginning postsecondary education with developmental courses at two-year colleges may harbor some hidden costs for the student. A 2008 study by Melguizo, Hagedorn, and Cypers of students enrolled in developmental education courses in California's community colleges who transferred to a four-year college suggests students who take developmental education courses at the community college and transfer to a four-year college ultimately pay more in terms of tuition and time to degree than students who began at four-year institutions and were not required to take developmental education courses.[24] Part of the reason is that students enrolled in developmental courses at the community college spend more time and money taking nontransferable credits, even after accounting for academic preparation. Further, students needing the lowest levels of developmental education courses paid nearly 44 percent more in tuition and fees than students who directly enrolled in college-level courses. Thus far, only financial costs of enrollment in developmental education have been discussed but there are other costs that must also be acknowledged: costs to society if developmental education is not offered.

Swail, Redd, and Perna, for example, include underpreparation and developmental education among the most pressing challenges of degree completion.[25] They also acknowledge that many students abandon their studies after the first or second year burdened by their lack of crucial skills and additional semesters of developmental coursework.[26] Students who abandon their college career risk a drastic differential in earning potential in comparison with those who complete a college education.[27] Along with individual gains, educational levels have also been linked to even greater benefits to society such as reductions in government health program costs and crime, along with improvements in technological advances.[28] These findings raise important questions about equity and extend well beyond state calls for effectiveness and efficiency.

Still, critics of college developmental education contend that these courses do not belong in postsecondary institutions, no matter the cost or potential benefits. Some concerns are that developmental education in public colleges and universities ostensibly requires taxpayers to pay double for academic skills that should have been learned in high school.[29] Concerns about costs have led some states to consider limiting developmental education to community colleges and/or outsourcing it to private companies. Community colleges are often targeted as the cost of instruction is lower than at four-year colleges, at least on the surface. As the Melguizo, Hagedorn, and Cypers study points out, students taking developmental courses are likely to pay more. Little is known, however, about the relationship between cost and effectiveness at both two- and four-year colleges or how outsourcing impacts students. Indeed, costs may be contained and benefits increased if four-year colleges continue to taking on the responsibility of educating students considered underprepared.

Locating the Responsibility of Educating the Underprepared

A major focus of President Obama's goals for higher education includes a reliance on community colleges to boost the US economy. At the same time, states and higher education systems have looked to community colleges to provide developmental instruction as a way of cutting costs while improving graduation rates. CUNY, for example, ended developmental education courses in all four-year institutions and designated its two-year community colleges as the sole provider of such courses.[30] More recently, Tennessee legislators, like other states before them, passed a state law restricting developmental education to community colleges. While these are only two examples of states and postsecondary systems that have reconsidered the placement of developmental education, similar trends have occurred across the country.

Implicit in this "redirection" is the belief that community colleges are best equipped to deliver this mode of instruction to students whose test scores suggest they are underprepared and that developmental education courses simply do not belong in four-year colleges. Because some studies have found that students who begin at a community college are less likely than those who start at a four-year college to earn a baccalaureate degree, there is potential danger in relying on the community college as the sole provider for developmental education.[31] While completing a degree, baccalaureate or otherwise, is not always a goal that community college students aspire to, many states and institutions continue to use degree completion as a measure of success. Further, President Obama's recent College Scorecard indicates that the White House is interested in using degree completion as a measure of quality.[32]

A policy brief by the American Association of State Colleges and Universities (AASCU) suggests that restricting developmental education to community colleges alone is a potentially ineffective strategy as community colleges are already overburdened with increasing enrollments and limited funding. Because developmental education equates to small percentages of higher education institutional budgets (1%–5%),

AASCU argued that states should "weigh the savings attained by [limiting developmental education to community colleges] against the costs of 'decreased tax revenue' and 'reduced productivity,' if students do not complete baccalaureate degrees."[33]

Given the community college's broad mission, open admissions policies, and relatively low cost, many students who may need more academic preparation begin their college careers at these institutions. Attewell and colleagues, however, showed that two-year colleges are more likely to require developmental courses than four-year institutions, even after controlling for academic preparation.[34] In other words, students with the same levels of preparedness are more likely to enroll in developmental education courses if they start at a community college than if they begin their academic careers in a four-year institution. This finding, then, raises important implications for academic progress and degree completion.

As previously mentioned, Melguizo et al. found students who took developmental education courses at a community college and then transferred to a four-year college pay more, in time and money, than students who did not enroll in developmental education courses.[35] The researchers concluded that while many factors contribute to the reasons students take longer to complete courses, colleges should "reexamine the procedures by which they currently encourage students to complete the [developmental education] process in a timely fashion" or review policies and methods of instruction to improve understanding of why students are not succeeding in a shorter timeframe.[36] This type of evaluation could be conducted at two- and four-year institutions.

Instructional practices and resources are indeed a concern when considering where developmental education should be located. A study by Callahan and Chumney found the lack of resources in most community colleges might limit the success of students who took developmental education.[37] In their qualitative study of two developmental writing courses—one at a four-year research university and one at a community college—Callahan and Chumney contended that access to resources related to course content, instruction, and out-of-classroom tutoring allowed the four-year college to be more successful in terms of course completion.[38] The researchers attributed the success of the four-year college to the instructor's emphasis on analytic skill development, instead of grammar; one-to-one tutoring; and an experienced, full-time faculty member. While Callahan and Chumney argued that some community colleges have the resources needed to be effective, most are under-resourced leaving the efficacy of developmental education "compromised."[39]

Given the history of higher education's efforts to shed itself of developmental programs, there is reason to examine whether the trend to shift developmental education exclusively to community colleges may effectively inoculate four-year colleges and universities from serving students who are considered underprepared.[40] In other words, if developmental education is deemed exclusive to two-year colleges, then four-year institutions are taken "off the hook" for educating students who may knock at their doors in need of academic support. Clarifying the responsibility that four-year institutions have toward students who are underprepared should be a consideration when policymakers deliberate whether to limit developmental education to two-year institutions.

McGrath and Spear, calling on research from the 1960s and the 1970s, suggested the growth of community colleges helped to "isolate traditional colleges and universities from the growing numbers of nontraditional students" as broad access did not equate to broad opportunities for students due to the fact that many community college students did not continue pursuit of a four-year degree.[41] McGrath and Spear continued this argument as they quoted Jencks and Riesman who described community colleges as:

> a safety valve releasing pressures that might otherwise disrupt the dominant system. They contain these pressures and allow the universities to go their own way without having the full consequences of excluding the dull-witted or uninterested majority.[42]

Indeed, community colleges play an important role in increasing educational attainment; however, all colleges, in particular four-year colleges, must work toward reversing educational disparities that continue to face the United States. Thus, with more high school graduates aspiring to a college education, it seems that if the nation is to meet its educational attainment goals, both two- and four-year institutions must shoulder the responsibility of educating students from all academic backgrounds, skills, and experiences.

Examining the Effectiveness of Developmental Education

As more states push developmental education entirely into community colleges, other states have recognized that regardless of where developmental education is delivered, the bigger issue is its overall effectiveness in increasing college success.[43] Policy debates centered on the educational outcomes of developmental education have generally defined effectiveness as degree completion and educational attainment. Critics often cite low-graduation rates of those who took developmental education courses to make the case that enrollment in developmental courses prevents students from earning a college degree. Recent studies, however, clearly show that simply looking at the completion rate of those who require developmental education is too simplistic a view of a highly complex issue. Bettinger and Long, for example, found differences in educational outcomes of those who take developmental education courses and those who do not often disappear when academic and social backgrounds are taken into account.[44] Research on the impact that developmental education has on educational outcomes thus requires a closer examination to better understand its effectiveness.

Some researchers suggest, for example, that enrollment in developmental education delays time to degree completion and that these students are less likely to graduate than students who did not take any developmental education courses.[45] Adelman found that 49 percent of students who took at least one developmental course graduated within eight years, compared to nearly 70 percent of students who did not take any developmental courses.[46] As previously stated, policy debates on the effectiveness of developmental education often end there. Adelman, however, extended the argument further and showed that the low graduation rates are more likely to be a function of inadequate high school preparation rather than developmental coursework itself.[47]

In a longitudinal study of developmental education in community colleges, Bettinger and Long found that community college freshman in Ohio earned fewer credits and were less likely to transfer to a four-year college or earn a degree.[48] Once they controlled for academic background, however, the researchers found students enrolled in developmental education courses completed degrees or transferred to a four-year college at the same or better rate than students who did not take developmental education courses. In a similar study of Ohio that included both two- and four-year college students, Bettinger and Long focused on students whose standardized test scores were considered marginal, that is, those students whose placement in developmental courses depended on the institution of attendance.[49] In other words, these students may have required developmental education in one college but not in another. In this study, Bettinger and Long found that when controlling for academic preparation, developmental education course-taking had a positive effect on persistence and degree completion.[50]

Because the Bettinger and Long studies were limited to first-time freshman of traditional age (18–20 years old), the impact of developmental education course-taking on adult learners or those students who attend college part-time seems unclear.[51] Additional research, however, showed that adult learners in community colleges are not as negatively affected by taking developmental courses as younger students in terms of

12 THE STATE OF DEVELOPMENTAL EDUCATION

degree completion.[52] The researchers suggest that the differences between younger and older students may be due to adult students needing to only refresh their academic skills after being out of school for a number of years. As more adult students seek postsecondary educational opportunities, there will be a growing need for research on their experiences with college developmental education.

Like Bettinger and Long's study, Attewell and colleagues ran a series of regression analyses to determine the impact of developmental course-taking on graduation rates, time to degree, and other outcomes.[53] This study, using logistic and propensity models to control for academic and family background, found that developmental course enrollment did not reduce a community college student's likelihood of earning an associate or higher degree. Low socioeconomic status (SES), poor academic preparation in high school, and being African American were instead found to be predictors of low graduation rates. When Attewell et al. looked at four-year colleges, however, students in developmental courses were only 6–7 percent less likely to earn a baccalaureate degree than students who did not take any developmental education courses.[54] Nonetheless, taking a developmental course did not prevent students from earning a baccalaureate degree, as more than 50 percent of developmental course-takers did complete the BA degree within eight years of entering college.

Still, critics maintain that too many students are taking too many developmental education courses.[55] As we illustrate in chapter 2, however, the percentage of students enrolled in developmental courses today does not significantly differ from developmental course taking 100 years ago.[56] Furthermore, the number of students taking multiple developmental courses is quite small. Attewell et al. found that only a few students (14% at community colleges and only 5% at nonselective four-year colleges) take more than three developmental courses.[57] This study also found community college students' chances of graduating are not reduced by taking multiple developmental courses. By controlling for academic preparation in high schools, Attewell et al. attributed low-graduation rates for community college students enrolled in developmental courses to academic background rather than to enrollment in developmental education itself.[58] Students taking multiple developmental courses in four-year colleges, in contrast, had a lower likelihood of graduating. In fact, "their graduation rates were between 12% and 15% lower than those of students with comparable skills and backgrounds who took fewer or no remedial courses."[59] Yet, approximately 33 percent of the few students who took several developmental courses in a four-year college nonetheless graduated within eight years.

While transfer rates and degree completion are important educational outcomes, it is equally important to take a step back to consider the extent to which students complete college-level courses. Bailey et al.'s work revealed that students in community colleges who are placed in developmental education often fail to complete developmental course sequences, in part because they never enroll in the assigned courses or because they skip courses within a prescribed course sequence.[60] Indeed, the study found that while many students in community colleges are referred to developmental education, less than one-third of the study participants actually enrolled in the appropriate courses. Similarly, many students who completed developmental sequences never enrolled in the college level, despite the likelihood of completing these gatekeeper courses.

While recent policy decisions seem to maintain that developmental education seals the fate of many students, the empirical evidence related to the effectiveness of the courses is not that simple. A great deal of students' success depends on academic preparedness, what subjects they take, and whether students enroll in referred or assigned courses. The evidence presented here signifies the need for more research related to the effectiveness of developmental education, as extant research does not sufficiently provide causal evidence between developmental education and educational outcomes. As Bailey explained, "There is in fact no strong consensus about how to carry out developmental education most effectively."[61] As a result, we are left with myriad approaches in various contexts in hopes of resolving the issue.

Overview of the Book

As states look to increase educational attainment for all citizens, it is important to understand why these policies—designed to meet state priorities and goals—succeed or fail. In the case of developmental education, a policy-focused discussion has largely been absent from the national dialogue. Whereas the focus has primarily been on placement exams, instruction, and student outcomes, understanding the policy context and the policies that emerge is equally important to comprehend the full complexity of the debate surrounding developmental education. As we previously noted, certain beliefs and values about the role of higher education influence the developmental education debate. This social construction about what is and is not the purpose of higher education—and by extension the continuation of developmental education in that context—permeates policy circles. These social constructions "become embedded in policy as messages that are absorbed by citizens...send[ing] messages about what government is supposed to do, which citizens are deserving (and which not) and what kinds of participatory patterns are appropriate in a democratic society."[62]

As we introduced in this first chapter, developmental education is fraught in controversy with vocal advocates in support and ardent opponents aiming to eliminate its presence in postsecondary education settings. Understanding the social constructs in which these policy positions reside is critical as they may influence not only the development of policy but also the behaviors enacted following a given policy change. Developmental education is fundamentally a social construct. Standards and benchmarks are set to differentiate between "college level" and "developmental." Placement tests reveal "competence" and sort students accordingly, assigning them a label that is indicative of each student's presumed abilities. Yet, as studies have shown, what is considered developmental in one setting may not be same in another. As such, uncovering these tacit and taken-for-granted assumptions about developmental education and the degree to which they influence contemporary education policy is an imperative social action as the success or failure of these policies, their interpretation at the campus level, and the impact they have on students must be considered within the broader debate.

In the second chapter, we examine the historical context of developmental education. In doing so, we demonstrate that many of the policy concerns of today are rooted in an historical debate about the purposes and beneficiaries of higher education. Understanding the history of developmental education and past approaches to serving students considered underprepared, therefore, provides a foundation for understanding the potential significance that developmental education can have today in meeting state and national goals related to college access and success. In the third chapter, we introduce the conceptual framework we used to guide our research. Developed following an extensive literature review and meetings with higher education policy leaders, our framework identifies specific elements that states can use to place developmental education into a coherent strategy to meet state priorities and goals including college access and degree completion. In chapters four through eight, we present our five comparative case studies conducted between 2010 and 2011. Within each chapter we use our conceptual framework as a guide to present a case study of each state. We provide the policy context for each state, examine the state's relevant developmental education policies, and explore the responses to these policies by system and institutional leaders. Namely, we explore the extent to which states and institutions placed developmental education within a larger strategy for college access and student success. In our final chapter, we look across all five cases to examine relationships between policy, institutional behaviors, and the implications policy has for educational outcomes, paying particular attention to equity issues that emerged from the five case studies. The concluding chapter thus holds particular relevance to policymakers, college and university administrators and faculty who are interested in improving developmental education policy and practice.

2

A History of Developmental Education

Developmental education is not a new concept in higher education nor is it an educational model that has always been relegated to the lowest tiers of postsecondary education.[1] Approximately 76 percent of higher education institutions offer developmental courses and 94 percent of institutions with high enrollments of students of color likewise provide developmental instruction.[2] As Merisotis and Phipps suggest, "those halcyon days when all students who enrolled in college were adequately prepared, all courses offered at higher education institutions were 'college level,' and students smoothly made the transition from high school to college simply never existed. And they do not exist now."[3]

Arguments in favor and against developmental education can be traced throughout the nearly 400-year history of American higher education. Because the founding and expansion of the colonial colleges predated public systems of primary and secondary education, many students admitted to institutions such as Harvard, the College of New Jersey, King's College, and others were inadequately prepared for a college curriculum. Yet, because the pool of students eligible for admission was so small, colleges accommodated their learning "deficiencies" and provided tutoring and other forms of developmental instruction.[4] Two hundred years later, President Henry P. Tappan of the University of Michigan railed against the "rudimentary courses... [that] ... were lowering educational standards by admitting poorly prepared students" and called for their removal.[5]

Despite the apparent need for developmental courses and the circumstances leading to that need, there was, and remains to this day, a debate over students whose academic profiles suggest underpreparedness and how the challenge they present should be addressed. Should higher education be reserved for the academically "superior" student whose capacity to excel surpasses that of the average student who "cannot expect to achieve more than mediocrity?"[6] Or should access be given to a broad array of individuals, whose inclusion will serve to further advance the needs of an increasingly complex society? The answers to these two questions can be whittled down to a perspective of responsibility. Whereas the former finds the bulk of responsibility for learning to rest on the shoulders of students, the latter presumes a more proactive role by colleges and universities to "facilitate student success by providing the necessary support mechanisms."[7]

The purpose of this chapter is to identify recurring themes found throughout the history of developmental education that speak to these ongoing questions about purpose and responsibility. In doing so, the longstanding practice of debating the causes of, responsibilities for, and effectiveness of developmental education is traced in the 400-year history of higher education. What we find is that the debate has changed little over time and as our case studies illustrate, some of the same conversations we are having today are similar to those of earlier eras in education.

Looking to the Past for Answers Today

The history of higher education is replete with anecdotes and drama describing the collision of forces surrounding the scope and purpose of postsecondary instruction. The founding of America's first colleges was driven by a vision to nurture and train the leaders of society who would "spell the difference between civilization and barbarism."[8] These colleges aimed to preserve cultural norms imported by Cambridge and Oxford-educated men, develop a learned clergy to uphold the Christian faith, and create an elite ruling class who would bring order to the colonies.[9] For these reasons, courses in rhetoric, classical scholarship, and biblical studies formed the curriculum of early colonial higher education. According to Brubacher and Rudy, the concentration of elite young men in the colonial colleges was intended for "preserving, not reconstructing" the established order.[10] Failure to do so meant:

> [T]he ruling class would have been subjected to mechanics, cobblers, and tailors, the gentry would have been overwhelmed by lewd fellows of the baser sort, the sewage of Rome, the dregs of an illiterate plebs which judgeth much from emotion, little from truth.[11]

In time, this vision was challenged by an alternate vision, one that was firmly grounded in revolutionary rumblings and a growth in religious diversity. The onset of the Revolutionary War and the colonies' break from England hastened a trend toward a more secular curriculum that included subjects in the sciences (including social sciences) and the arts. Consequently, the role of education shifted from the training of an elite populace to one that resonated greatly with the spirit of democracy. The new optimism that characterized the nation after the Revolutionary War catapulted the development of a distinct American educational system that was funded by taxpayers and welcomed a broader segment of society.[12] No longer would the colonies rely on England for goods and other needed services; instead, they would rely on their own ingenuity and skill to make the fledgling nation much more self-reliant and prosperous.

The spirit of democracy and self-reliance is one that still characterizes America today. In a time of global competition, advanced technology, and scarce resources, America is looking to harness the strengths of its citizens to retain its global prominence. The need to improve the educational skill level of US citizens cannot be understated given the dire economic conditions currently crippling the nation. As such, our country's leaders look to colleges and universities, from the smallest community colleges to the most elite universities, to provide the education and training that will develop the necessary workforce of the twenty-first century. In these times of tremendous challenge, the country's postsecondary institutions are being asked to once again assume the mantle of opportunity, open its doors, and ensure that a broad spectrum of the population will receive the education needed to safeguard the economic and social prominence of the country.

Yet, questions remain that underscore the tension-filled debate surrounding developmental education: What is the purpose of higher education? Who will benefit? What roles do postsecondary institutions assume in preparing students whose academic profiles suggest a need for developmental education? Historical responses to these questions provide a foundation for understanding developmental education policy and institutional responses today. One of the primary purposes of higher education is to foster economic development by training a skilled workforce. Whether it was the Morrill Acts' expansion of higher education to include applied studies, the GI Bill's extension of higher education to returning veterans after the Second World War, or court rulings that opened college and university doors to those who were previously denied entry, increasing college access has been a primary means for growing the nation's economy and by extension, increasing the social mobility of its citizens. Thus, developmental education, as a pathway to college access, can be viewed as an opportunity for economic development.

While historical evidence points to the vital role that developmental education has played in promoting access to higher education, there are likewise many instances where higher education leaders have identified developmental education as a basis for contention and very often a threat to academic excellence.[13] Despite its presence on American college campuses since the opening of Harvard in 1636, questions concerning the appropriateness of these courses have been asked repeatedly, yielding a debate that pits student access and postsecondary quality against one another as if they are two mutually exclusive considerations. Consequently, this intricate balancing act between access and excellence is too often construed as a policy "problem" that threatens postsecondary opportunity. We suggest that proponents for and against developmental education need to reframe the question such that the focus begins to shift away from, but not ignore, fruitless debates of access and excellence. Instead, they must begin to thoughtfully examine the benefits of investing in developmental education to achieve both.[14]

College Access and the Role of Developmental Education

The enrollment needs of the colonial colleges following the Revolutionary War, the growing number of colleges that were established before the civil war, and the broadening mission of higher education due to the Morrill Acts resulted in an increase in the number of students with varying levels of preparation accepted into postsecondary education institutions. The practical realities of expanding access to fill the growing number of seats available in colleges and universities was also combined with a moral purpose to expand access to knowledge. Lyman Beecher, a Presbyterian clergyman, expressed this sentiment well by observing that the moral purpose of colleges and schools was to

> break up and diffuse among the people that monopoly of knowledge and mental power which despotic governments accumulate for purposes of arbitrary rule, and bring to the children of the humblest families of the nation a full and fair opportunity... giving thus the nation the select talents and powers of her entire population.[15]

Francis Wayland, president of Brown University (1827–55), echoed these sentiments and developed an extension division that would meet the needs of farmers, mechanics, and industrialists, despite the objections of the Brown Corporation. For a period of four years, the division provided courses in applied science to a smattering of students. In 1854, the experiment was shuttered due to convincing evidence of the proliferation of a "less-skilled student body" in addition to the seemingly "widespread objection to [Wayland's] 'lowering of the standards' of the bachelor's degree."[16]

Still, the broadening access to higher education led to a range of strategies employed by postsecondary education institutions that laid the foundation for our present-day model for providing academic support and developmental education on college campuses.

The Conditional Admissions and Preparatory Programs

The diffusion of knowledge to individuals from humble and prosperous origins whose academic abilities and preparation varied greatly, often necessitated the inclusion of so-called preparatory programs that would bring students to the requisite skill level to succeed in postsecondary settings. This was more a result of a lack of standardization among secondary schools and private tutoring practices than due to students' academic competencies.[17] Though compulsory education laws had been in effect in Massachusetts since 1642, most learning took place in the home. Only those with sufficient capital could afford to send their children to the Latin grammar schools, hire private tutors, or receive instruction from a local minister.[18] Consequently, as Casazza and Silverman indicate, only 36 and 123 students were enrolled in Yale and Harvard, respectively, in 1710.[19] Less than 500 students in total graduated from Harvard in the seventeenth century.

Moreover, the colleges themselves had little consensus as to what constituted adequate preparation or the subject matter that students should master prior to admission. At one point, Columbia University required both physics and chemistry while Princeton required neither. Though Latin was a common entrance requirement, there was little agreement as to which texts, verses, or authors the students should have been exposed.[20] Consequently, as Brubacher and Rudy concluded, "[I]n part the failure [or preparation] was due to excessive variety of requirements. Further, the colleges themselves were often at fault because of the discrepancy between the requirements they announced and the ones they actually enforced."[21] The lax enforcement of entrance requirements was in many cases directly tied to a college's survival. In a time when nearly 700 colleges were founded and failed before the civil war, colleges were dependent on students seeking a collegiate education—irrespective of preparation.[22]

Inconsistent actions and practices by the colleges and existing K-12 systems yielded the admission of students who were referred to as "conditional," students who were very often the norm on college campuses, and whom required some form of preparatory or so-called developmental support and instruction. Harvard, for example, found more than half of its freshmen students needing tutoring in Latin to improve their verbal fluency and written competency to succeed at the institution.[23] By the late nineteenth century, Harvard continued to admit half of its incoming students as conditional admits.[24] Similarly, Vassar's president lamented a student body whose "range of student achievement extends to a point lower than any scale could measure."[25]

To bridge the gap between "conditional students" and postsecondary expectations, preparatory programs or preparatory departments were institutionalized on many college campuses.[26] Preparatory departments, viewed as secondary schools within postsecondary settings, provided some level of "preparation" to entering college students who lacked basic competence in the subject areas, including reading, writing, and arithmetic.[27] Students enrolled in preparatory departments often took six years to complete their studies. Whereas in some cases these programs were housed directly on the college campus, other institutions developed relationships between feeder schools to provide the preparatory work, thus freeing the university from directly providing this level of instruction.[28]

The University of Wisconsin (UW) is credited for forming the first formal preparatory program in higher education. Established in 1849, the Department of Preparatory Studies instructed students in study skills and provided developmental courses in reading, writing, and math.[29] In 1865, of the 331 students admitted to the University of Wisconsin, only 41 students were enrolled in credit-granting college-level courses.[30] The UW program served as a model for other programs across the country, and by the end of the nineteenth century, nearly 40 percent of all first-year students in the nation were enrolled in developmental education courses and approximately 80 percent of postsecondary institutions had preparatory departments.[31] These numbers do not differ greatly from today, where approximately 30 percent of first-year students enroll in developmental education courses in 76 percent of postsecondary institutions.[32]

Postsecondary expansion into the western states further necessitated the inclusion of preparatory programs. Between 1862 and 1890, the federally supported Morrill Acts expanded the reach of higher education ensuring the teaching of agriculture and mechanical arts as well as barring the funding for states where discrimination persisted.[33] The less-selective requirements for admissions found institutions to be faced with a student population ill-equipped to meet the rigors of higher education.

Early into the twentieth century, 315 colleges were reported to still have preparatory departments on their campuses.[34]

Arendale proposed that, at the time, preparatory schools served very distinct functions in higher education in addition to their primary purpose of preparing students for college-level work.[35] First, they enrolled students who could afford the tuition and therefore supplemented the financial support provided by federal and state governments. Second, preparatory programs served as "surrogates" by providing a model for instruction to secondary schools that were slowly developing. Third, the changing requirements for college admissions and graduation made it too hard for the developing secondary schools to keep pace with the new demands. Finally, exposure and greater reliance on print resources contrary to the almost-exclusive use of lecture and recitation of the past heightened the need for these departments.

Post–Civil War America and Access for Students of Color

Urbanization, industrialization, increased immigration, and the emancipation of African Americans from slavery characterized post–civil war America.[36] The greater concentration of families in urban areas facilitated the growth of schools and the expectation that college attendance was a distinct possibility. Industrialization changed the apprenticeship of the past, introducing new occupations requiring more complex training and skill development that "fostered a greater exigency for education."[37] The infusion of 25 million immigrants between 1881 and 1925 underscored the importance of education to address language differences, poor schooling backgrounds, and assimilating the numerous cultures into one unified "American culture." Finally, the emancipation of slaves forced the country to face the effects of involuntary servitude and deliberate illiteracy imposed on 3 million people.

Greater federal involvement in higher education in the nineteenth century foreshadowed present federal action. The Morrill Acts of 1862 and 1890 not only served to broaden access to postsecondary instruction, but they also served to introduce a more vocational orientation to the purpose of higher education.[38] That is, students were able to take courses in agriculture, home economics, engineering, and other scientific fields. Moreover, business leaders further challenged the traditional scope of higher education, demanding a curriculum that emphasized practical knowledge over a "classical and literary emphasis."[39] Similarly today, business leaders look to higher education to provide the skilled workforce of tomorrow but are often left to wonder at the worth of a college education that does not adequately prepare students for said workforce. In delineating the costs associated with developmental education, the Alliance for Excellent Education stated that "[t]here are additional costs, such as the cost for employers who either provide training programs to teach basic skills to employees or must purchase technology which substitutes for the lack of basic skills among employees."[40]

These challenges, combined with the preexisting obstacles noted in the previous sections of this chapter, were addressed through the use of developmental instruction. Missionaries from the Baptist Home Missionary Society of New York and the American Missionary Society of New York founded colleges devoted to the higher education of blacks beginning in 1864 and freed slaves following the Emancipation Proclamation. Realizing that students had little to no knowledge of letters and numbers, primary departments within these colleges were put in place to introduce reading, writing, and arithmetic. Gradually, additional subjects were introduced such as agricultural and industrial training. Over time, a formal academic course of study modeled after the traditional New England colleges was introduced and offered to students sufficiently versed in the secondary materials. As Brubacher and Rudy remarked, "The dominant policy of the time seems to have been one of groping, testing, and experimenting, rather than stubbornly seeking to impose an artificial stereotype on unprepared students."[41] In the 30 years since the conclusion of the civil war, more than 1,100 blacks had graduated from Historically Black Colleges and Universities (HBCUs), which were largely established after the passage of the Second Morrill Act in 1890.[42]

Access in the Twentieth Century

At the start of the twentieth century, courses in developmental reading and study skills were fairly common as 350 (of fewer than 1,000) colleges offered courses entitled "How to Study."[43] A 1929 survey identified nearly 25 percent of postsecondary institutions offered developmental instruction and others mandated enrollment in such courses (e.g., Ohio State University).[44] The University at Buffalo initiated a precollege program in 1926 where students who performed poorly in high school but planned to enroll at the university were asked to take part in a three-week summer study course. Some of these students were either "debarred" from admission as a result of their performance in the study course, while others identified as "doubtful" were given a reduced course load during the academic school year.[45]

Addressing the gap between secondary preparation and postsecondary expectations continued to be a concern despite the presence of developmental education on four-year college campuses. The demarcation of higher education was widely discussed at the conclusion of the nineteenth century and early into the twentieth, with prominent educators such as college presidents Charles Eliot of Harvard and Nicholas Butler of Columbia making such recommendations as reducing the number of years spent in college from four to three and moving algebra from the college to the high school classroom.[46] It is during this period in time that the development and "mushrooming" of the junior college came about.[47] In a quest to become "true research and professional development centers," university administrators sought to drop the first two years of instruction, which often consisted of developmental instruction, and place it within another setting.[48]

A further push for the development of junior colleges came from William R. Harper, president of the University of Chicago, who believed that the "weaker" colleges should become junior colleges and offer courses that were collegiate or preparatory in scope. This idea had been proposed earlier by other educational leaders who worried that the first two years of college were secondary in nature, leading such institutions as the University of Illinois, the University of Michigan, and Stanford University to consider dropping the first two years of college on the "theory that the university should not be engaged in secondary instruction."[49] The junior college would thus attract more students to postsecondary education, to include those who had not previously considered a college education. The short span of the college may likewise make it easier for students to "respectfully terminate" their college attendance after only two years of study. Finally, as President Harper rationalized, graduate and professional schools would be supportive of these "terminal facilities" for they would be the recipients of a more selective student body prepared for advanced academic work.

Though these aims are given a positive connotation, Casazza and Silverman observed that junior colleges often provided a "sorting" function in education, counseling students away from further education after two years.[50] Nonetheless, these colleges thrived, providing opportunity to students previously denied access to higher education. The exponential growth of this innovation was such that by 1930, over 70,000 students were enrolled in 450 junior colleges instituted in all but five states across the country.[51]

The Second World War, the GI Bill, the launch of Sputnik, and the Civil Rights Act of 1964 all served to promote the notion that education is a national imperative to ensure national security, economic stability, and global competitiveness. Even more importantly, these events and subsequent state and federal actions ushered in a belief system that all individuals, regardless of background, age, or station in life could access postsecondary education. The GI Bill, for example, provided educational and vocational opportunities to returning servicemen, of which, nearly 8 million participated in some form of postsecondary education or training program. Of those who were able to take advantage of the GI Bill, as many as two-thirds did not have the requisite study skills to succeed in a postsecondary environment.[52] As a result of the influx of these new students, guidance centers, reading and study skill programs, as well as tutoring services were instituted and made available on college campuses.[53]

The historical record plainly shows the extent to which developmental education courses were a necessity on college campuses. Whether it was due to inconsistent precollege requirements in the eighteenth century, the need to enroll as many students as possible to guarantee the survival of emerging institutions in the nineteenth century, or fear over national security and global competitiveness in the twentieth century, developmental education has been employed to attain those goals. However, as the next section illustrates, the inclusion of developmental education on college campuses has cast a shadow over postsecondary settings.

The Branding of Developmental Education and the Debate Over the Purpose of Higher Education

Testimony from an angry and embarrassed constituency over the need for developmental instruction can be found throughout the annals of higher education. From the late 1800s to the present day, developmental education has been described as an "embarrassment" to colleges and universities that offer such courses.[54] The Yale Report of 1828, a document intended to reaffirm the role of postsecondary institutions to provide a classical and not a practical education, intimated that not all individuals would have the intellectual acumen to engage in this kind of training. Indeed, the future president of the University of Michigan stated, "We have cheapened education so as to place it within the reach of everyone."[55] In 1830 Ezra Cornell, founder of Cornell University, inquired as to why faculty did not teach students "what they didn't know," to which the faculty responded, "If Cornell wanted the faculty to teach spelling, he should have founded a primary school and not a university."[56] Given the controversy across the country surrounding the student who was conditionally admitted, steps were taken to eliminate the need for developmental instruction. It was suggested by some that students with "defective preparation" should no longer be admitted.[57] Instead, as Rudolph recorded "The 'laboring classes' would be introduced to what they needed to know by 'men of superior education.'"[58]

Still, the rise of both the common schools and public high schools led to greater numbers of students with aspirations for college attendance. The first public high school opened in Boston in 1821 and the *Kalamazoo* decision by the Supreme Court in 1874 upheld the use of taxes to support public education.[59] By 1890, over 2,500 high schools could be found across the United States. Despite their proliferation, public secondary schools were still not specifically organized to prepare students for college; rather, as Cohen noted, "Their net effect was to elevate the desire for more schooling and to hold the younger students away from college so that the median age of entrants increased."[60] Thus, postsecondary systems eager to rid themselves of their preparatory programs could not do so until matters at the secondary level could be resolved.

The Committee of Ten led by Charles Eliot, president of Harvard, convened in 1892 to standardize the high school curriculum and bring an end to questions concerning the role of secondary education within American education at large. Their recommendations made clear the divide between secondary and postsecondary instruction, lending a more college-preparatory orientation to the high school curriculum. The recommendations called for higher expectations of all students, who should be required to take four years of Latin, history, English literature and composition, and German or French. In addition, the committee recommended requiring three years of Greek, algebra, and geometry, and one year of physics, chemistry, botany, geography, astronomy and meteorology, and anatomy and physiology.

While these recommendations should have brought an end to questions of preparation, a great deal of criticism was levied against the committee (comprised primarily of university presidents) for ignoring the more comprehensive responsibility of high schools to educate the majority of students who would not necessarily continue on to a postsecondary education.[61] Postsecondary institutions, many of which had begun to eliminate their preparatory programs, were thus forced to reinstate these programs as few secondary school students actually took the college preparatory curriculum recommended by the Committee of Ten. Moreover, institutions were still faced with the dilemma of maintaining their enrollments, and as such, continued to enroll students who were not adequately prepared for college-level expectations. To some extent, colleges in the northeast curbed this need by admitting only those students who attended private secondary schools with college preparatory curricula. Still, some of the country's most illustrious institutions such as Columbia, Princeton, and Yale were forced to include developmental education courses in their curriculum as more than half of its incoming first-year classes did not meet entrance requirements.[62]

The junior colleges, therefore, provided the opportunity for greater numbers of students to pursue postsecondary studies, which allowed many colleges and universities to accomplish their aim to serve a select student body capable of doing advanced work.[63] Yet, the junior colleges, from their inception, did not see themselves as "less-than" institutions, but rather saw themselves to be on a corollary tract with four-year colleges and universities, where their primary function was transfer.[64] In fact, Knoell and Medsker found that college graduation rates of junior college transfers were equal to those of their four-year counterparts.[65] Their research suggests, as McGrath and Spear point out, "the community college's mission of access could be realized without danger of eroding academic standards."[66]

Over time, the function of the junior college evolved to include a multiprong mission to deliver a number of new programs such as vocational education and other terminal credentials in order to serve an increasingly diverse student population.[67] The expanded mission of the community colleges led them to work through challenges they were initially unequipped to address. This is especially true with the advent of students who were underprepared arriving on campuses across the country after passage of open door policies of the 1960s. According to Cohen and Brawer,

> The community colleges reached out to attract those who were not being served by traditional higher education: those who could not afford tuition; who could not take the time to attend a college full time; whose ethnic background had constrained them from participating; who had inadequate preparation in the lower schools; whose educational progress had been interrupted by some temporary condition; who had become obsolete in their jobs or had never been trained to work at any job; who were confined in prisons, physically disabled, or otherwise unable to attend classes on campus; or who were faced with a need to fill increased leisure time meaningfully.[68]

Moreover, the urging by the Carnegie Commission on Higher Education for junior colleges to open their doors to all graduating high school students and other qualified individuals meant that their mission and offerings changed substantially.[69] As the junior college took on the role of providing developmental education, it had to confront its own capacity to do so. Junior college administrations' response, or lack of a coordinated response, impacted the perception of developmental education as an undesirable part of the higher education enterprise.

An example of how community colleges were unprepared to serve the influx of students needing developmental instruction was revealed in early studies of developmental education in community colleges that found them to be housed in traditional departments that offered little more than "watered down" curricula by faculty who had no training, experience, or commitment to developmental instruction.[70] Roueche's review of the research concerning open-door policies and students who were considered underprepared revealed that 55 percent of developmental education instructors in California had less than two years experience, which confirms other research indicating that the least experienced instructors were likely to be found in developmental education settings.[71] Instructors who taught developmental courses interviewed by the American Association of Junior Colleges felt that graduate school courses must be offered to help potential instructors learn effective teaching methods in open-door institutions. Changes over time to developmental instruction could be seen, such as a more developmental approach to learning that did not fault the students for their prior educational experiences. Instructors in an evolving developmental education program viewed "the current education process as transformational, taking the student from one state and developing his or her abilities into those of a more capable, self-confident, and resourceful learner."[72]

Undoubtedly, the perceptions of developmental education, from the student to the deliverer of courses, hold implications for the ways the general public and elected or appointed officials view the effectiveness and efficiency of developmental education. Recent policy debates, for example, raise concerns about increasing numbers of students who are academically underprepared. The Alliance for Excellent Education questioned whether the high costs associated with developmental education was essentially "paying double" for students to learn content that should have been learned in high school:

> Individual states, and the nation as a whole, are not only paying to academically remediate thousands of young adults, but they are also facing future financial loss because students who need remediation are more likely to leave college without a degree.[73]

Strong American Schools likewise questioned the high costs of developmental education and extended their argument further to address the "hidden costs" of placement in developmental education, notably the effect on students' feelings of efficacy.[74] Of the students polled for the report, 37 percent indicated feelings of frustration after discovering they were deemed unprepared for college-level work.

Still others argued that the current percentage of students enrolled in developmental courses was far too high. Two studies in fact argued that the percentage of students enrolled in developmental education might be even higher than reported as some institutions, fearing the negative stigma of developmental education, would not report offering such courses.[75] Although studies in recent years have made great strides to measure the scope and impact of developmental education, Kozeracki concluded, "Advocates of developmental education have not yet done enough to generate reliable regional or national data about the value of offering developmental education."[76] Without such reliable data, reforms enacted will have widespread, potentially negative effects on systems and students without fully understanding the depth of the problem.

Balancing Access and Excellence in Higher Education

Foundational to this work is a discussion of the constant struggle that American higher education institutions have faced throughout their histories to provide access while ensuring excellence. Soliday provides a particularly apt description of this seeming crisis, observing:

> Crisis is also cultural, and within the economy it involves conflicting aspirations that higher education has addressed for a century: the desire to create a meritocratic culture through democratic access to the B.A.; and the desire to create an insular, exclusive research tier that promotes our spectacular economic and technological expansion.[77]

As higher education became more diverse in terms of the curriculum of the academy and the class and race of its students, a number of policymakers and higher education leaders facing dwindling budgets and low retention rates, came to believe that the goals of access and excellence were mutually exclusive.[78] While we argue that the access versus excellence debate is unnecessary, we recognize that a certain vision of postsecondary education permeates the popular imagination—a vision that seemingly does not tolerate the thought that students may not be prepared for college-level work. Moreover, as McGrath and Spear suggest, "compensatory programs threaten the perceived traditional function of higher education—to be a center of learning rather than a center of 'social and community action.'"[79] Moreover, increased access to postsecondary settings beginning in the 1960s and the increased need for developmental education put into question the legitimacy of the college or university as a signifier of exclusivity and excellence.

To rest one's ideological stance on such a notion, however, is to subscribe to what Soliday referred to as a "peculiar historical amnesia surrounding postsecondary remediation in American culture."[80] The presence of developmental education on college campuses served a variety of functions, both for the improvement of student ability and skill, as well as for distinct institutional functions such as stable enrollments. The institutionalization of student support services, such as tutoring centers and reading skills laboratories, over the course of the 400-year history of higher education underscores the recognition over time that students enter postsecondary settings with an array of preparation levels and an array of needs. And it is the college's obligation, as noted by the National Education Association in 1918, to serve the students "whose needs are no longer met by the secondary school and are disposed to continue their education beyond that point."[81]

3

Developmental Education as a Strategy Toward State and Institutional Goals

Public policy largely remained outside the contentious developmental education debate taking place on college campuses. It was not until the last decade of the twentieth century that public policy began to take a more aggressive stance on the placement of developmental education in American higher education and lawmakers became concerned about who was responsible for paying for developmental courses. With the understanding that community colleges were designed to provide wider access to students with diverse academic backgrounds, public policy often focused on reducing or eliminating developmental education in four-year institutions and on improving it in two-year institutions.

Yet, given the recent pressure on higher education institutions from the White House and the private sector to produce degrees and other credentials, it is imperative that both the two- and the four-year sectors become increasingly skilled at serving students considered underprepared as they represent nearly half of the college-going population. Because students who enroll in developmental education tend to have lower graduation rates or longer time to degree than those who do not enroll in such courses, state policymakers have aimed to improve effectiveness and efficiency of developmental education programs. They have done so by placing restrictions on where and how developmental education instruction can be delivered, which tests to use to assess college readiness and place students into developmental education courses, how to fund developmental education, and what measures to use to hold institutions accountable.

With this increased focus on developmental education since the mid-1990s, it is important not only to examine the ways in which these policies developed, but also to understand how institutions responded to these policies that do not always account for the diversity of student learning. Indeed, how policy is implemented is largely determined by institutional response and attendant behavior.[1] In some cases, institutions may prioritize public policy priorities that eclipse institutional priorities and mission. Other institutions may respond, instead, by following state policy to a minimal degree to preserve mission and to achieve their own institutional goals.

In this study we hope to further understand the implementation of policies related to developmental education in five states by examining how policies enacted influenced institutional behaviors. While the community college system was included in our data collection, our primary interest was in four-year colleges and universities. Data from the community college systems were used to help us understand how four-year institutions interacted with the two-year college sector to meet its own priorities and/or those of the state.

In an effort to understand the ways institutions responded to public policies related to developmental education, we used a nested conceptual framework to account for the varying policy contexts: the state,

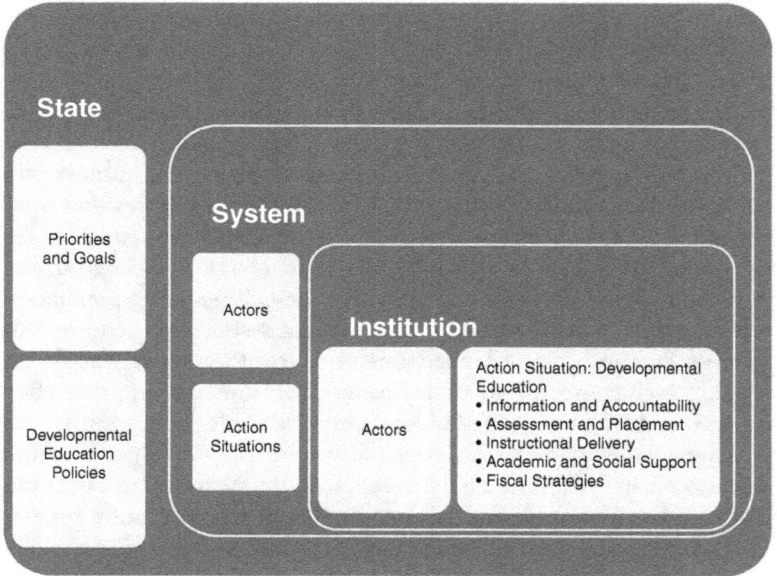

Figure 3.1 State developmental education policy and institutional behaviors

the university system, and the institution. As indicated by figure 3.1, institutions are nested in at least two levels of policy[2]: the state policy environment—which includes state priorities/goals, contextual variables (demographics, developmental education rates, and other higher education measures)—and the state's higher education system. Together, the state policy environment and the higher education system influence individual institutions.

The Getting Past Go (GPG) project, a collaboration between the Education Commission of the States, the University of Massachusetts Boston, and Knowledge in the Public Interest was designed to leverage developmental education as a critical state strategy for improving degree completion and academic success. After reviewing state developmental education policies and meeting with policymakers and developmental education leaders who comprised the GPG Advisory Board, a conceptual framework was developed to help clarify which policy levers influence institutional behaviors and outcomes. The framework posited that states used five policy levers to increase the effectiveness of developmental education, including (1) data collection and reporting, (2) assessment and placement, (3) program delivery, (4) funding, and (5) accountability and performance incentives. We used this initial framework to guide data collection for our case studies.[3]

As we conducted the research, however, the need to refine and modify our initial framework became apparent. The purpose of the GPG framework was to examine policy levers that may increase the effectiveness of developmental education and therefore assist the state in increasing educational attainment.[4] The initial framework, however, did not account for the ways individuals within the institutions, those responsible for carrying out policy, respond to policy. More specifically, we found the GPG framework to be missing a critical piece in the policy process. We therefore considered the extent to which institutions responded to state priorities and goals and the strategies and behaviors they undertook to meet educational attainment goals of the state as well as their own institutional goals.

Our focus, then, is on behaviors that take place within institutions of higher education. In other words, we focus on institutional behaviors as the outcome and posit that state policy can most effectively impact developmental education and its outcomes, if considered within institutional contexts. Our emerged framework, therefore, allowed us to identify patterns of behavior and will allow us, in future work, to link these behaviors to outcomes. The framework accounts for the way institutional actors interpret and implement policy. Borrowing terms from Ostrom's Institutional Analysis and Development Framework[5] and Richardson and Martinez's framework for comparing state higher education systems,[6] we identify the institutions of higher education as the action arena that includes the institutional faculty, staff, and administrators (actors) and their behaviors related to developmental education or serving students who may be underprepared (action situations).

Actors and Institutional Leaders

Actors and institutional leaders are those responsible for implementing policy at the institution or system level. Actors may be single individuals or a group (such as a department's faculty). Whether they are system and institutional leaders, faculty members, or staff, the actors are decision-makers who select "actions from a set of alternatives made available... [during] the decision process."[7] Actions taken are often a result of how the actor interprets and understands solutions, constraints, and incentives for decision making. As a result, actors may impede or promote policy implementation.

Action Situation

Action situations are where these actors interact with each other and the policy. More specifically, they exist "[w]henever a set of individuals are faced with a set of potential actions that jointly produces outcomes."[8] The action situations of interest within the context of this book are those areas where actors strategized or interacted around developmental education and responded to state policies. These specific strategies and interactions centered around policies related to

- Information and accountability
- Fiscal strategies
- Assessment and placement into academic courses
- Instructional delivery
- Academic and social support.

The Use of Information and Accountability

Information and accountability focus on the data that institutions collect and report to the states, as mandated by the state. These data may include participation rates, student success outcomes, and the cost of delivering developmental education. State policies can create accountability structures by using these data to measure student and institutional performance to report to the legislature and/or the general public. These accountability structures can have fiscal elements, which usually take the form of performance benchmarks or performance funding.

Fiscal Strategies

State policy may serve as an incentive or disincentive for innovation in developmental education, especially if states place financial or structural limits on developmental education delivery. Some states, like Oklahoma, allow four-year institutions to offer developmental education courses, but do not permit state funds to be used for such courses. Thus, institutional actors will have to make decisions about how to offer developmental courses or whether to offer them at all. While decisions made about funding developmental education at public colleges and universities influence institutional behaviors in terms of course offering, they may also impact enrollment if policies require students to pay fees or higher tuition for these courses.

Assessment and Placement

While higher education systems and institutions often develop assessment and placement strategies, states may influence institutional behaviors in these areas through specific policies. Indeed, some states use policy to determine assessment tests and common cut scores for placement as well as methods of instruction. Some states, like, Colorado require institutions to use one or more specific exams, while other states allow institutions to decide if or how they will assess students for college readiness. Other states, North Carolina for instance, are more restrictive with two-year colleges as their assessment and placement policies only apply to the state's two-year colleges.

Instructional Delivery

Similarly, most institutions determine how courses are taught and when. Increasingly, however, states are interested in where, how, and when institutions offer developmental education. States may choose, for instance, to require students requiring developmental education to take these courses within the first two years of their enrollment in college. State policy may also determine where and if developmental education is offered and in what institutions. Some states, like South Carolina, choose to limit developmental education to the two-year college sector.

Academic and Social Support

Institutions use academic and student support services to either supplement or replace formal classroom instruction. Examples of widely used academic supports include summer bridge programs, supplemental instruction, tutoring, and writing or math labs. Student support may also include supporting students more holistically through intrusive advising and more creative ways to support the student beyond academics. These strategies can be a particularly important avenue through which institutions can respond to more restrictive state policies while still attempting to achieve their own institutional priorities.

Our Study

Using our conceptual framework as a guide, we conducted a three-year national study with the intent to examine state policies of five states and explore the impact of policy at public four-year higher education institutions. In doing so we examined the formal state policies that exist within each of five selected states and the ways in which college and university faculty and staff responded to enacted policies.

To locate our states, we relied specifically on the GPG policy national database,[9] which details state policies related to developmental education. This database served as the starting point for identifying a cross-section of systems from which to cull additional information about developmental education policies and their impacts. We chose five states that reflected a continuum of contrasting strategies to address the issue of developmental education. These states—Colorado, Kentucky, North Carolina, Oklahoma, and South Carolina—represent various contexts including governance structures (state or institutionally controlled), geographic regions, college participation, and when possible to determine, various rates of developmental education enrollment and completion. They also represent varying levels of policy intensity as defined by the number and type of state policies related to developmental education.

Each state had at least one written policy (statutes, agency regulations, memoranda of agreement) on developmental education that was implemented at least five years before data collection. In other words, written policies had to have been implemented in 2005 or earlier. While we reference policies that were approved and/or implemented after 2005, these more recent policies were not considered when selecting states. All selected states also had to have policies that held specific implications for four-year colleges. It is assumed, for example, that policies limiting developmental education to the community college impact *both* sectors of postsecondary education. Thus, states with such policies (i.e., South Carolina) were eligible for selection.

We began our study with a review of documents and publicly available records to understand the context of the state, its policies, and its institutions. Next, we conducted a series of individual and group interviews with state, system, and institutional personnel to understand the extent to which institutions altered practices and behaviors in response to state policy. Participants were recruited to offer insight into how higher education systems, institutions, departments, and individuals responded to state policy changes. The only criteria for participation were to have held a publicly elected or appointed state office, a senior position of responsibility at the state or system level, or a faculty/staff position during the time of policy implementation. While this study focused on institutional responses to policy, state-level policymakers and administrators were included to help us better understand policy development and implementation strategies or goals.

While we recognize that community colleges play a critical/crucial role in this issue, we primarily focused our attention on the institutional responses of four-year colleges and universities in an effort to build upon what has already been extensively detailed in the literature about developmental education at community colleges.[10] Our study enabled us to understand the ways public policy influences public four-year institutions that are similarly charged with maintaining student access and success. Sometimes these goals are viewed by higher education leaders as competing goals and "the prescription offered by policymakers differ from the judgments of professionals who work within higher education."[11] Thus, this book reveals how institutional actors seek to accomplish goals within the constraints of sometimes conflicting state policy.

4

South Carolina

South Carolina maintains some of the most restrictive developmental education policies in the nation, as four-year institutions within South Carolina are not permitted to offer developmental courses. Despite this restriction, racial and economic disparities, as well as inequities within South Carolina's elementary and secondary schools across the state suggests four-year institutions will continue to face challenges to serve students who are underprepared. This has led faculty and staff to develop creative ways of offering course-based academic support without using the terms "remedial" or "developmental."

State Context

The state of South Carolina, with 4.6 million people, is the 24th most populous state in the nation and has witnessed continued population growth. Approximately, 66 percent of the population is white, 28 percent is African American, 5 percent is Latino, and 1 percent is Asian American.[1] While South Carolina continues to be a diverse state, a historical racial divide continues to shape and challenge educational as well as social and economic matters in the state.

Public institutions in South Carolina are governed by their own boards of trustees and all institutions are overseen by the statewide Commission on Higher Education (CHE). The South Carolina Technical College System (SCTS) serves as the governing board for all 16 community colleges. The CHE, by statute, is responsible for submitting an omnibus annual budget request to the governor's office for all 33 public institutions (including the University of South Carolina, 10 comprehensive four-year, and 16 two-year technical [community] colleges). They are also responsible for reviewing new academic programs and maintaining accountability systems by monitoring student progress at each college or university including private institutions. Despite its statutory authority, the CHE lacked the ability to create a coordinated vision for higher education in the state. In fact, in 2007, the governor appointed nine members (including former members of the CHE) to the Higher Education Study Committee to develop a statewide strategic plan for higher education.

Historically, South Carolina had numerous manufacturing jobs available that did not require an advanced education. Because well-paying jobs were available in plenitude, a high proportion of the state's citizens traditionally did not invest their time and money into pursuing higher education. A state policymaker revealed how the textile industry had an interest in keeping people undereducated "because you don't stand in front of a bobbin machine for 10 to 11 hours a day if you have any other option." As a result, many young people today have parents who do not understand the types of jobs one can access with a college degree and the importance of pursuing higher education.

Throughout the state, at various levels of governance, many individuals voiced concern about insufficient public recognition that manufacturing jobs are not returning. One state higher education leader explained:

> For years we've been trying to say to students the textile industry has gone. Don't plan to drop out when you turn 16 and get a job in the mill. There is no mill. We have huge numbers of people that had their careers planned who are now in their 40s and 50s and 60s and they're unemployed and they're desperately poor. We try to have these conversations about trying to bring in people who still have some work life left in them and get them off public services. Turn them back into taxpayers.

An administrator within the South Carolina Technical College System (SCTCS) further explained that many middle-aged adults planned to "go work in the mill and… have a nice life. And then that changed. Someone changed the rules in the middle on them."

South Carolina's high unemployment rate illustrates this change in the rules. In 2011, the state's seasonally adjusted average unemployment rate was 10.3 percent, down from 11.2 percent the previous year. This compares with a national average of 8.9 percent in 2011.[2] Having an undereducated and underemployed population presents large challenges in the state's efforts to decrease reliance on public assistance, increase tax revenue, and attract new industry. Respondents bemoaned the existence of a high unemployment rate at the same time employers are unable to find enough skilled workers to fill available positions. A higher education leader repeated a story once publicly told by the president of the South

Carolina Chamber of Commerce in 2009. According to this higher education leader, the president of the chamber pointed out how the state had "250,000 unemployed South Carolinians at the same time there were over 200,000 jobs unfilled." The president of the chamber attributed this to the fact that the unemployed "didn't have the skills...didn't have the education...didn't have the background" to fill these jobs. Similarly, an SCTCS leader lamented, "It's depressing when...a good industry locates here and then you find out a certain percentage of the people they employ they've had [to] import from out of state because we didn't have the skilled workers that they needed." Another higher education institutional administrator explained that the inability to attract employers also leads to an inability to retain college graduates who "have to move out of the region" to find jobs. A state higher education leader summed it up this way:

> We want to make South Carolina a stronger state and make the economy stronger through education and so we know that if we want to be able to compete nationally and internationally, we are going to have to become more educated citizens.

Statistics confirm the story told by these higher education leaders and administrators. The 2012 American Community Survey reported that while only 29.1 percent of the adult population nationwide had earned a bachelor's degree, only 25.1 percent of South Carolina's adult population (age 25 or older) had done so. The adult population with a bachelor's degree varied widely by county and ranged from 7.9 percent in Dillon County to 38.4 percent in Charleston County.[3]

Of the full-time students entering South Carolina four-year universities in the fall of 2005, 57 percent graduated by 2011. Of diploma/certificate-seeking students entering two-year colleges in the fall of 2008, 12.6 percent graduated by 2011. Graduation rates varied significantly by race and ethnicity as illustrated in tables 4.1[4] and 4.2.[5]

Table 4.1 Six-year graduation rates for full-time, degree-seeking freshmen entering four-year universities in fall 2005 (in percentage)

Asian American or Pacific Islander	65
White	63
Latino	59
American Indian or Alaskan Native	50
African American	40
Total	57

Table 4.2 Three-year graduation rates for associate, certificate, diploma-seeking students entering two-year colleges in fall 2008 (in percentage)

Asian American or Pacific Islander	14.3
White	14.1
Latino	12.6
American Indian or Alaskan Native	11.9
African American	10.1
Total	12.6

State Priorities and Goals

While South Carolina is like many other states with goals of boosting its economy and growing its workforce, it has not made higher education a key component of achieving those goals. Indeed some at the state and institutional levels questioned both the governor's and the legislature's commitment to higher education. Perhaps as a result some also questioned priorities of the state's citizens as higher education leaders indicated the need for a shift in culture to make higher education a public and private priority.

A clear indicator of higher education as a low priority was the decrease in higher education's share of the state budget. Not surprisingly then, concern about the lack of adequate educational funding was a theme expressed more frequently than any other when we spoke to people across the state. While state leadership demonstrated support for improving the economy through increased educational attainment, funding levels did not match the rhetoric. One higher education administrator argued:

> You hear the Chamber of Commerce talking about wanting to improve the state of South Carolina, the economy...but then when you talk on the other side with the legislative group about supporting education, they defund us at a very rapid rate.

Similarly, one university faculty member argued, "South Carolina was the first to secede and has been the last to succeed...according to a lot of conventional metrics. We've failed to transition our economy to the changing market...so education is the obvious way forward for this." While higher education commissioners and campus leaders expressed dissatisfaction with the legislature's lack of commitment toward education in general and higher education in particular, the state like others around the country, had to endure a fiscal crisis. South Carolina legislators have faced significant financial challenges in recent years. One state higher education leader explained:

> The biggest issue that this state faces over the coming year and for the foreseeable two or three years after that is the same budget crisis that most states in America face right now...On a five billion dollar budget we are facing a one billion dollar shortfall next year. So fully 20 percent of our existing state programs...will have to be cut in the next budget cycle.

When we visited the state, we noted a wide sense of frustration about policymakers' "short-term thinking" that does not align with the reality of the current economy and fear that the state is "losing ground" in its ability to compete with other states by not investing in education. One state educational policymaker explained, "Everything we're doing is mitigating against trying to improve ourselves as a state to get people into the knowledge economy." Many higher education leaders pointed out that the lack of financial support in K-12 schools can be seen most vividly in the predominantly black, low-income communities along the Interstate 95 corridor. The inadequate funding of schools in this region led to the creation of a 2006 film, *The Corridor of Shame: The Neglect of South Carolina's Rural Schools*, to document the deplorable physical conditions of these schools.[6] With disgust in her voice, the same state educational policymaker bemoaned the "dreadful" conditions in these schools "that have raw sewage leaking out the backs of them" and children "sitting in a classroom with their coats and their mittens on."

In 1993, these reprehensible conditions led 40 rural school districts (representing nearly 50% of all districts in the state) to sue the state for inadequate funding of public schools. This legal case, *Abbeville County School District et al. v. The State of South Carolina et al.* made it to South Carolina's Supreme Court in 2008 where it was ruled that South Carolina provided a "minimally adequate" level of education as required by the state's constitution.[7] One higher education leader described the decision as, "just mind-boggling." Another argued, "We have a state constitution that is not friendly...it is deplorable...It's embarrassing, it's a shame." A university faculty member pointed out how the phrase "minimally adequate...should tell you all you need to know about what South Carolina thinks about education." He further argued that there is "a Senator who introduces a bill every year to change that from minimally adequate to excellent or something better than minimally adequate." The bill, however, would require two-thirds of the state's General Assembly just to get the proposed constitutional amendment on the ballot for public vote. Thus far, the bill has been held up in a senate subcommittee on the judiciary.

Higher education leaders on campuses and of the state coordinating board aimed their anger about inadequate school funding directly toward the legislature. One professor expressed his outrage by contending, "They [legislators] don't understand any of this... They... have no clue what it is to the actual people living and dying, paying taxes, in their counties." A state higher education leader described the way legislators "vote the party line," which means they are focused on saving money and keeping taxes low. During election season, "they pass out these little slips of paper that say I, fill in the name of the new legislator, promise I will not raise taxes. And they all sign those little slips of paper and they have tied our hands to solve problems." Overall, many at the institutional level believed the legislature was primarily focused on not raising taxes at the expense of education.

Not only is the K-12 sector constrained financially, but higher education has also faced declining state financial support over time. A state higher education leader argued that South Carolina's public higher education institutions have shifted from being state institutions to state-supported institutions to state-located institutions. As a result, funding of higher education is now primarily through tuition and fees paid by the students and their families.[8]

The decrease in funding is not due to a lack of advocacy by education leaders. One respondent emphasized,

> Daily, we have people down there trying to spend time... talking about what we're [higher education] doing, talking about why we need to do it. It would be nice if you had a state that supported education enough that you didn't have to spend effort... convincing them that we need to be educating our public.

This advocacy for funding is especially clear in a 2009 report of the legislatively appointed Higher Education Study Committee entitled, "Leveraging Higher Education for a Stronger South Carolina." The first page of the report expresses a sense of urgency around educational funding, arguing "South Carolinians with a minimal level of education will continue to see wage levels and job stability decline as employers outsource work... other states are also moving swiftly and South Carolina must do the same or risk being left behind... South Carolina must act now."[9]

It became clear, in South Carolina, that there was significant tension between higher education leaders (including the South Carolina CHE) and the General Assembly around public higher education tuition and fees. One state higher education leader explained:

The general assembly gets a lot of political pressure from constituents who say my child wants to attend the University of South Carolina...or whatever institution but tuition just went up from $9,000 per year to $10,000 per year and that $1,000 differential will keep my child from being able to afford it, so you just priced me out of the market. The general assembly has been talking about imposing a cap on tuition increases...in order to say that politically they have done what they can to rein in the cost of higher education.

Higher education leaders, on the other hand, believe capping tuition does little to solve the problem as they are already operating efficiently and are being asked to educate more students with less money. One state higher education leader expounded that the governor at the time, Mark Sanford, and the general assembly seemed to believe that

> The problem is that the institutions are renegade. They are spending too much money. They don't need all that they are asking for. They need to shut up their whining and just live within their means. The perspective of the institutions, of course, is quite the opposite. They are running efficiently. They are achieving their missions. They...are already doing more with less.

Perhaps given these sentiments, the South Carolina legislature enacted "performance funding legislation" in 1996. The legislation included 9 critical success factors and 37 performance indicators upon which public higher education funding is allocated.[10] Most relevant for our purposes were indicators 6A and 7A. Indicator 6A refers to the "percentage of first-time freshmen who meet or exceed Commission-approved target scores on the SAT or ACT" and applies only to four-year institutions.[11] Indicator 7A refers to the "percentage of first-time, full-time, degree-seeking undergraduate freshmen receiving degrees within 150 percent of normal time."[12] As a result, performance-based funding essentially served as a disincentive for South Carolina higher education institutions to enroll students with lower SAT scores or students less likely to graduate in a timely manner.

One final priority of the state also relates to accountability. The Education and Economic Development Act (EEDA) of 2005 (Chapter 59 of Section 59 in the Code of Laws) is an effort to improve transitions between secondary and postsecondary education. The EEDA, also known as the Personal Pathways to Success, "focuses on the need to increase the number of high school graduates who are well-prepared for college."[13] Along with increasing opportunities for dual enrollment, the EEDA "calls for the coordination of the study of the content and rigor of high school courses in order to provide a seamless pathway to postsecondary education."[14]

Barriers to Academic Success

Many people we interviewed offered their insights on why South Carolina students do not pursue and persist in higher education at higher rates. The barriers most frequently mentioned were the cost of higher education, lack of academic preparation, a culture that does not promote education, and the difficult adjustment faced by some students as they enter the culture of higher education.

Cost of Higher Education

Tuition rates in South Carolina's public higher education institutions have increased dramatically in recent years from an average public four-year tuition rate of US$5,502 in 2001 to US$10,691 in 2012. With the increasing cost of higher education, money has become a significant factor for those considering higher education. At the same time that tuition has increased, there has been an expansion in merit-based scholarships available for the state's most high-achieving students. A state higher education leader pronounced, "There are many, many, many students or families that just simply...have been priced out of the market...If they don't qualify for the merit-based scholarship, cost is a huge barrier. If you do qualify, cost is not a big barrier. So we have a growing haves and have not population." Moreover, while merit-based scholarships grew, need-based scholarships did not. This same state higher education leader articulated that "implicitly the legislature for these last 10 years has therefore said we are doing for higher education all that we can do. There has been very little funding for need-based scholarships." He went on to say that need-based support was particularly lacking for students who will need "remedial work."

Low-income students who do initially earn a merit scholarship can find themselves losing the scholarship if they are unable to maintain the required grade-point average. One higher education administrator who works directly with supporting the academic success of low-income students reported, "Fifty percent of our scholarship recipients lose those scholarships in the first year. Fifty percent of those don't come back because they can't afford to come back." As a result of seeing this frequent occurrence, some administrators believed that policies should be more flexible around maintaining merit scholarships to prevent first-generation and low-income students from losing their scholarship funds as they adjust to college life.

The high cost of college also requires many students to work full time to pay for college. One university professor shared his experience of how he meets with students to enquire about their poor class performance despite their demonstrated strong academic ability. He explained that the students tell him, "I've worked all last night then had to get up and come to class," and "I didn't have time to study because I was working and I have to pay for my education." Clearly the lack of college affordability has also impacted students' academic experiences.

Poor Academic Preparation

Another significant concern for education in South Carolina is reportedly poor academic preparation that incoming college students receive in secondary schools. A state higher education leader questioned the "quality of graduates coming out of the K through 12 system and whether they really are prepared for the rigors of higher education." Similarly, a university administrator revealed that the expectations are higher in college:

> When the students get to us at the university the rigor is so much more demanding than it was at the high school level and most of our students will tell you they are shocked at the difference of the expectations.

Teacher quality was one issue that was used to explain the inability of some schools to prepare students for higher education. Some state policymakers, for example, explained that it is difficult to find teachers willing to teach in rural schools, particularly along the Interstate 95 corridor, because of inadequate facilities and the extreme poverty conditions of the communities. Some teachers simply do not want to live there. Along with the difficulty in recruiting knowledgeable teachers, schools were often unable to provide an adequate college preparatory curriculum. A state higher education leader recalled:

> I was talking to a counselor yesterday from one of those counties, and his problem was, "how can we possibly get our students to meet college entrance requirements?...I don't know what to tell people, because you're requiring three lab sciences, and we can only offer two. We don't have the capacity to offer a third lab science."

An administrator at the SCTCS described how this lack of academic preparation led to a need for developmental education and subsequent dropouts because "if you come in at that very lowest level and keep working, especially if you're a part-time student and only taking a couple of courses each time, there's a lot of opportunity to fall out."

Culture

Some believe that the academic success of students in the state is inhibited by a culture that does not prioritize education. One interviewee lamented:

> It just seems to me like there is so much energy and effort put into Friday night football, Friday night lights. Why can't we have some of that energy and money and attention paid to...math people...science people...

Others believed that the rural nature of South Carolina means many students have not been exposed to higher education and the jobs that can be accessed through pursuing higher education. One administrator conveyed that, as a result, more has to be done to make higher education a viable alternative: "It's not just academic preparation, but it's a mindset. How do you transform a mindset to help them believe that they can aspire to become more than what they see in their communities?"

A state higher education administrator shared the story of a recent conversation with a middle-school counselor. After a few minutes of dialogue about the many first-generation students attending the school, he realized there was a discrepancy in what was meant by "first generation" and how it was understood among those in higher education. He explained:

> When we at the commission talk about first generation students, we're talking about first generation college students...I have this feeling that's not what you're talking about. And [the counselor] said, "No. I'm not...I'm talking about first generation eighth graders."

Given the low levels of educational attainment across the state, students may experience a sense of culture shock when they arrive at the college campus. One higher education leader explained how culture shock can be a significant barrier to academic success:

> A lot of it is culture shock. That's why we lose a lot of students, because you have students coming from very rural areas of the state, and they go to a large university, and with expectations that they never thought about before. So, there's a culture shock, but also they're surrounded by a lot of new things that they've not been exposed to in the past.

Relatedly, a university faculty member explained how expectations for African Americans in high schools can impact whether college is even considered. He explained, "South Carolina is a fairly racist state still so what you find a lot of times, the African American students in the high school, they don't even consider talking to them about going to college...they don't make any effort to encourage them to go."

State Developmental Education Policies

South Carolina is home to a number of public policies specific to developmental education. Most notably, the state does not permit developmental education at four-year colleges and universities. Of the five states we studied, South Carolina was therefore the most restrictive in terms of public policy.

In 1988, the South Carolina state legislature passed legislation authorizing the CHE to establish "provisions, procedures, and requirements" as well as a funding plan for "developmental education programs and courses" in the state of South Carolina. The law also required that each public institution create a plan consistent with the policies put forth by the CHE. This became Section 59–104–30 of the South Carolina Code of Laws.[15]

During the 1993–94 and 1995–96 state legislative sessions, legislation was proposed to further amend the Code of Laws by adding Section 59–104–35 to limit the "allowable maximum expenditure of state funding for developmental education by the four-year state-supported institutions of higher learning in South Carolina beginning with fiscal year 1995–96."[16] While this section was never added to the South Carolina Code of Laws, the CHE did implement a policy in 1996 that phased out state funding for developmental education courses at four-year universities in a similar manner to that originally proposed by the legislature.

Many of the people we spoke to largely viewed the decision to remove developmental education coursework from four-year institutions as financially and politically motivated. The decision enabled legislators to demonstrate cost savings by avoiding "duplication" of services in high schools and colleges while improving the perceived quality of four-year public institutions. One state higher education leader described the prevalent view at the time among legislators in this simple way: "We're not going to pay for educating them twice." This leader questioned the validity of that line of thinking in stating, "You're not educating them twice. If they got the skills, we wouldn't have to be teaching them." Another state higher education leader explained:

> The legislature did not like the fact and does not like the fact or the thought that students might be going into a four-year institution...and that the institution is having to essentially be funded to have the students brought

up to speed so that they can do the work they should be able to do coming into the college.

This leader also pointed out that in 1987, Carroll Campbell (former South Carolina governor) questioned, "How much money can we save by not doing this [developmental education]...at the four year institutions?" Although shifting developmental education from four-year colleges to two-year colleges was predicted to save $1.73 million annually, no one that we spoke to at the state or institutional levels believed any follow-up analysis had been conducted to study whether this prediction has been realized.

Since removing developmental courses from four-year institutions, only two-year colleges in the state of South Carolina are permitted to offer these courses. State funding strategies were not used as a policy lever in other aspects of developmental education. While developmental education is still permitted and funded at two-year technical colleges, the state still maintains policies related to assessment, placement, and the number of credits that students can take in developmental education.

Assessment and Placement Policies

While South Carolina legislation requires assessment of students to determine whether they should be placed in developmental education or college-level courses, they do not mandate the cut score of the exam itself. Nonetheless, the 16 technical college campuses all use the COMPASS and ASSET placement tests to determine academic preparedness of incoming students. Each institution may determine its own minimum scores necessary for placement in entry-level college courses. Throughout the technical college system, all incoming students who scored below a minimum level on the reading assessment were advised to enter adult basic education courses before taking developmental education courses.

Interestingly, four-year colleges and universities do not have a common assessment to determine college readiness. In fact, four-year institutions vary so widely in their use of placement exams that some institutions may not clearly know whether a student would benefit from a developmental education course. One university faculty member described how his college was reinstating a placement test, but "we did away with it for a period."

This variation results from the nature of South Carolina's CHE and its inability to mandate change at the institutional level. According to a study participant, the state's CHE is, "at best a coordinating body. There is not the breadth of power to enforce policy changes." Although some have tried to change this power dynamic so that the commission has more of a voice in decision making, they have been unsuccessful in their efforts. One state higher education leader argued:

> The guy who was an executive director [of CHE] about eight years ago who tried to force the issue of giving us more power in the commission, got fired. Everybody that's followed him has figured it out. You don't push that issue. We are a legislative dominated state.

Information and Accountability

State policymakers were also interested in holding institutions accountable for developmental education. Section 59-101-350 of the South Carolina Code of Laws states that the CHE is responsible for collecting "the percent and number of students enrolled in remedial courses and the number of students exiting remedial courses and successfully completing entry-level curriculum courses" to be included in the CHE's annual report to the General Assembly.[17] Despite this policy, there is no developmental education data in the annual reports or the Higher Education Statistical Abstracts between the years of 1996 and 2012.[18] For a few limited years, the annual reports included the heading, "Success of Students in Developmental Courses," which was followed by the statement:

> Students are usually enrolled in developmental courses because they have been determined by the institution to lack certain skills that are needed for college level work. None of the research or teaching universities provide such courses. Several senior institutions contract with a nearby technical college to offer some developmental courses. Students who complete such courses at technical colleges are not included in this report.[19]

Institutional Responses

Institutional reactions to eliminating developmental education courses in South Carolina's public four-year institutions were generally neutral or positive. Because the policy had been in effect for so long and perhaps because institutional leaders found other ways to serve students whose academic backgrounds suggest a need for developmental education, it was widely reported that the policy is barely noticed at this point. Further, many believe that ending developmental courses simply made sense. Subsequently, many institutional leaders did not devote nearly the amount of time talking about the end of developmental education as they did to discussing inadequate educational funding for supporting their students.

There were, however, a few people who mentioned negative aspects of the developmental education policy. One institutional leader expressed concern that a student might be less likely to succeed if beginning at a two-year college first: "the research says the odds are a kid that has those problems is going to wind up in a situation where he's less likely to even graduate from a two-year school." There was also concern about whether a student might be biased against beginning at a two-year college. In other words, some students may not see two-year colleges as a viable option and, therefore, might forego pursuing higher education altogether. Finally, one professor expressed frustration about the policy as it prevents four-year institutions from legally utilizing a tool that might be beneficial to some students:

> I guess the biggest disadvantage is that we can't legally help students who need help. You have to think of a round the mulberry bush to do it. You can't just directly say you're remediating students, you can't do that. That would be great if we could do that.

The majority of those we talked to had no issues with the policy or felt it was a worthwhile change. The neutral to positive reaction also likely relates to the fact that the two-year system is highly regarded among institutional administrators and most do not believe it is detrimental for students to enter the technical college system before transferring to a four-year institution. One campus administrator directly stated, "I don't know that there were any real disadvantages. I think we presumed that it would have a negative impact on our enrollment, but it really did not. In fact, it gave us an opportunity to do some solidifying of our entry level, freshman level courses."

The most frequently reported advantages of this approach, however, included greater mission differentiation among the state's public higher education institutions and the ability of the two-year system to specialize in the delivery of developmental education; greater consistency in curricular content of developmental education and entry-level courses; cost savings to students; and the creation of alternative forms of course-based academic support at four-year institutions.

Mission Differentiation

According to many institutional leaders in South Carolina, the elimination of developmental education courses at four-year institutions has led to clearer mission differentiation among educational sectors in the state. One administrator of the technical college system put it this way:

> We do have...a much clearer idea of the role of the four-year institutions, the role of research institutions, the role of two-year colleges and I do believe that we have a lot more transfers than we used to have.

As a result of the policy, the technical college system now views developmental education specialization as a central aspect of its mission. Another administrator within the technical college system stated, "I think if you look at the faculty that teach the developmental courses they are trained and they attend conferences and workshops that are geared to teaching developmental education students. I think that that probably would be a huge advantage because those faculty members go into the classroom knowing exactly what they're bumping up against." A state higher education leader stated, "If a student is really needing remedial education, it is probably better that they get it in an environment that's in part designed to take students at every level...the technical college expertise...has been taking students at every level...I think they're probably better at that than a four-year institution would be."

Administrators and faculty at four-year institutions, however, seem to take a different approach. One higher education administrator bluntly stated, "I don't think it [shifting developmental education to community colleges] saves money." Moreover, many university staff and faculty explained that it was important for them to serve the students they admit—and their admitted students often come with varying degrees of preparedness. One faculty member in particular argued that all sectors of postsecondary education in South Carolina serve similar students:

> I recognize there's been a variety of piecemeal, competing, imperfect solutions to this. Whether it's the relative strata of educational institutions...Moving beyond the high schools, we've got this sort of community college and the shift from technical to community college. We've got lower tier four-year universities...Then you've got your kind of upper tier flagship institutions. I think all of these institutions respond to a similar population of students in a variety of ways...Institutions like ours have this very mixed bag. Some of our students could fall into your middle of the road kids. The sort of kids you expected to be there as a student [at this university]. The sort of student whose GPA and SAT scores generally conform to our mean and median. Then you've got your kids who for a variety of reasons...can fall off significantly below that in their [academics]. And then you've got kids who can fall far above that...Now at the flagship institutions at first it can seem as if they don't have a whole lot of

contact with these students who are the topic of our conversation and yet at many of the institutions...the faculty the administration are committed to meeting them in some capacity.

In efforts to meet the needs of their students, a university administrator pointed out, "it gave us an opportunity to do some solidifying of our entry level, freshman level courses." Although developmental courses were removed, the curriculum needed to be adapted to continue to serve students who entered needing academic support.

Instructional Delivery and Academic Support

Many administrators and faculty frequently described how the inability to legally provide developmental education courses to students at four-year institutions did not change the fact that students still entered the universities academically underprepared and that administrators, staff, and faculty remained committed to supporting student success. A state higher education leader explained that even though developmental coursework has been "eliminated from the four year programs...that isn't to say that student support for students who need help has been eliminated...every institution has learning labs, math labs, different things." One state higher education leader recognized, "Doing remedial work without calling it remedial is part of the challenge we face." To meet this challenge, one university administrator described "a myriad of programs that are offered out there...to fill in gaps...for whatever reason that [developmental education] was cut out I'm sure many other things have filled in." Further, a faculty member emphatically stated, "My philosophy is that if you take them in you need to try to do something to push them forward to the next level." Another administrator described the need for campus support staff to work extra hard on behalf of students in arguing:

> I needed to get everything I could get out of the people—because you know our budget is in the toilet, so I kept thinking how can I—we have got all of these kids we need to help. How can we do this and not add personnel?

The continued existence of students with an academic profile that suggests a need for developmental education and no additional funding has led many institutions to find creative ways to offer course-based academic support without identifying the support as developmental. To meet this challenge, one university administrator described "a myriad of programs that are offered out there. Maybe I shouldn't say this—but I'm going to because I've always been a risk-taker—it's to fill in gaps for, what might be the premise of that issue, is that we had remedial and now we no longer have it but we still have the need for additional help." While many faculty and administrators talked about the supplemental academic support provided to students in the wake of an end to developmental education, another administrator at the same university provided another perspective: "Students aren't really any worse off because other things have been put into place and that didn't exist when we had the remedial courses and sometimes the remedial courses aren't taught in a great way and [the students] really don't get a whole lot from it." This administrator's statements suggest that students were getting better support from the variety of programs and initiatives that replaced traditional developmental education courses.

A widely used, course-based form of support is the addition of a supplemental lab section for students who need extra assistance. One university that we visited turned to enriched course where lab classes were added to different sections of college-level courses in math and English "for students who have lower placement test scores... so students who place into those courses will meet more often during the week... those extra class meetings are geared towards catching up on the basic math skills that they must not have had for their placement scores to be where they were." An administrator described how adding supplemental instruction "was the best they could do" after developmental education was eliminated. He went on to say, "I guess that was kind of a compromise" to balance the state policy with the institutional needs at the ground level. A faculty member further explained:

> What we've attempted to do in [this enriched] class is bridge the distance between [the lack of funding for developmental education] with the recognition that not all of our students are prepared the same... All that we can do here at [this university] is deal with the resources we have and the student population we have.

The faculty member further explained that the course was a part of a national movement toward "mainstreaming, which is why the enriched courses are not designated differently they are the same college-level course with different sections. These enriched course sections are capped at 15 although the faculty try to keep them at 12." Other sections of the same course are capped at 20. With smaller class sizes and additional lab time, the faculty have "plenty of time in those additional two sessions to meet with each one of [their students] individually." Thus, students who may find themselves with developmental needs will get the attention they require.

Another university that we visited was also planning to offer similar courses. One campus administrator indicated, "We're going to pilot... we're going to designate some of the sections [of first year writing]... as... supplemental instruction... where groups of eight to ten students get together outside of class either with an instructor... or with a peer tutor or graduate student." Another higher education administrator at the same institution described how the University 101 courses are generally taught by professors in a way that goes "way beyond" to offer a "remedial type program."

These alternative forms of instructional delivery and academic support are perceived by most institutional administrators and faculty more positively than developmental education courses because they do not carry the same stigma for the students. One faculty member argued, "I don't know if these students even recognize that they're in a[n] [enriched class] as opposed to [the other]. And for our [next course level], of which there's only one, we don't have a [lab] designation for it. It's just [the course]."

Perhaps as a result, professors have also found students to be more motivated in credit-bearing courses than noncredit courses. One faculty member recalled, "I think the big advantage is that when we had the remedial course, it was not for credit; it didn't count towards credits for graduation... some students are less motivated because of that." He expressed preference for the new enriched course structure because of how "these courses are going to satisfy their... requirements."

Along with changing courses and academic support services to meet student needs, there are also many individuals working hard to ensure students are adequately supported. With great passion, one faculty member described himself and his colleagues in this way:

> We are 100 percent dedicated to the performance of our students... our faculty, staff, and administration recognize that we teach the students we have, not the students we wish we had... [we] hire teacher scholars who are dedicated to our student population... it is our department expectation that... if they [an underprepared student] needs to meet with you every day after class for an hour then that's your job.

A professor at another university conveyed how "[e]very faculty member in the department works in the writing center at least one hour a week." Similarly, an administrator who directs an academic support center also expressed the need "to get everything I could get out of the people [employees]... because... we have got all of these kids we need to help." Certainly, the faculty, staff, and administrators at the institutions we visited maintained a commitment to serving students, regardless of the students' academic backgrounds and despite state policies that suggest those students who are underprepared do not belong at their universities.

While full-time faculty and staff have had to work diligently to support students, there was concern about the increased reliance on part-time faculty. A state higher education leader explained how the "abysmal" amount that adjunct faculty get paid provides significant cost savings "and the legislature loves that. They love that!" This "savings," however, has costs elsewhere as explained by a faculty member: "If we're relying on people who are only partially committed to us then we can't really count on them to be fully committed to our students."

Fiscal Strategies

As a result of these expanded programmatic and curricular offerings, it is questionable whether eliminating developmental education courses from four-year institutions has really decreased costs for the institutions in the manner intended. While faculty and staff were clearly committed to continuing to support students, they also recognized the financial cost it takes to do so. One faculty member at a school offering enriched courses explained how the courses are "a bit of a burden for us. Since faculty staff [these courses] for two sections, we end up paying them twice as much to teach fewer students. So there are some financial burdens to this approach."

Institutions justified the expenditures, however, because they recognized that providing the necessary support is an investment. Indeed, they found that the programs paid for themselves through increased student retention. Even at the state level, one administrator demonstrated how supporting students is cost-effective:

> It's seen as an enrollment management vehicle...I'm asking you to hire one person for $32,000 full-time in a math lab...every student that comes in the door who's a full-time student, living in the dorm...is $18,000. You only need two [students]. We only have to save the two [students] to cover the cost of that [instructor]...The more astute presidents are starting to get interested in enrollment strategies that maintain [their] student base.

Another institutional administrator argued:

> It's [academic support is] expensive but...we've done analysis. If we can improve our retention and graduation rates by this percent, what revenue does that mean to us?...The revenues that come through, if we can improve retention and graduation rates, offsets the cost of doing anything on the other side; so we believe in student success. We're putting money towards that.

Collaboration

The EEDA has the potential to decrease the need for developmental education due to greater collaboration between four-year colleges, two-year colleges, and K-12. The most pertinent aspect is a recently developed course alignment project between postsecondary institutions and secondary education. In an effort to ease the transition from high school to college, the South Carolina CHE has worked extensively with the Oregon-based Education Policy Improvement Center to develop a course alignment project. A leader of this initiative explained:

> What we're trying to do is get the entry level college courses, and the exit level high school courses aligned with each other, and the effort, of course, is to change the way the high school courses are being taught, so that when students go into college they don't get shocked by the fact that they don't get extra credit, by the fact that the homework is not checked every day... that's required a lot of contact between the colleges, the college professors, and high school teachers, which is pretty unique.

This state higher education administrator explained that the initiative has had very positive reactions:

> We had one woman who had been teaching twenty some years who said, "In my twenty years of teaching, I've never had an opportunity to sit down with my counterpart at the college and say hey, what do you find when you see my students come in? What do you see? What's successful? What's not successful?" So these partnerships have proved very beneficial.

Administrators at higher education institutions also spoke positively about collaborative efforts. An English faculty member said, "It is just kind of a natural coming together. I don't know why we didn't think of it years ago. But it really did help us to be able to say to the high school faculty these are the things that your students need to do in order to be competent when they get to the [college] level. Conversely, the high school faculty would say, well how is it that we can teach this... So real opportunities for exchange of information."

Information and Accountability

Although the course alignment project has the potential to decrease the need for developmental education in the state, there will be no certainty around this because of a lack of data collection. This lack of data is in noticeable contrast to our other case study states and is particularly interesting given that Section 59-101-350 of the South Carolina Code of Laws requires that data outlining the future academic success of students exiting developmental courses be collected and reported annually by the CHE. As previously mentioned, the CHE annual reports have not included developmental education data. Similarly, the CHE includes limited data on developmental education, and the SCTCS web site did not include any at the time of our study.

State higher education leaders consistently reported to us that the state has not been able to study developmental education in a meaningful way or they were uncertain whether the state had. When asked whether the state's developmental education policy has had any impact on academic success, one state higher education leader stated, "I have to admit that part of the reason that we haven't noticed is because that's not been something that we've been able to really study." Another stated, "I don't know that we've ever run the numbers specifically looking at whether there was an increase after the last group of colleges could no longer offer developmental, I don't know." Similarly, those we spoke to reported that there had been no follow-up to investigate whether the state had experienced the anticipated cost savings from eliminating developmental education courses at the four-year colleges and universities.

A number of explanations were offered for the paucity of data. One individual attributed this to lack of time in stating, "I'm not sure that we have time to have any tracking data, any effective tracking data, anyway." The lack of data analysis was also attributed to a prioritization of other topics as another person explained, "frankly in the current environment the trend data we've been looking at all has to do with funding." Others thought that because so many changes were happening simultaneously, it would be impossible to directly and quantitatively measure the effects of any specific policy change. "It is hard for me to distinguish because we have had several things going on simultaneously. Again, the effort to bring more students into the pipeline, the advent of the scholarship program, has caused many students who might not have ever attempted higher education before to get into the system...it makes it hard to analyze and say that the challenges we face in regard to remedial education are due to the policy. I don't know that you could ever trace cause and effect and isolate them at one policy," explained one state higher education leader. Finally, the lack of data analysis was attributed to a lack of staff and money. A CHE staff member expressed a real desire to do more research on the effectiveness of course alignment efforts, but regretted that funds simply are not available for this. Similarly, the SCTCS office also would like to have data more readily available on their web site and regretted being unable to do so as a result of limited staffing. An SCTCS administrator stated, "We're moving in the direction of trying to put more [data] online, it's been kind of an ongoing discussion and most other states have and so we're trying to head in that direction."

Through directly contacting the Institutional Research office of SCTCS, some developmental education reports were made available to our research team. These data were limited to descriptive statistics including the number and proportion of students enrolling in developmental education courses; the number of developmental courses taken; the proportion of incoming students requiring developmental courses in math, reading, and English; and the ethnic and gender breakdown of students taking developmental education classes. Data available indicate that the proportion of incoming students taking developmental education classes has increased from 33 percent in 2006 to 38 percent in 2010. The subject in which students are most frequently enrolling in developmental education is math, followed by English, and then reading.

There were also some institutional data and anecdotal reports offered to our research team related to the success of students who had received extra academic support through developmental education or lab courses. One four-year institution had tracked the grades of students enrolled in lab courses and traditional courses and found that the final class grades were relatively comparable between the groups. A university faculty member stated, "So by the time these kids come out of [a lab section] many of them, most of them, can go toe-to-toe with whoever was in a regular class. In fact, some of them exceed what those students can do."

In 2010, the state did receive US$14.8 million through the Statewide Longitudinal Data Systems grant from the federal government to create a data management system that would enable the tracking of student success from K-12 to postsecondary. One of the major anticipated outcomes of the grant is to use these data to "inform policy and practice." Therefore, there may be increased use of data in upcoming years.

Conclusion

It became clear from our case study that leaders in South Carolina did not view developmental education as a strategy that can be used in state efforts to improve academic success and thereby expand economic development. Rather, developmental education seemed negatively perceived by many in the state. Legislators viewed developmental education in terms of the cost of paying for the same instruction twice. Professors in four-year universities complained that students were not motivated to put effort into a class that offered no course credit. Administrators disagreed with how students "use up" their financial aid dollars on courses that offered no credit. For all of these reasons, it is not surprising that South Carolina decided to eliminate developmental education courses in four-year institutions. What has occurred in South Carolina following this decision, however, offers valuable lessons for other states to consider in developmental education policy development.

Inconsistency in institutional policies around assessment and placement means that sophisticated students can potentially find ways to "work around" developmental education requirements. Students can do so by attending a four-year institution where they can access lab courses/supplemental instruction instead of developmental education courses or by choosing an institution that does not require placement exams. Students attending two-year institutions can do so by choosing a college with higher "cut" scores. This becomes a question of fairness as students with the same skills at different institutions may face differing developmental education requirements. This may inadvertently impact lower income students who need to attend a two-year institution near their homes in order to reduce costs or who are not as knowledgeable about how to "beat" the system. Thus, inconsistency in institutional policies may unintentionally hinder the educational attainment of low-income students and subsequently widen income inequality in the state.

Deciding to eliminate developmental education courses from four-year institutions has not eliminated the need for course-based academic support. Instead, higher education institutions have found other avenues through which support can be offered without using the name of developmental education. As a result, it is questionable whether the elimination of developmental education courses in four-year colleges and universities truly saved state money or better served students. In the political climate of the state, however, the policy change has allowed legislators to tell their constituents that they are not "paying for the same thing twice."

The most prominently used forms of course-based, academic support in four-year institutions were enriched courses and supplemental instruction, including the addition of a lab section to college-level courses. Both of these approaches offered the benefits of reducing stigma, increasing student motivation, and enabling students to receive course credit. Because these approaches to academic support were viewed more favorably than developmental education courses, the decision to eliminate developmental courses in four-year institutions was not viewed negatively by most.

Another positive result of the policy change has been the technical college system's embrace of its role as the developmental education provider in the state. SCTCS has supported faculty specializing in the teaching of developmental education courses and has created a developmental education curriculum that provides consistency in courses across campuses. If effective, this specialization could improve institutional capacity to support students entering community colleges underprepared.

Perhaps the most significant insight offered by South Carolina is the example it provides of how important it is to utilize data in the decision-making process. With the limited funding available to support public education in South Carolina and the urgent need for a more educated citizenry complicated by severe racial and ethnic soial inequities aross the state, it is essential that all funds be allocated in the most useful manner possible. Data analysis at the institutional level indicates that adding lab sections to courses for academic support may be quite effective in supporting students to complete college-level courses. Anecdotal evidence indicates that the alignment project may prove to be a valuable tool in reducing the need for developmental education and the quest to improve college attainment rates. South Carolina's ability to know this with certainty, however, is limited by a lack of statewide analysis around how to support academic success among students who enter college less academically prepared. Further, given the educational disparities in the state, disaggregating the data by race, ethnicity, SES, and perhaps geographic region will be critical to understanding the effectiveness of any efforts in this regard.

5

Oklahoma

Reform has played a prominent role in education in Oklahoma, leading to the development of multiple initiatives aimed to increase access and success in higher education. Yet, despite this commitment to raise the standards of learning, assess the readiness of precollegiate students, and hold schools accountable for these increased expectations, nearly half of all first-time freshmen were identified as needing developmental education. The consistency of underpreparation among Oklahomans prompted system and college administrators and faculty to raise critical questions about the decades of reform and reconsider how closer alignment with their feeder institutions, greater collaboration between systems, and increased support may yield a decreased need for developmental education on the front end and improved education attainment on the back end.

State Context

The state of Oklahoma, with 3.7 million people, is the 28th most populous state in the nation, witnessing a nearly 9 percent growth change from 2000 to 2010.[1] Close to 76 percent of the population is white, 8 percent is African American, 9 percent is Latino, 2 percent is Asian, and 9 percent is Native American or Alaskan Native.[2] Nearly a third of the state's population is under the age of 18 and only 23 percent of those 25 years and over hold bachelor's degrees, which is 5 percentage points less than the national average of 28 percent.[3]

At the time of this study, Oklahoma saw a slight decrease in the state's unemployment rate dropping from 6.9 to 6.2 between 2010 and 2011.[4] Employment opportunities largely rest in office and administrative support and sales, with food preparation and serving, production, and transportation and material moving rounding out the top five occupations.[5]

Though these employment opportunities are perhaps the most plentiful in the state, they are also among the lowest paying, as the median income for office positions is less than US$30,000 and food preparation and serving pays less than US$20,000 per year. The highest paying positions lie in the health, engineering and technology fields; and all require some form of postsecondary education.

In fact, job-growth projections for Oklahoma make clear the need for postsecondary credentials. In Northwest Oklahoma, for example, nearly 70 percent of all jobs by 2020 will require postsecondary training; yet as of 2012, more than half of Oklahomans 25 years and older only have a high school diploma as their maximum education attainment level.[6] Given the changing labor demands of the state, and the increasingly important role that higher education must play to ensure that Oklahomans are prepared to meet the demands of the twenty-first century workforce, a 36-member Citizens' Commission on the Future of Oklahoma Higher Education was created to offer recommendations that would "serve as a long term guide...to direct higher education in the promising but uncertain decades ahead."[7]

Released in 1999, the Citizens' Commission presented a report that contained 41 recommendations, among which were specific calls for higher education to "respond effectively to the changing demographic location, age, race, and origin mix of Oklahoma's population,"[8] and to specify policies that will ensure programs are preparing employable graduates. The Citizens' Commission recommended that higher education should do more to adjust curricula, counseling, and other factors to be more targeted to existing industries and become more attractive to expanding business enterprises. At the same time, however, commission members were cognizant of the criticisms levied at higher education by the business community for "failing to produce students with problem solving abilities, and writing and math skills." They suggested that these deficiencies could be corrected, not by adding additional resources or courses, but rather through "a change in pedagogy—the way knowledge is taught."[9] Without such a change, institutions of higher education were at risk of producing college graduates "who verge on being functionally illiterate."[10]

State Priorities and Goals

The Citizens' Commission on the Future of Oklahoma Higher Education was just one in a series of efforts aimed at improving education, a top priority for the state. House Bill 1017 in 1990, for example, has been widely acknowledged as "Oklahoma's landmark education reform legislation"[11] for the wide-ranging reforms addressing school funding, administration, curriculum, assessment, and teacher quality. Of note in this bill was the establishment of new statewide curricular standards that spelled out what students needed to know in preparation for employment or postsecondary education. Specifically, school districts were charged with preparing students for enrollment in the state's research institutions without the need for developmental education. Post-1990s reforms included passage of the Achieving Classroom Excellence (ACE) Act, which initiated reforms to the high school curriculum, assessment, and graduation requirements, such as the expectation that all students had to satisfy a college preparatory curriculum if they were to graduate from high school.

Senate Bill 1792 was signed into law on July 1, 2006, and resulted in two programs of study for Oklahoma high school students: the ACE Act College Preparatory/Work Ready Curriculum or the Core Curriculum. The former is the default college preparatory curriculum for all students entering Oklahoma high schools, and the latter gives parents an alternate path toward high school certification for their children. While both curricula lead to a standard high school diploma, there are clear distinctions as to the level of preparation students receive for postsecondary options. Parents are required to complete an opt out form if they choose the alternate noncollege preparatory curricular pathway. Although too new at the time of the study to be able to trace impact of the new requirements, data show that few students actually opted out of the college prep curriculum: 11.8 percent in 2006–7, 10.4 percent in 2009–10, and 8.8 percent in 2011–12.[12]

Other key initiatives guiding Oklahoma education at the time of this study were many, including Oklahoma's Promise, OK EPAS, Brain Gain, the Oklahoma High School Indicators Project, and Complete College America. Each of these initiatives was designed to help and prepare students to access higher education. Oklahoma's Promise helps students pay for college, and Brain Gain aimed to increase the number of Oklahomans earning college degrees and keep said graduates in the state. OK EPAS is a voluntary series of assessments and reporting measures geared to providing students in eighth and tenth grades with sufficient information so that they will take more proactive measures to become college-ready. The Oklahoma High School Indicators Project evaluates the performance of individual K-12 schools using several markers, including the tracking of high school-to-college going rates and developmental education rates of current graduates. Most recently, the Oklahoma State Regents for Higher Education (OSRHE), Oklahoma's system of higher education, joined Complete College America's Alliance of States and committed to setting state- and campus-specific degree completion targets, developing aggressive action plans to meet those targets, and collecting and reporting data to measure progress.[13]

Despite these wide-ranging initiatives designed to increase degree completion, Oklahoma still faces preparation and access needs in higher education, especially as it relates to developmental education. In fall 2010, 281,359 students were enrolled in Oklahoma's public and private institutions.[14] Of those students enrolled, 39,608 were first-time freshmen[15]; 19 percent enrolled in research universities, 24 percent in regional universities, 47 percent in community colleges, and 10 percent in private colleges. Among first-time freshman, nearly 42 percent of students were required to enroll in developmental education courses[16]; 7 percent at research universities, 39 percent at regional institutions, and 56 percent at community colleges. Data show an ebb-and-flow in the need for developmental coursework as 37 percent of students required it in 2003–4, nearly 43 percent in 2008–9, and 45 percent in 2011–12, the year this study concluded.

Whereas a system-level administrator commented on the reality that the need for developmental education was not likely to ever go away, there was nonetheless a sense of frustration that the dollars directed at reform have not achieved the desired objectives. This administrator observed, "In my 20 years in Oklahoma higher ed, the more money we put in K-12, we have not seen the results." Another system-level administrator remarked, "I almost see [developmental education] as a necessary evil…it's one of those things that if we want to get to that goal of completion, this is just the kind of thing we have to do to prepare those students so they can get there." Yet, to do otherwise, as some states have done by eliminating developmental courses from certain postsecondary sectors, would not be in the best interest of Oklahoma. As a system-level administrator commented:

> I was curious to [know] how these kids [in developmental math and non-developmental math] did and it turns out [they did] pretty well…I wanted to point out that if we turn these students away because they just needed [developmental education] we'd be making a huge mistake for them and for the state.

The question for these administrators thus lay in the flexibility and effectiveness of policy to address a highly diverse student population with developmental education needs. As a system-level administrator concluded:

> What are we going to do with people [e.g.], who have been out of college for years and are coming back? How much Algebra do they remember from

high school? I hope the assessment policy is allowing space for the institutions to have different levels of remediation... It's enough to deter them from pursuing their degree, and then we think the economic cost [of losing them] is way too high, so we're supportive of developmental ed at the higher education level because it's needed.

While four-year institutional administrators expressed a desire and need to do more, many times these sentiments came into conflict with the purpose, value, and place of developmental education on the college campus, especially at the research and regional universities. A system-level administrator defined developmental education as "polarized" because how individuals felt about the subject depended on the population being discussed. She went on to explain:

For the direct high school population, I think it's seen very negatively and an indictment on our public school system. And I think that does cause some concern on a lot of those different constituencies of paying for the same instruction twice. That [the public is] supposedly paying for it in high school and then they're having to pay for it again at a college level.

In contrast, when applied to the needs of a returning adult population, there is a greater sense of tolerance given that these individuals have been out of school for some time and may be a bit "rusty" and could "benefit" from developmental instruction. In fact, assessment policy supports exemption for "students admitted under the special adult admission provision... consistent with the institution's approved assessment plan."[17]

Cost of Higher Education

According to the Education and General Budget Summary Analysis for FY10,[18] the total system-wide budget increased by 2.1 percent over FY09 for a total of US$2.163 billion. This budget increase enabled modest institutional budget increases of 2.6 percent and student assistance increases of 0.7 percent. State appropriations for higher education decreased by 3.5 percent, from a high of 18.5 percent of the state budget in FY08 to 15.4 percent in FY10. Tuition and revenue increased by 1.6 percent and received US$68.8 million in federal American Recovery and Reinvestment Act (ARRA) stimulus funding.

At the time of our interviews, Oklahoma Question (SQ) 744 was on the ballot which, if passed, would require the Oklahoma State Legislature to fund public education to at-least the per pupil average of neighboring states.[19] Many of those interviewed, however, expressed concern about potential passage of the bill, as it would lead to an approximate loss of 25 percent of the states' services, including a significant decrease to appropriations for higher education. A system administrator noted, "If 744 passes...how you see education in Oklahoma today cannot survive that. So all they are going to be doing is treading water. You want to talk about innovation? All they are going to be trying to do is keep their doors open." SQ 744 was overwhelmingly defeated by a majority of the voters in November 2010, 81 percent to 19 percent.

While the financing of higher education did not come across as strongly as a barrier to academic success, it is worth noting that in FY10 and FY11, tuition and fees represented 38 percent and nearly 42 percent, respectively, of total revenue generated for higher education.[20] This means that tuition and fee increases have largely been borne by students and their families while state-generated revenues in support of higher education decreased. For students enrolled in developmental education courses, an additional financial burden is placed on them as they are required to pay more for developmental courses at state system institutions, which are individually set.

A system administrator commented on the highly sensitive challenge of developmental education in the public consciousness and the expectation that developmental coursework should not be supported by public funds. Annual reports documenting Oklahoma's Promise, Oklahoma's scholarship program aimed at working families earning less than US$50,000 annually, show that approximately 35 percent of students receiving funds in 2010–11 required enrollment in at least one developmental course.[21] Though these students demonstrated financial need, they were still held responsible for paying any fees assessed for developmental course-taking. In addition, as a system administrator reported, the system is regularly monitored to ensure public funds are spent as they were intended. She explained:

> Most of the inquiries we get through our office from the state legislature is to double check to make sure there are no tax payer dollars and there is no tax revenue going to pay for remedial courses, because the view is they have already paid tax payer dollars for the student to be able to pass an Algebra I test. So that is more of a political issue than it is a financial issue.

In 2007–8, institutions generated approximately US$2.2 million to offset costs for providing developmental courses,[22] though it is difficult to assess what that offset is given the lack of information as to the true costs of providing developmental instruction. Fee variability can be seen across institutions: Northeastern State University, a regional institution, charged, for example, undergraduates US$186.40 per credit hour, which included a fee of US$55.90 for developmental courses.[23] Oklahoma State University, one of two research institutions, charged Oklahoma residents US$107.80 per credit hour plus an additional US$10 per credit hour for developmental education.[24] And Oklahoma City Community College charges US$13.00 for developmental education on top of the US$77.50 per credit hour resident tuition.[25]

The "Annual Student Remediation Report 2007–2008" in its conclusion suggested that the costs of providing developmental education are slight when the expected increase of first generation and adult students to Oklahoma higher education are considered. The report stated:

> Although critics of remediation complain that the costs drain valuable state resources, such costs are negligible when compared to the alternatives, which can range from falling levels of degree attainment to employment in low paying jobs. In Oklahoma, remedial education at two- and four-year institutions currently serves students needing remedial courses without placing a financial drain on state appropriated funding for higher education.[26]

Indeed, as a system administrator argued, the costs for providing developmental education had actually been a benefit to postsecondary institutions. Because of the standard practice of using adjuncts to provide instruction, the administrator suggested, "some institutions [have done] very well."

State Developmental Education Policies

The state system of higher education comprises 25 colleges and universities—including 2 research universities, 11 regional universities, and 12 community colleges—and 11 constituent agencies and 1 higher education center. The system is coordinated by OSRHE, and each institution is governed by a board of regents. The role of the regents is that of a coordinating board and not a governing board, thus, as a system administrator described, "We govern by persuasion and policy more or less." While this administrator recognized that "it would be great if [they] could exercise a little more muscle at times," innovation is more likely to take root and succeed when it is spearheaded at the institutional level rather than enforced from the top down.

OSRHE adopted and implemented a policy in 1991 titled, "Policy Statement on the Assessment of Students for Purposes of Instructional Improvement and State System Accountability,"[27] requiring higher education institutions to administer comprehensive assessment programs for the appropriate placement of students in courses. In 1993 the policy was modified to make mandatory the development of underprepared students and require a minimum cut score of 19 in the American College Testing (ACT) subject tests in English, mathematics, science reasoning, and reading as a "first cut" to determine whether a student needs to enroll in developmental education courses. For students scoring below the required ACT minimum, students will either immediately enroll in developmental courses or attempt a secondary assessment.

The State Regents Assessment Policy, adopted in October 1991, mandates the administration of five different assessments to "maximize student success." In adopting this policy, institutions are allowed to charge students up to US$1 per credit hour to support the assessment effort, which includes "the systematic collection, interpretation and use of information about student learning and achievement to improve instruction."[28] The results of these efforts are transmitted to the state regents and publicly disseminated in the "Annual Student Assessment Report" as a means to "demonstrate public accountability by providing evidence of institutional effectiveness."[29]

The purpose of the entry-level assessment is to "assist institutional faculty and advisors in making course placement decisions that will give students the best possible chance of academic success."[30] These assessments gauge the basic academic skills of all incoming students in addition to collecting data on "student attitudes and perceptions of college life," which facilitate the delivery of support programs including orientation, computer-assisted instruction, tutoring, and learning resource centers. Study participants were generally positive about the assessment policy, noting that as long as the policy was serving the best interests of students, then policy was ultimately beneficial.

Institutional Responses

Study participants had various responses as to the impact of policy. On one hand, there was a sense among participants that policy as currently written was both dated and had a "one size fits all" approach to developmental education. A community college administrator pointed to the fact that the policy "was written prior to most of us that are in the system right now." A community college faculty member called the old policy a "hindrance because it doesn't accept things that are changed in the last 20 years." And perhaps worst of all, the questions the policy raised at the ground level yielded answers that were unsatisfactory, or as a faculty member observed, "very unscientific; very uncoordinated."

Despite the challenge of a policy in need of review, the participants nevertheless felt that it provided sufficient flexibility to the institutions such that they could respond and innovate in ways that were specific to their context. A system administrator described the situation on the ground in the following way:

> I don't necessarily think it's a bad thing that they're still following the same policy, they still have to have some assessment. If they have curricular deficiencies they still have to figure those out. If they have performance deficiencies, they still have to do something about that.

In addition, institutional leaders recognized the value of even having a policy in place that recognized the issue and the proactive steps they were taking to address the challenge of developmental education. One administrator argued, "Having something which is what some people don't even have anything, old or otherwise, is great. It recognizes that we've got a remediation issue, that everybody coming to us is not going to be prepared." And still as another administrator stated:

> I think that's the benefit that [developmental education policy] is not being pushed by a legislator or any other agenda. We're being proactive using all of the data and information and people available to us. I think that puts the elements in place to have a better product in the end because we're not just looking at one particular issue that someone's pushing.

Others commented about the opportunities to not just raise the visibility of underpreparation, but connect it to institutional priorities of retention and completion. In this regard, developmental education was seen as a strategy to facilitate success, despite the negative public perception.

> Retention efforts are definitely a high priority... we have to be able to show we are making progress on graduation rates and retention... remediation is what helps you retain these students. I mean anybody with any common sense is going to recognize that, but the white noise that is out there [about remediation], it is just such a hard message to get across.

The impact of policy, while restrictive in some regards, could be seen across multiple domains as institutions and their representatives had to reconsider new and innovative ways to meet the demands of reform and still meet the needs of their students.

Instructional Delivery

The tension surrounding developmental education in Oklahoma could be seen with regard to institutional mission, the role of faculty, and the appropriate placement for the delivery of instruction. A regional institutional administrator commented on the interplay between mission and action, observing, "Our faculty really embrace [developmental education], they know it's part of our mission and they want to do the best job [they] can for that student." However, as a community college administrator suggested, mission and even policy guiding the delivery of developmental education is not enough, but rather has "to be something you believe in" and knowing that it is a benefit to students.

The contrast in the language used between representatives from the community colleges and the regional/research universities was telling as the former often spoke about the student as being the primary focus of their work whereas the latter spoke about importance and fealty to the discipline. A senior community college administrator discussed his work and that of his counterparts as follows:

> At the very top is the student and that's who we're here for and I think, like I said, speaking for most of the two-year school vice presidents for academic affairs, that's how we feel about it. Sometimes our four-year partners don't necessarily see it that way but then again it's not in a bad light, it's just not their mission.

This assessment was reinforced by a research institution administrator who remarked, "The perception from many faculty members is, 'when the students get to my course they should be prepared for what I want to teach them and I don't want to teach them this stuff they should've learned in high school.'" He went on to say that faculty are more keen on teaching the higher level courses because they are more "exciting," much more on the "cutting edge," with greater alignment to their independent "research," and students are "easier to teach" because they are much better prepared.

This distinction and how it is translated by the administrative and faculty ranks yielded reflection and questions for consideration. A regional administrator was absolutely certain that upper level faculty were not the best choice to teach in developmental courses, saying:

> We would use senior faculty that taught upper level calculus courses to also teach our developmental courses and it was a recipe for disaster. [Developmental education] students are obviously the ones that need the

very most help... [so] you would have students that know absolutely nothing about algebra trying to be taught by somebody who didn't really feel like it was their place to come down to their level.

So while the policy directive has been to largely remove developmental education from the research and regional institutions and place it solidly within the purview of the community colleges, there nonetheless remain questions about whether the system is doing what is truly best for students. A regional institution faculty member reflected upon their practice to recommend that students go to a two-year college for preparation before returning to the four-year university. He said, "Occasionally we'll see them again later... but I'm afraid, by looking at the statistics in our part of Oklahoma, that a lot of them just stop out forever and they don't go back to school."

Though it is a "tougher sell" for the research and regional institutions to embrace developmental education, there is acknowledgment by study participants that a cultural shift, and a reconsideration of policy, has to occur to better serve the needs of Oklahomans and reach the goals laid out in reform. A community college administrator observed:

> There's no really clear-cut place for one institution to stop and one institution to start if you're not getting graduates; which of course is one of the major goals of the state of Oklahoma. If you're not getting graduates, it goes back to retention. It goes back to preparation.

For this administrator who has a partnership with a regional institution to provide developmental education to students, he remarked, "it just all has to tie together" if they are to be effective in preparing and moving students from the time of entry all the way through to degree completion.

Assessment and Placement

System and institutional administrators stated that they have integrated assessment results into multiple areas of institutional review, sharing vital information with faculty and students as a means to "tie [everything] together." The "Annual Student Assessment Report," however, gives rise to concerns that the latitude given to institutions to administer secondary assessments and determine their own cut scores yields considerable variation across the systems. This variance "diminishes the ability to compare practices across the state or with institutions in other states."[31] A system administrator observed, "We're very prescriptive... but on the secondary, it's all over the board. And we've really tried to encourage [the institutions] to standardize." A research university administrator acknowledged the wisdom of standardization, and while generally supportive, nonetheless acknowledged that institutions may not respond well if told what to do.

Until such time that this variance of placement can be addressed, study participants shared ways in which they are looking to perfect the system to ensure the placement of students is accurate for their developmental needs. A regional institution administrator shared, "Connecting entry level testing and remediation with retention is a big interest...how do we get to that point where we help students progress through this process so that they're ready for what they need to be learning?" This includes options for retesting, experimenting with study aids, software, and other methods to prepare students for greater success at the time of assessment.

ACT scores provide institutions with a baseline measure of readiness in reading, mathematics, English, and science. Those scoring below the requisite 19 on the ACT are immediately referred to secondary testing for proper placement. Study participants had a great deal to say about this particular cut score, from concern about the system's "over-reliance" of the cut score in lieu of other measures for more accurate placement. A research university administrator commented:

> It's one of the things I think that I'm a little concerned about that we focus too much on the ACT and lose sight of some of these other things that are also important for students to be aware of and to be tracking [so] that we make sure that they're going to be successful not just because they have the academic preparation, but also because they understand how to learn in a classroom, how to engage, are motivated, [and] have the support they need.

This over-reliance is likewise expressed by others as they remarked on the notable lack of information the ACT actually provides to support accurate placement. A regional university administrator noted, "One of the things [the ACT] doesn't do very well is it doesn't give you very good diagnostic information about the students." As such, developing a truly comprehensive and robust diagnostic assessment is critical for the success of policy, both for guidance and enforcement. As yet another regional university administrator stated:

> It's really difficult to sit across the table from a parent in particular and have the parent say "Why is my child not placing into college level course work?" and the only response that you can give them is "they didn't meet

the cut score"; and really, that's a meaningless conversation to have with a parent.

At the time of the study, this policy was currently being revised by the Council of Instruction, which is comprised of academic vice presidents, that meets once a month and advises the entire state system in the review of current and recommended academic and related policy and procedures. According to a system administrator, the council was currently on a "fifth draft" of review and was benefiting from the expertise of individuals currently working at the institutional level. As this individual stated, "We've pulled in people who are dealing with assessment on a day-to-day basis at the institutional level because the State Regents pretty much has the 30,000-foot view. We set the parameters for the policy and the institutions have some latitude how they cut scores." As a result of this inclusion, "there's so much new information on students' success and evaluation and preparation for college that it's almost a paradigm shift away from what [they've] been doing."

Until the review process is completed—which was estimated at about 18 months from the time of our interviews—individual institutions, within their approved assessment plans, have the option to establish higher standards by requiring additional testing. Students who are required to enroll in developmental courses must receive a grade equivalent to a "C" or better to successfully "remediate" the identified deficiency.[32] Students are further required to correct their identified "deficiencies" within the first 24-college-level hours attempted, but may be allowed to be continually enrolled beyond the 24-hour limit and must remove deficiencies in a discipline before taking college-level work in that discipline. However, as it is noted in policy:

> The president or the president's designee may allow a deserving student who failed to remediate a basic skills deficiency in a single subject to continue to enroll in collegiate level courses in addition to remedial course work beyond the 24-hour limit providing the student has demonstrated success in collegiate courses to date. Such exceptions must be appropriately documented.[33]

The policy, as previously noted, permits greater flexibility for returning adult students and whether they need developmental courses. While adults must demonstrate competency in the curricular areas to the "satisfaction of the admitting institution," they are exempt from the specific ACT subscore requirements.

While the policy allowing individual institutions to exercise greater flexibility makes sense as each institution is different, a system administrator nonetheless expressed concern over the variance this inevitably led to institutions and the potential impact this has on articulation and transfer agreements. He noted:

> We had a situation where the cut score for the same test at the research institution was lower than at a community college. It was just all over the map and we thought that was pretty inconsistent especially since we have an articulation effort that tries to match courses on campuses so that they transfer and if we're talking about your first year college algebra and to get to that course, you have to have a high score at one institution and a low score at another institution? Are those courses really equal?

In addition, there is anecdotal evidence that students, realizing the differing requirements, will "shop around" for schools, particularly at the community college level. As a result, as one individual observed, "We've heard four-year universities indicate that a lot of [transfer] students can't even write and so there's kind of a tension between the two-year and the four-year with regard to remediation and how effective it is at the two-year level." The fact that no data are collected from this population of students once they have transferred further adds to the tension because there are no data to prove or disprove the anecdotal information that have led chief academic officers to vociferously voice their concerns.

Even so, as individuals spoke of the upcoming revisions to the assessment policies, there was the hope that institutions would still have some leeway to at least "customize" their offerings in ways that address the diverse needs of students—from those who need more intensive instruction to those who simply need a "refresher" to remind them of what they may have temporarily forgotten. In doing so, institutions could exercise judgment about practices and innovations that would best support their unique contexts.

Faculty Development and Academic Support

How institutions provided developmental education varied across the system; yet, it was abundantly clear that institutional commitment to delivering effective developmental education programs has led to changes to hiring practices and professional development for faculty. Above all, critical questions about articulation between the two-year and four-year institutions have been raised not only in an attempt to improve alignment and consistency of rigor and learning, but also as a means to separate fact from perception.

Institutional administrators have taken a much more intentional approach to the hiring of instructors who do not just meet the requirements to teach content, but to hire individuals who demonstrate an affinity to working with a population of students that requires a different approach to learning. At one community college, a faculty member leading the department's hiring efforts asks explicit questions of working with students who are more akin to high school students than college-level students. Another community college faculty member, echoing the previous remarks, stated, "The tenure process really has nothing to do with [teaching in developmental education], but I take the most qualified math teachers and have them doing the remedial because they know where the student is supposed to go." The individuals he hires are very often instructors with high school credentials or have experience working at the precollegiate level.

Given the unique pedagogy required to be successful in a developmental setting, another community college faculty member described the changed professional development provided to faculty across all levels so that they have a better understanding of good teaching practices and not just content knowledge. She remarked:

> What I'm doing with our professional development right now is I'm back filling instructional design. I'm back filling pedagogy, all of those kinds of things for our faculty because they don't know it coming in or after they've been here for a while because we don't have them going through colleges of education. That's not how we hire and that's a handicap performance.

Due to these changes to hiring and professional development opportunities, as well as earlier reference to the use of more appropriate diagnostic tools to identify student course placement, participants remarked about the changing conversations taking place in their campuses. A regional college administrator observed a new-found curiosity among his faculty after the implementation of the diagnostic portion of their secondary assessment. He said:

> The faculty are very curious as to what it is exactly that the students are not prepared on... [and] it's led to additional conversations about the course work that the students are experiencing in the remedial courses. The faculty are very engaged in conversations to make sure that the remedial course work really does in fact prepare them for the college level courses that the students are going to be taking.

These more robust conversations have perhaps led to more vocal questions about articulation and preparation at feeder institutions.

Several student participants described a climate where faculty are more willing to vocalize discontent over the preparation of their students in developmental courses at the community colleges. The inconsistency between schools and the different levels of developmental education taught before transitioning to college level courses means that articulation and transfer between institutions is far from seamless. One faculty remarked that not all institutions are able to hire the most "qualified instructors," thus compromising the preparation of students. Others question the strict enforcement of the 24-hour requirement, suggesting that students did not always complete developmental coursework before transferring to the four-year institution. And finally, there is the perception that grade equivalency between the two-year and four-year institutions cannot be assured because, as a research university administrator stated, "There's a perception at least from faculty at [the research institution] that an A in a [community college] course should be equivalent to a B [because] our standards are higher."

Even where partnerships between institutions are formalized, there remains a sense of unease as to the preparation of students. The partnership between Oklahoma State University and Northern Oklahoma College, and the partnership between the University of Central Oklahoma and Rose State College means that the responsibility of developmental education is in the hands of the community college, and the student taking those courses retains his or her status as a four-year college/university student. A regional administrator describes this collaboration as having multiple positives especially as it relates to students. He said:

> There won't be very many [students] that will say, "well I'm planning on going to a two year school," especially some of the more elite high schools in the state that it would be a stigma to say that. But the nice thing about having them on campus is the students can live in the dorms, they can feel like an OSU student even though they're participating in NOC's programs they can live in the dorms, they can do some of the other activities that OSU students can do.

And although this kind of partnership should allow for a seamless transition between the precollegiate and college-level coursework, a faculty member who is part of one of these partnerships remarked, "I've heard that the faculty that are teaching the college algebra classes don't feel like the students are being as successful as what we thought they were, and so I'll be talking with that dean this semester and see if it's really true or see where that's coming from."

Given these challenges of articulation, equivalence, and latitude, a faculty member from a regional institution noted that in keeping their developmental program in-house, they are able to control for these challenges. He observed:

> I think it's a luxury for us to have [remedial education] students in house. I think it's not a luxury for the other schools to have to hire out or outsource because our developmental—as far as the Math Department goes, there are developmental math faculty that also teach the upper level classes so we bring these developmental math students along with us as we teach higher courses. They often follow with us so they become familiar with the faculty here whereas at other schools, they don't know. They don't have any connections.

As can be seen in the examples above, innovation in faculty development and academic support is not without its challenges, raising concerns that extend beyond variance among institutions, but about how these variances are understood and worked through with the support of evaluation and information sharing.

Information and Accountability

Browsing through the OSRHE website reveals a wealth of information collected and made available for public consumption. From information about high school preparation to tuition impact analysis, there appears to be a commitment at the system level to collect as much data on a wide array of indicators to inform decision making at the system and institutional level. A system-level administrator noted:

> Because we have a widely dispersed audience, diverse audience I should say, legislators, Regents, the media, as well as the institutions. We have a lot of constituents so we have that in mind whenever we are developing [reports]. We don't want them to be so dense and wordy that the people give up because we think that the information we have to report is important and it's only important though if people take advantage of that.

In addition to these reports, efforts are undertaken at various levels to share the data resources with feeder institutions such that there can be greater alignment and collaborative efforts to minimize the variance between systems. Moreover, institutions are regularly encouraged to "monitor and evaluate" their progress or any changes to institutional processes. A system-level administrator remarked, "We ask them to tell us how they study their test scores and how they modify their remediation and how they go about that."

Unfortunately, this encouragement is received with mixed results, wherein some institutions may be more responsive than others. The reasons for this are several, with participants commenting that in some sectors there is "significant opposition to share information," to the concern that information "can be used against us." And finally, there is the sentiment that perhaps the data are simply not comparable considering the latitude given to institutions and the varying levels of developmental education provided.

To monitor progress against identified state goals, institutions submit annual reports, two of which are the "Annual Student Assessment Report" and the "Annual Student Remediation Report" that provide detailed information into the status of students in the system. According to one administrator, "Monitoring takes place with these reports." Because the OSRHE is a coordinating board, and not a governing board, these reports allow them to see not only where problems lie and begin to address them, but also what new and innovative things are happening across the system that they may not immediately be privy to. As one system administrator remarked:

> Right now we do not have an office for developmental ed that can oversee and monitor all these things. Monitoring takes place with these reports. Built into the policy is the requirement that they report certain things to us so sometimes that's our first glimpse at what is actually going on and they're annual reports.

Participants likewise spoke of the value of data for information sharing and decision making. A regional university administrator talked about developing reports specifically intended for a faculty audience so as to "help inform their decisions and conversations" about student progress and outcomes. Above all, respondents made clear that the data are not only used for the purposes already articulated, but that there is a sense of accountability throughout the system to enforce the requirements of policy equally so that the outcomes of placement and developmental education are trustworthy across the system. A regional university administrator shared his frustration when he stated:

> I think that the Regent's policy is enforced very subjectively from institution to institution. We're all supposed to be playing with the same rules, but what we see are many, many students... [that] can only get

to a certain point at the [feeder schools]. We operate under the premise that the 24-hour policy is enforced and we do enforce that here and I'm the guy that has to do it unfortunately, which makes for some pretty uncomfortable conversations each semester. At the end of the semester...if [students] can't pass, then we actually limit them to zero level math only and it's very uncomfortable. Other schools don't do them any justice by allowing them to continue that far [because] then we have to be the bad guy.

Indeed, what was especially concerning for college administrators was the fact that they could point out to specific high schools that were doing a good job preparing students for postsecondary success and those that were not. An administrator from one of the research universities remarked:

I was visiting with the engineering associate dean the other day and he said when he looked at their feeder schools there were some high schools in the state that they had not had a single student complete the engineering program. There were just some schools in the state that they knew if they had a student from that school that they weren't going to make it...It was kind of an interesting thing that he even knew which schools were providing the most successful students and which [schools] were really—hadn't done much at all in terms of preparing students.

This comment is noteworthy because it yields questions about the data being collected in the state and the action that takes place as a result of analysis. Looking at the ACE Opt Out numbers, it is clear that in some counties, higher percentages of students were opting out of the default college preparatory course of study. For example, in 2011–12, nearly 70 percent of entering freshman in an Oklahoma City charter school opted out and 26 percent of students in a Tulsa school district did the same.[34] Other information sources, largely a result of the Oklahoma High School Indicators Project, provide data that point to the level of preparation of students by high school, such as mean ACT scores and college-going rates of recent graduates that should facilitate increased preemptive action. One regional college administrator remarked:

Well we point fingers, isn't that what the papers say, that we all point fingers? The high schools say we expect too much and we say that high schools aren't doing their job. But really it's because we fail to meet in the middle. We have a good relationship with our feeder schools but it can definitely be better.

Echoing these comments, another regional college administrator noted that the importance of collaboration and coordination between systems to reduce the need for developmental education is vital, yet postsecondary educators have to tread lightly so as not to appear as if it is telling K-12 what to do. In addition are the reality of turf battles, which as one system administrator suggested, "You have pockets of cooperation where if [local entities] don't want to [cooperate] they'll say, 'the Superintendent says no' or they'll say, 'our local board says no.' So those are significant external challenges for higher education as a whole to impact." This is especially true for policies enacted by the state system of higher education that may have no direct impact on K-12, which, as a system administrator argued, "It's very challenging to push anything at the K-12 level even though we're participating in efforts both nationally and state initiatives to bridge the two."

However, there remains hope that collaboration and coordination to address differences in quality of courses, patterns of course-taking, counselor guidance, and teacher effectiveness, to name a few, will occur to abate the need for developmental education. A system administrator remarked:

> I think there's the underlying hope that the new state superintendent opens up the opportunity for greater collaboration between the common education as well as higher education because...the disconnect of communication and collaboration between the two is the creator of high levels of developmental education within the institutions of higher education.

This spirit of collaboration is particularly critical for institutional actors who encounter students who "come right out of high school experiencing four levels of remediation yet finding evidence [after the fact] that they struggled throughout high school," or as another college administrator pointed out, the high proportion of very small feeder schools who are producing valedictorians and salutatorians yet who are only scoring a 15 on the ACT. A system administrator concludes, "We're wanting to do things that are in sync, or at least complement what we're doing on the ACE curriculum so that [high school graduates] are coming out with a little better preparation. And as those numbers shrink, if we could do more interventions and more things for these students, provide more supports, then maybe that will kind of help us move along."

Conclusion

While the policy guiding developmental education in Oklahoma does not place restrictions as to which institutions can or cannot offer these courses, it nevertheless raises questions about process, practice, and impact. The state, through its various reforms and initiatives, has made it abundantly clear that its priority is to ensure that all Oklahomans are given every opportunity to access higher education, both through preparation in K-12 to financial and academic supports in higher education. This goal, however, is challenged by the increase and variance of cut scores that limit access to certain sectors of higher education.

Increasing cut scores on the ACT, for example, means that students needing developmental education are more likely to be found in the regional and community colleges than they would be in the research universities. In fact, between the 2002-3 and the 2003-4 academic years, enrollment in developmental education rates in the research institutions dropped nearly 50 percent, from 13.2 percent to 6.8 percent. This drop coincided with changes in policy that made admission into the research universities significantly more challenging with increased entrance requirements. Most recently, as a regional institution administrator recalls, cut scores were revisited. "The [math faculty] requested that we increase the cut scores... it didn't quite get past the provosts so it is still the same."

This action suggests that while the goals to increase access to higher education are paramount, that access will only be granted to those who seemingly "fit" in the mold of a traditional college student. This same assessment can be made with regard to the financial support provided for developmental instruction. Oklahoma's Promise provides scholarships to the most financially-in-need students so that they can attend college. While research demonstrates that students from families with minimal financial resources are more apt to require developmental education, the practice of requiring students to pay out-of-pocket additional fees levied for developmental education course-taking seems to counter the "promise" of the scholarship program.

How Oklahoma addresses these challenges to reach its objectives for an increasingly educated population remains to be seen. Despite the challenges connected to policy, there nonetheless appears to be a clear understanding among those we spoke to that developmental education is critical to the state's goals to achieve the degree attainment goals set out for Oklahomans. A system administrator observed that "developmental education is an integral part of Oklahoma's Brain Gain initiative[35]—we feel it's too bad that it's necessary, but if it's necessary, then we must do it." Given the sheer size of the state and geographic location of postsecondary institutions, all institutions, from the four-year research and regional colleges and universities to the two-year community colleges, have a role to play. Whereas the regional and research institutions are most likely to not have the same levels of developmental courses as their community college counterparts, the responsibility to educate local populations with limited access to different types of institutions means that some of the four-year institutions may be the only ones to provide said education.

6

Colorado

The state of Colorado has the dual distinction of having some of the most educated residents in the country, while experiencing a "leaky education pipeline" that prevents students from moving from PreK–12 and through higher education. With ambitious goals laid out for increasing the graduation and degree attainment rates of Coloradans, a sweeping reform has engineered a new vision for education, one that sees developmental education as a vital component of its strategy. Yet, policy restrictions that impact higher education institutions and lack of financial support raise the question of whether Colorado's goals can be achieved.

State Context

The state of Colorado, with 5 million people, is the 22nd most populous state in the nation, with a nearly 17 percent growth change from 2000 to 2010.[1] The vast majority (88%) of Colorado's population is white, 21 percent is Latino, 4 percent is African American, 3 percent is Asian, and less than 2 percent is Native American or Alaskan Native.[2] Thirty percent of the state's population is under the age of 18 and 36 percent of persons 25 years and over hold bachelor's degrees, which is 8 percentage points higher than the national average.[3]

Between 2010 and 2011, Colorado's unemployment rate remained flat as there was a minute drop from 8.9 to 8.3 percent.[4] The most numerous employment opportunities can be found in office and administrative support, followed by sales and related occupations. The remaining top five occupations in Colorado are in food preparation and serving, business and financial operations, and education, training, and library occupations.[5] The availability of these positions point to a higher than average education preparation and attainment of Colorado residents. Job growth projections in the state indicate that 74 percent of all employment opportunities by 2020 will require postsecondary credentials.[6] The greatest growth between 2010 and 2020 will be in the education sector at a rate of 38 percent, with arts and entertainment at 33 percent, management of companies and enterprises at 32 percent, and health care and social assistance at 28 percent. Positions in manufacturing, construction, and trade will see growth rates of less than 10 percent.

The educational attainment of Coloradans ages 25 to 64 shows that 68 percent hold postsecondary credentials.[7] Between 2007 and 2012, the average annual growth rate of degrees awarded to Coloradans was 5.6 percent.[8] To meet projected growth rates by 2020, Colorado's institutions of higher education will need to produce at least 200,000 more bachelor's degree holders, or, 1,000 credentials annually, a 2 percent increase above existing production. Workforce trends suggest that Colorado is in a unique position in that the state is slowly returning to prerecession employment figures and has the opportunity to "exceed previous economic accomplishments"[9]; to do so, PreK through higher education will need to play prominent roles to attain its objectives. Yet, while this goal appears to be within reach, data show that Colorado "has a leaking educational pipeline, producing 22 postsecondary degree holders for every 100 students who enter a Colorado high school."[10] Likewise, retention from the first year of college through the second year is low, and the number of students who achieve credentials within six years of enrollment is very low. Put another way, for every 100 ninth graders in Colorado schools, 70 will graduate and 44 of those will go on to college. Of those 44, 29 percent will require some level of developmental education. Only 22 of this group will graduate from college within six years.

Moreover, the significant education attainment disparity between whites and people of color will have long-term detrimental economic impacts if the gaps are not reversed. Attainment rates of Colorado adults aged 25 to 64, by race and ethnicity, demonstrate this disparity as 53 percent of whites and Asian Americans hold a college degree while only 32 percent of blacks, 18 percent of Latinos, and 28 percent of Native Americans have the same.[11] Among the graduating high school class of 2011, 57 percent of students immediately enrolled in college in fall 2011. Broken down by race and ethnicity, Asian American and white students represented the highest enrollments at 69 and 63 percent, respectively, and African Americans at 54 percent. Latino students had the lowest enrollment rates at 42 percent, a gap of 15 percentage points from the state average of 57 percent.[12] Of further note are the retention rates of students. Asian American students had the highest overall retention rates at 87 percent, with the lowest being those of Latino students at 71 percent, representing a gap of 16 percentage points.[13] These statistics point to what has been referred to as the "Colorado Paradox,"[14] wherein transplants to Colorado inflate the state's degree levels but Colorado high school graduates are less likely to complete their education journey all the way through college degree attainment.

Guiding higher education in Colorado are the Colorado Commission of Higher Education (CCHE) and the Colorado Department of Higher Education (CDHE). The CCHE was established in 1965 by the state legislature and was given charge to address all matters relative to higher education. As a coordinating board, the CCHE consists of 11 members appointed by the governor and, with the consent of the Senate,[15] serve a term of four years. In 1985, the role of the CCHE was further defined by giving them authority over governance procedures such as reviewing and approving degree policies, establishing institution-wide admissions standards and enrollment policies, and determining institutional roles and missions, amongst other responsibilities.[16] Its authority was further augmented by HB1187 in the same year, which called for "institutions of higher education [to] be held accountable for demonstrable improvements in student knowledge, capacities, and skills between entrance and graduation."[17] The CCHE was given oversight of the development, implementation, and measurement of institutional goals related to student learning and growth. The results of these accountability provisions would be reported to the governor and the General Assembly on an annual basis.

Senate Bill 08-818[18] in 2008 further clarified and defined the role of the Department of Education separate from that of the CCHE, and in certain instances, responsibilities originally assigned to the CCHE were reassigned to the CDHE. The bill specifically delineated the role of the CDHE such that their primary responsibility was to implement the "duly adopted policies of the Colorado Commission on Higher Education."[19] In so doing, the CDHE became responsible for such items as review of new institutional programs, evaluation of existing programs, the administration of extension and continuation programs, and the submission of analysis of institutional progress. Where defined, as in the case of review of newly proposed institutional programs, the CDHE would review submitted proposals by institutions of higher education and submit to the CCHE its recommendations. One of the most critical functions of the CDHE was to work closely with the public system of education to develop policies, procedures, and practices that would "facilitate the transition of students between systems."[20] In doing so, the CDHE would work with institutions and their governing boards to set up reporting mechanisms with the secondary system and facilitate relationship building between faculty and teachers.

State Priorities and Goals

Colorado has taken aggressive action to herald innovation and change in education through state policy. Reforms beginning in the 1980s and continuing through the present day have focused on the broad themes of access, rigor, accountability, and alignment[21] to ensure seamless pathways between K–12 and higher education. The Postsecondary Enrollment Options Act of 1988 made it possible for juniors and seniors to enroll in college courses at public and private institutions free of charge and have the capacity to graduate in five years with both a high school diploma and an associate's degree. In 1993, Colorado was among the states leading the standards reform movement with the development of Colorado's Model Content Standards in the content areas of reading, writing, mathematics, science, history, and geography. These standards, along with the statewide Colorado State Assessment Program (CSAP), measure student progress against state-level benchmarks that clearly articulated what students should know and be able to do at the time they leave high school.

In the new century, increased attention was given to the preparation of students to pursue higher education opportunities post high school graduation. In 2001, the Colorado legislature mandated that all students in their junior year must be assessed to (1) determine achievement and readiness to pursue postsecondary options and (2) "identify potential areas of academic weakness before graduation."[22] The ACT college admissions exam was therefore selected by the Colorado Department of Education (CDE) to measure said preparation toward higher education and has been administered to juniors since the time of adoption. With the implementation of the ACT as a readiness indicator, several objectives were achieved, as the test would serve as

> a measure of the extent to which high schools were preparing students for college, a tool for pushing high school curriculum into better alignment with college requirements, and a way to help students overcome a barrier to college acceptance.[23]

Because the ACT, otherwise known as the ACT for Colorado, was administered exactly as the national college entrance exam, students attained concrete knowledge and experience with a tool widely used by colleges and universities across the United States for the purposes of admission.

The preceding reforms that began to address questions of standards, preparation, and alignment seemingly paved the way for the large-scale reform in 2008 known as the Colorado Achievement Plan for Kids (CAP4K). The CAP4K required the PreK–12 system to work closely with higher education to reconsider the system of education as one continuous journey beginning in early childhood all the way through postsecondary degree attainment. Building off of the work of the P-20 Coordinating Council established by then governor Bill Ritter in 2007, this landmark legislation thus required the CDE to collaborate with the CDHE to

> align the public education system from preschool through postsecondary and workforce readiness [to] ensure that a student who enters school ready to succeed and achieves the required level of proficiency on standards as he or she progresses through elementary and secondary education will have achieved postsecondary and workforce readiness when the student graduates from high school if not earlier. As such, the student will be ready to enter the workforce or to enter postsecondary without need for remediation.[24]

The process for implementation of reform was significantly long, with 2014 as the identified year for full implementation. In the years between the passage of CAP4K and the duration of this study, two efforts took place simultaneously. First, the Graduation Guidelines Council was charged with developing high school guidelines that articulated a shared vision for the "value and meaning of a high school diploma"[25] and delineated the minimum expectations, components, and resources that would support students to attain that diploma. Second, Colorado developed postsecondary and workforce-readiness "endorsements" that affirm a student's readiness for postsecondary education and which would give students "priority consideration for admission in Colorado's selective and highly selective institutions."[26] Underlying the development of these guidelines and endorsements was the belief that "seat time" and the accumulation of credits was insufficient to determine college-readiness, and guidelines instead focused on proficiency, or a "floor of competencies regardless of work interests."[27] Finally, the Colorado State Board of Education adopted the Common Core State Standards in 2010. This adoption of the standards, toward which Colorado played a critical role, sets not only clear educational expectations that are common across the states, but also ostensibly indicate a student's readiness for college and career.

In the same year, the CCHE released Colorado's Strategic Plan for Higher Education,[28] which identified the challenges facing higher education and offered key recommendations for the path forward in the areas of affordability, access, quality, and accountability. Recommendation number three reflected the broader themes of alignment and coordination evident in CAP4K; at the same time, the goal acknowledged that changes will not happen overnight as students leaving K–12 will not all be fully prepared for postsecondary work. The report states:

> We need to better prepare students for college-level work when they arrive at college. To do that, we need to start earlier in their education to get them on a path toward college. We also need to support the best approaches to remedial education in higher education, as many students will still need that support out of high school.[29]

This recommendation was particularly apt given the state of education at the time of its development.

The data presented earlier are borne out at one of our institutions under study:

> Students coming from the front range—Colorado Springs and the Pueblo area. They probably do better but surprisingly they don't persist to graduate at the same rate as local students. We lose about 40% of freshmen and that has been consistent. About 30% never graduate. We have a high % of first-generation students, highest percentage of Pell students among Colorado 4-years, about 80% are Pell-eligible, 50% are Pell grantees, and about 30% are Hispanic.

This goal to improve the delivery of developmental education and move students into credit-bearing courses was echoed in the 2012 revision of the Colorado Master Plan, which, among other directives, calls for the improvement of students' trajectories through postsecondary education by improving basic skills education, providing enhanced support services, and decreasing the amount of time required for students to complete a degree.[30] Specifically, the revised Master Plan challenges higher education to first, eliminate disparities of outcome between those assigned to developmental education and those that are not; second, take steps to improve persistence from one year to the next; third, increase the number of credit hours accumulated by students in the first year; and last, decrease time to completion.

State Developmental Education Policies

The Statewide Remedial Education Policy guiding Colorado institutions of higher education was adopted on November 4, 2004. Though this policy was revised on December 5, 2013, and went into effect in fall 2014, the revision will not factor into this discussion as it was not in effect at the time of the study.

According to the statewide developmental education policy, upon admission and enrollment, students in Colorado's colleges and universities are assessed in the areas of mathematics, reading, and writing.[31] To successfully place in college-level courses, students must (1) score a 19 or higher in math, 18 or higher in writing, and 17 or higher in reading on the ACT; (2) score 430 or higher on the SAT Verbal for reading, 440 or higher on the SAT Verbal for writing, and 460 or higher on the SAT mathematics; and (3) score 85 or higher on the Elementary Algebra test, 95 or higher on the Sentence Skills test, and 80 or higher on the Reading Comprehension test on the Accuplacer assessment. Students who do not qualify for enrollment in college-level courses are required to enroll in developmental education classes in the first semester following the placement test and complete said coursework within the first 30 semester hours of enrollment. Students who fail to meet the 30-hour threshold must meet with an academic advisor before enrolling in additional courses.

Section 4.02.02 of the Statewide Remedial Education Policy prohibits four-year colleges and universities from receiving general fund support for developmental education courses. Each of these institutions, however, "may offer basic skills courses by contracting with a Colorado public community college or on a cash-funded basis."[32] The exception to policy are two institutions that serve a two-year function within the system of higher education and are approved to receive state general funds for the delivery of developmental education courses. State policy further requires all institutions to collect and submit to the CCHE data on students enrolled in developmental education courses. Data to be collected include demographics, school districts of origin, year of high school graduation, areas of developmental instruction, and credit hours earned. These data are shared with the education committees of the state legislature, the Department of Education, and the school districts across the state.

Institutional Responses

Institutional leaders discussed at length the natural tension that exists between the rhetoric of public policy and the reality of their institutional contexts. The aggressive reform in Colorado over the past several decades implies a commitment to a new vision of education that identifies developmental education as a vital component of the college completion agenda. Institutional administrators, however, were not fully convinced that developmental education was a clear priority for state legislators. One university administrator, for example, remarked:

> We articulate as a monolith that [developmental education] is important to us, but if you look at the priority we set in terms of dedicating resources in an intentional way to developmental education, I think that message is

a little different, and I think it's true for most institutions. People will say it's exceedingly important for us, but you'll see that with resources it might not be consistent.

This reference to funding support was shared by others at both the system level and across the colleges and universities. The lack of resources may in part be due to the financial challenges experienced by Colorado during the recession. In 2007, for example, the share of higher education expenditures was 14 percent; higher than the national average of 10.2 percent.[33] Between 1991 and 2007, funding per full-time equivalent (FTE) remained relatively stable at an average of about US$8,000. Postrecession expenditures, however, showed a dramatic decrease as higher education expenditures, as a share of total state expenditures, went down to 9.1 percent, falling well below the national average for the first time in many years.

Information and Accountability

Colorado's sweeping legislation requiring PreK–12 and higher education to work together makes "information and accountability" unique to that of the other states in this study. Beginning with the roll-out of the CSAP, information and accountability have been a thread in the fabric of reform in Colorado. In 2001, the state legislature ordered the development of a statewide data system that would make it possible to trace student academic progress. In 2006, a unique student identifier was created that not only made it possible to track students over time, but allowed stakeholders to follow students even if they changed schools or districts.[34] Higher education soon followed as they were required by the legislature to use the same student identifier no later than 2009, thus making it possible for Colorado's Departments of Education and Higher Education to share data for the very first time. In doing so, systems could match students' histories and perhaps begin to identify academic weaknesses long before students entered college.

In fact, a system administrator discussed the importance of this development in a report that was issued in 2011. In this report,[35] a collaboration between the Departments of Education and Higher Education took CSAP and ACT results from the graduating class of 2009 and matched students enrolled in Colorado colleges who required some level of developmental education. The results of their analysis indicated that students who ultimately were required to enroll in developmental education could have been predicted as early as the third grade. The predictive utility of the ACT and the CSAP, they found, suggested that while not perfect, could help to identify students with identified weaknesses and target intervention efforts well before they entered higher education.

While the potential for the sharing of information is great, there still seemed to be a lack of common understanding about how best to utilize these data sources. As one of the administrators responsible for the report remarked, "We struggled with getting the message out. It was DOA. It got no press. A few legislators were interested, and wanted to do more, but what?" Another administrator noted that they produce a number of reports on developmental education, the most recent of which included high school information. Still another administrator described the system's ability to "share data with P-12, [which is] a pipeline to develop a longitudinal database" but as with the previous administrator, there loomed the question of "what's next?" Another administrator affirmed, "We have not looked carefully at all of the ways in which the data intersect, and frankly, that's one of the things I want to accomplish in terms of retention and completion."

Assessment and Placement

Interestingly, while the broader issues of information sharing between systems elicited a fair amount of discontent, the same could not be said about the assessment and placement policies enacted by the state. Recall, all postsecondary institutions are required to enroll students in developmental education if they do not meet identified ACT, SAT, or Accuplacer cut-off scores. In some institutions, administrators adhered to a strict interpretation of policy. One four-year college administrator, for example, remarked, "We place students in the appropriate level and make sure they pass or don't go forward in their sequence." Another administrator observed, "We don't have a limit on remedial course taking...it reads that if students haven't completed the remedial courses successfully, we start limiting the classes they take so they can focus and be successful."

There are, however, other institutional administrators who recognize the limitations of the cut scores, placement guidelines, and for some, the definition of developmental education itself. One such administrator explained, "Developmental education used to be called 'remedial,' [which] implied that students have seen it before. That's not true. I'm first generation myself and I didn't really have a model." For this administrator, the precollegiate experience did not prepare him nor did it expose him to a system of selection and sorting at the college level. Building off of this premise, another administrator said, "We know assessments are blunt instruments and we can't distinguish between 'I knew it, but forgot it,' or 'I never learned it.'" Because of the uncertainty of what the cut score really means in regard to its diagnostic capacity, another administrator commented:

> The state set the minimum scores for ACT that determines [placement] in developmental education. Students are supposedly supposed to complete developmental education in one year, but practically, that is not the case. I am glad that the state has not been very strongly regulatory about this—they're not giving us money on it, so it's good they're not regulating the crap out of us.

Instead, as this administrator implies, institutions must adhere to the cut scores as laid out in policy, but seemingly have the flexibility to design programs and advise students into the most appropriate coursework or course format that will be met with success. If there was dissatisfaction with aspects of the policy on assessment and placement, it seemed to be more about what can be done to lessen the need for developmental education—and that led to additional comments about information sharing across the CDHE and CDE.

Thus, while the potential for information sharing between systems and data-based decision-making exists, there remains a lack of coordination that permeates the education enterprise. Unsurprisingly, participants talked a great deal about the need for greater collaboration that extends beyond rhetoric but gets to the heart of the issues plaguing education. An administrator observed, "K–12 has been promoting students all along knowing they are not at grade level. The assessment data being used was unrelated to student ability. It's strange how it's not being used for student progress. It's hard not to point fingers." Another college administrator reflected on the current state of collaboration:

> There is a verbal commitment to addressing the issue of developmental education but I don't know of a real concerted leadership or financial commitment to get K–12 and higher education on the same page and really work through some goals. It's fortunate to see K–12 and higher education at the table today, than was the case three to five years ago, but [we] haven't tackled really difficult issues [yet].

Consequently, because the hard issues have not been "tackled," there is the sense among institutional administrators who we talked to that they are still working in silos and that the commitment to developmental education, by default, remains at the institutional level. An administrator at a rural institution argued:

When they tell us that "you're not going to get money for teaching remedial classes," my opinion is in the noise. We have to respond not by saying, "then we're not going to do it," but respond by saying, "it still has to get done." Success of students depends on this piece.

Not only does it have to be done, but there are serious consequences that result from not tackling the tough questions, notably the policy on not funding developmental education on certain campuses. Another administrator remarked:

> [Developmental education policy] hurts a lot of students, especially in the southern schools. We're a commuter school. [We] serve a lot of small towns and minority students, students who are nontraditional and have not taken math class in over 20 years.

While these realities raise tough questions about local controls over graduation requirements, the continued underpreparation of students and who should foot the bill for developmental education, there is reason for optimism as administrators recognize the potential for collaboration and growth. One administrator remarked, "Have you seen the strategic plan? [It's] the first time remedial education is in a strategic plan...first time remediation got acknowledged as a challenge and a priority instead of a complaint." Still another administrator acknowledged not only the potential of the legislation but where responsibility for action lies when he said:

> CAP4K [is] developing [the] P-20 pipeline; [it's] landmark legislation [that] the state took very, very seriously. Individual responsibility for relationships with high schools lies with the colleges. Some have phenomenal relationships, pockets of great relationships, but at the highest level, not so good.

Ultimately, until the issues of information sharing and collaboration are resolved, accountability will rest with the schools and their adherence to mission and sense of purpose. As an administrator resolved:

> In our philosophy, and as stated in our strategic plan, we're an access institution and we want to provide excellent learning and teaching opportunities for all students. The reality is that some students come in where no one wants them to be. Some students do surprisingly well, [and] some well-prepared students flame out because they are not used to so much freedom.

Administrators acknowledged that in most places, developmental education is viewed from the point of view that it is a "sink or swim" perspective, but for these institutions that seek to fulfill their institutional missions, despite public policy, they do what they can with what they have to shepherd their students through their college careers. One administrator concluded, "We know that it is a sink or swim process but we want to give them every support we can."

Instructional Delivery

How institutions provide developmental education varied based on what they are able to do. As previously noted, policy dictates that only two-year institutions can provide developmental education programs; though the four-year institutions are not prohibited from doing so, they are not eligible to use state funds to support its delivery. The realities of their environments, however, make it near-to-impossible to not consider how best to provide this course of study. One college administrator observed:

> Coming from a science background, I am surprised that the highest failure rates are in art appreciation, history, and government. Usually by the end of the first semester, [students] will have a D average because of all of the writing requirements.

While he referred to students who did not need developmental education, this administrator recognized that the transition from high school to college has not always left recent high school graduates prepared to be "college students," even those who have been identified as being college-ready. As a result of this lack of congruence between preparation and a definition of "college-readiness," postsecondary institutional leaders must be acutely cognizant of the methods, strategies, and supports that can make students enrolled in developmental education courses successful.

The four-year institutional administrators we spoke with described the many ways they undertake to deliver developmental courses. Administrators alternately talked about three college programs: Portfolio, Move Forward, and the Academic Transitions program.[36] These innovations resulted from the recognition that something "different" needed to take place to promote increased success through the developmental sequence. In addition, the sheer volume of students in developmental education likewise prompted action in a different direction. As one administrator described:

We struggle with what classes to put them in when 40% of students need developmental education. We have three levels of developmental math. We're a writing and reading intensive liberal arts college, so we have to read and write a lot. [But] if you're in two or more developmental education courses, then we have a sequence of courses to help get them up to speed.

Because of the challenge of students who come to higher education with a high need for developmental instruction, one institution developed the Academic Transitions program to give students who are required to enroll in two or more developmental courses the opportunity to move through the program with additional supports, including access to an academic success strategies course. According to institutional administrators, students who complete this program have higher than average retention rates and higher grade-point averages (GPAs) than typical first-year students. At the time of the study, administrators were exploring the option of offering the Academic Transitions program as concurrent coursework during students' final year in high school. One administrator observed, however, that such an approach to developmental education "brings up a related question about resolving if it's the college's responsibility to be teaching developmental education while students are in high school—it just adds another level of complexity."

Similar to the Academic Transitions program is Move Forward, a summer bridge program that gives students the opportunity to take developmental education courses during the summer while living on the college campus. Moreover, the program makes it possible for students to retake the Accuplacer at any point during the course of the summer, thus giving students the opportunity to place in college-level courses in fall. Like Move Forward, the college Portfolio program is a 5–9-week session wherein students can sign up to take two to three developmental education courses at a nominal fee and receive discounted housing and meals. At the time of the study, this was a new program, but given the success of other programs like Move Forward and Academic Transitions, institutional administrators were confident they would get the numbers to fill their spaces.

Learning Communities and Supplementary Instruction were other innovations referenced by institutional leaders, noting that these programs are connected to content courses such as psychology, sociology, and government. In these, "University 101" is included, where students receive a combination of academic and learning success skills. Another model described was an online program, which allowed students to move at their own pace. As described, students self-select to participate in the online course that has an instructor available with office hours like all professors.

Using this as a model, the institution at the time of the interview was looking to launch a pilot beginning in middle school wherein students would be able to pass into a college-eligible math course by their senior year.

Given the collaborative nature of reform in Colorado, administrators likewise talked about concurrent enrollments that enable high school students to acquire college credit on the road to graduation. One administrator said, "Legislation has made opportunities for concurrent or dual enrollment for high school students in the postsecondary sector, and while most of the activity is on the public school side with the community colleges, some four-years do it as well." This gives students not only the benefit of accessing a higher level of learning but also receiving an introduction to what it means to be a college student and the demands associated with that new identity.

Having these courses on campus, for many of these administrators, was akin to a badge of honor. One administrator noted:

> It's nice that we have developmental education in a high school setting because students have the rest of the college experience [to] use their financial aid to pay for these opportunities, get residential life experience, and other enrichments available to college students.

In taking ownership of these programs, postsecondary institutions expose students to the possibilities of what it means to be a full-fledged college student, with all of its privileges and responsibilities.

Finally, there is a sense that developmental education is more than just a focus on basic skills. Rather, higher education leaders seemed to view it as an interdisciplinary effort that requires ongoing engagement with other departments. An administrator noted:

> Our integration and articulation with faculty and curriculum and the 100-level coursework—we work very much with other departments like psychology. [We ask] "What does reading and writing ability look like to you? What do your students need to have so they're ready for comp?" Also [we] need to have connections with middle and high school teachers.

Similarly, another administrator noted the importance of understanding the overall function of developmental education within the larger vision of the institution and her own personal role in guiding the departments. This administrator reflected:

> I am doing academic work but not necessarily college level academic programming so that model of having a stand-alone developmental education

department didn't really fit here. Developmental education here is an interdisciplinary effort coordinating among multiple departments. We are working with the testing center, student engagement and success.

Given this new perspective, greater attention is given not just to who is hired to work in these departments but who is most appropriate to work with the unique population of students. Although an administrator responsible for the coordination of developmental education at another institution was pleased to announce, "And they fund my position, which is something," she ruefully admitted the need to do more. She said, "[The institution] could do more...all five of [the department's] positions are not tenure track instructors and are paid $35,000 a year which is very low and they don't have the protection associated with tenure." Moreover, as another administrator remarked, "A typical Ph.D. may not be geared towards [developmental education]...we need special instructors...they need to have a lot of compassion."

Clearly, developmental education was not just an academic endeavor for these institutions, rather developmental education was viewed much more holistically to address all of the varied needs students bring to the classroom.

Fiscal Strategies

Financial shortfalls after the recession had some real implications for Colorado postsecondary institutions. One university administrator put it this way: "The total higher education budget in FY12 will very likely be about $519 million for all of higher education. When you think about that and how it is spread over the campuses that we have, less than 10 percent of the total budget comes from the state. At some institutions, it's five percent." The reality of providing services to students under these tight financial conditions prompted a college administrator to remark, "The state is in some ways more constructive than it has been in the past, but they're searching for the magic pill."

For developmental education, this "magic pill" is particularly elusive as institutions had to grapple with the restrictions placed upon them by the state legislature. More specifically, they had to come to grips with the developmental education policy that either permits or limits the use of general education funds to support instruction for students considered not yet college-ready. This lack of funding for developmental education, combined with the reductions in support arising from federal changes to student aid, is especially hard on institutions with missions to maintain open-access and/or serve a geographical location that is likely to have a large population of students who are in need of additional supports, both academic and financial. Yet, the profile of students one institution serves—"80% Pell-eligible, a large first-generation population, located in a region that serves an economically depressed area, and a large number of students who are high need financially and academically"—means that any loss of financial support will have an immense impact on the institution. For students, that impact will be tragically detrimental, as another college administrator observed:

> Reducing Pell awards will have a huge impact on students and in turn on institutions. State cuts will lead to higher tuition rates. We've always been the least expensive residential four-year. If the Pell piece goes away and need-based state aid is cut, there will be kids who won't go to college.

In light of the goals of the 2010 Master Plan and the revised 2012 edition, wherein "restoring fiscal balance" is a priority to ensure enrollment demands, the lack of funds and the resulting consequences compromise the objectives laid out and the ultimate success of the plan for Colorado higher education.

To make up for the lack of state funds earmarked for developmental education, and decreasing federal funds for state aid, institutions have had to identify new strategies to support the college-going ability of students. Depending on where one stood in the debate of developmental education, an administrator commented, "One party is, 'we should collect money from K–12 for not doing their job and not admit those students.'" One institution we visited once charged students more for developmental courses, explaining

> For a period of time we were adding insult to injury, charging an additional $50 fee to students needing developmental education. Now they are basically another general fund course. For any course that has disposable materials they may pay a little extra. There is a so-called fund tied to the lottery that the community colleges get a slice. We get a sliver of a slice. Last year it was $36,000. It ain't enough to do anything with.

These additional dollars collected from students were described as a kind of "tax" that were not always specified to be used to support the delivery of developmental education through administrative advocacy, These dollars, however, are now being used for the purposes of tutoring and additional faculty support. The latter is particularly relevant because as an administrator noted, "We don't have professional development set aside for faculty teaching developmental education; [those students are] a different population with different needs in the classroom."

Given the challenges above, many of which are often unfavorable to students, the administrators commented about the various strategies they have employed to lessen the burden that students and families assume to afford enrollment in higher education. A system administrator remarked:

> Community colleges can use state funding for remediation but baccalaureate institutions cannot. It does not mean that the baccalaureate institutions are not doing it, but it's done on a cash or private support basis. The four-years are clever at securing funding, stacking courses, embedding remediation in credit courses.

Another administrator talked about their distance education program, which as a cash program, has helped to generate revenue for over a decade. An administrator from an institution that is geographically isolated and serves a high proportion of students with academic and financial needs, described trying out a new tuition model that offers a flat rate for 12–20 credits as a means to encourage students to take on more courses and potentially even pursue a minor. This particular strategy aligns with research that suggests that students who pursue a course load of "high academic intensity" are more likely to persist from one year to the next.[37]

For many of these institutional administrators, the use of Federal Title V funds and private dollars from philanthropy helped to support the bulk of their work in moving their initiatives forward. The institution referenced above, with the unique dual role to serve the two- and four-year function, actively sought out these dollars to support the high volume of students it enrolls with high needs. In seeking out these funds, they are able to support programs that move students quickly through the developmental education sequence. Others were able to hire tutors or offer summer programming for students who demonstrated higher academic achievement and do not need to enroll in a traditional semester-long program of developmental education. As an administrator observed:

> We have had a series of Title V grants to launch some first-year programs. Each of those necessarily may not have had a 100% success [rate] but students engaged in those programs...are making it through the first year at a higher rate than before. We've [been able to] institutionalize what we started and have several other [programs] in various levels of development and institutionalization.

Another administrator talked about using funding in a slightly different way, wherein the student is looked upon from a more holistic perspective, rather than just from the standpoint of academic need. This administrator said, "Title V funds two student advocates who work as case managers to help students get child care, domestic violence [counseling], transportation—if we can get students in our class with regularity I know we have the best instructors who are helping students [to be successful]."

These fiscal strategies are just some of a number of tactics Colorado institutions employed to ensure increased success among students in developmental education. Though they are conscious of the harsh realities of this proposition on the campuses, many nonetheless recognize they have no choice—they have to deliver these programs. Whereas one administrator remarked:

> Remediation is a financial issue, an efficiency issue, an effectiveness issue, a pipeline issue. We're devoted to students successfully completing a postsecondary credential, but remediation gets in the way of that. It hits everything we do. In addition to the $19 million the state pays, there are the $10 to $15 in student monies that go towards remediation. Remediation is a costly conversation.

Another administrator, however, noted:

> Right now we have a Title V program that gets Wal-Mart Grant [funding]—both fund [two support programs]. The Wal-Mart grant is ending next year. This is a very successful program and we are hoping the university will be able keep the program despite the cuts. There is lot of faculty buy-in; they have a lot of power, so they might be able to keep it.

The commitment, the buy-in, and the advocacy demonstrated by these administrators (despite the cost) is also indicative of the various levels of academic and social support they endeavor to provide to their students to facilitate greater success in and out of developmental education classrooms.

Academic and Social Support

A great deal of time was spent by administrators discussing how their sense of mission fed their sense of responsibility to deliver programming that addressed the affective domain—those areas that can substantially contribute to a student's success or failure in the academic environment. For the four-year institutions, this was especially important given the constraints of policy and the creative lengths they went to hone in and meet the needs of their unique student populations.

One administrator talked about the supports necessary in and out of the classroom; not from the point of view of academic prowess and the know-how of faculty, but rather in regard to environment and what elements of that environment would foster engagement and cultivate success. In describing a new approach to tutoring, an administrator remarked:

> The math tutoring is unique—students meet one-on-one with tutors for 50 minutes so that really helps students who have lower skills to bond and trust with tutors and get the time they need to improve. We take the access responsibility very seriously and make sure those who haven't had the opportunity to get those skills [do].

Similarly, another administrator observed:

> These students need small classes and intrusive advising; [they] need constant care and attention on a regular basis and we'll get some amazing success stories. "I was in developmental education and came here just to party." But now they are in a Ph.D. program [or] a med program in Denver. We are working on intrusive advising and we want to improve.

Further building on this thought, another administrator connected these practices with the completion agenda being promulgated by the state. The "irony" of the completion agenda, she remarked, is that it forces institutions to consider not working with students who may need developmental education but may go on to earn advanced degrees. The state's mandated admissions index, which is a score based on GPA and performance on a standardized test, will identify student admissions eligibility. As schools raise the minimum index for eligibility, more students with developmental academic needs have fewer choices as to where they can attend college. The move toward greater selectivity challenges the state's commitment to increase the number of degree recipients, as a community college system administrator observed:

> The irony is that the goal of the completion agenda was to increase the number of degrees; and if we look at the percent of the population who need degrees, the lowest students who need remediation [come] from that population."

For administrators, the verbal commitment made by the state legislators does not resonate with the realities on the ground of college and university campuses. As such, campus administrators talked about how they frame their discussions related to developmental education within and outside the institution to ensure that the needs of their students are understood and supported. One college administrator explained:

> When I have the opportunity to talk with legislators, I tell them that our little [developmental education] program has three [high school] valedictorians, people who are best in their class, 4.0 high achieving students who are for whatever reason [in this program]...Someone has to cover that gap.

Moreover, institutional administrators wanted to make clear that their commitment to their students is not a drain on resources, but an opportunity to help students reach their full potential. Another administrator remarked:

> There are cases where fantastically talented individuals come in ill prepared or something. Talented students will be working on some form of scholarship...there will be talented students who need remedial work. As students realize "I can be successful in my chosen field and be a scholar, it may be I will need remedial work in writing or math, but I can still be excellent."

To deny these students the opportunity to cultivate their scholarship because of a presumed deficiency is, according to the institutional administrators we spoke to, a violation of social justice that cannot be ignored, either by institutional covenant or personal belief. For one administrator, whose students are "more than one-half Latino, many minorities, Pell-eligible, athletes, lower SES," to do otherwise is to essentially "whiten the graduating class."

For colleges within distinctive geographical constraints, the challenge is just as great, if not greater. As an administrator explained:

> We have a unique mission in this part of Colorado and our population. We are a Hispanic Serving Institution and nearly a Minority Serving Institution, but we also have a unique relationship with the town. The town is not going to respect us if they're sending us their students and they don't leave here as better-educated individuals. We need to recognize there is a bit of a hole in your portfolio, and how we can fix it. It's a responsibility.

Given the responsibility these institutional administrators face, the approach they take in the classroom, in their advisement centers, and in their centers of student support must adhere to their academic and social support portfolio of the whole.

As such, this much more holistic perspective applied to all of their students, and not just the students enrolled in developmental education courses. An administrator observed:

> Sometimes students don't need academic support but they need support because they're first generation. They might keep a GPA of 3.4...[and while] they might not have academic needs [they] are looking for a place to belong, to connect with, social support.

Another administrator commented on the importance of looking at the strengths of the student, building on that strength, and being able to articulate how either math or reading would contribute to the development of that strength. She explained:

> I look at students holistically, but don't know that we do that as an institution...It isn't so much as pigeonholing students, but to turn the story around, and say, "to be successful you need a strong foundation, and here are various levels of preparation." You can be successful as a musician, but you need college algebra, and if you're struggling with math, it will be hard to mature as a musician, especially in theory.

Another administrator discussed the importance of identifying career paths early on to ensure retention of students from one year to the next. This was especially true among first-year students whose high attrition rates have raised questions. The administrator explained:

> The first year is where we have the highest dropout rate for high school students. They're trying to figure out if they really belong. Taking courses they don't like, don't really see the prize. Career exploration, guidance, understanding labor market info, shadowing—connecting with a career goal is critical because they have to get through remediation but need to see, "is this suffering worth it?"

Finally, a college administrator noted that for some of his students who are among the most underserved in the entire state, the needs they have are perhaps those that many in the rest of the state take for granted. He argued, "For developmental education students, it's not just academic, they're worried about transportation, health problems, someone to watch their kids, food on the table. We try as an institution to help them as much as we can."

The underlying theme across these efforts is the attention paid to the whole student and not just the academic proficiencies they have upon enrollment. The "case management" approach to developmental education, which may include strategies such as early alert systems and more intensive advising, helps to ensure that students receive the attention they need and that the institution is aware of their progress. An administrator who talked about the increased use of online resources to serve the high numbers of students needing developmental education noted that, in these settings, it is difficult to provide this level of support. He said, "Wraparound services are so important for developmental education students, but hard to provide to online courses."

Although acknowledging the challenges placed upon them by policy and by sheer volume of need, administrators proudly extolled the value of their programs and the successes they encountered. These success stories, in their eyes, are those that need to be shared with a skeptical public that questions the value, the expense, and the placement of developmental education in higher education. In doing so, they raise awareness of the benefits of developmental education to students, notably the opportunity to access higher education. As an administrator concluded:

> I want to take a photo of a graduating class and identify the developmental education courses—students who make it through developmental education are more likely to graduate, even more than those students who didn't need developmental education. It's important to tell those stories in this economic climate. There is blaming of students [who] are not seen as entitled to a college education. [We need to] remind them they're not dummies.

Conclusion

Colorado has made extensive efforts to utilize public policy as a lever to stimulate educational innovation related to developmental education. The 2004 Statewide Remedial Education Policy attempted to ensure that students enroll in and complete the required developmental education courses early in their college career. Furthermore, this policy prohibited funding of developmental education courses in four-year colleges and universities. In 2008, the CAP4K attempted to reframe education as one continuous journey beginning in early childhood all the way through postsecondary degree attainment with the intention that developmental education would no longer be necessary. The 2012 revision of the Colorado Master Plan attempted to address student trajectories through higher education and eliminate disparities in outcomes between those taking developmental education courses and those that did not. Extensive data collection related to developmental education has also been required by state policy.

A tension however, remains between the rhetoric and the reality of state policy as it is implemented at higher education institutions. While there is a verbal commitment between the K–12 and postsecondary sectors to work collaboratively, some feel there has not been effective leadership to tackle the most difficult issues and get beyond finger pointing. While state policy leaders promote increasing college attainment rates, the reality of restricted funding for developmental education courses challenges the ability of four-year institutions to effectively support those students considered underprepared for college and ultimately to fulfill their institutional missions. While the extensive amount of data collected means the potential for data-based decision-making exists, a lack of coordination between educational sectors and lack of common understanding of what to do with the data has prevented this potential from being achieved.

The degree to which data are being collected and shared between the CDE and the CDHE is impressive. Not only do the data address rates of enrollment, persistence, degree attainment, and other critical factors, but the data also show where in the state students are doing well and where improvement can occur. These data sources can be used for more effective decision making with regard to early interventions targeted toward students in the early and the middle grades, but also to assess the use of innovative instructional practices such as those used by our study participants. Moreover, the relative flexibility of policy regulation means that postsecondary settings can address the needs of students in developmental education with supports and services that are best tailored to their unique contexts. The fact that the state covers a wide expanse of urban, rural, and suburban environments, however, means that there cannot be a one-size-fits-all approach to the question of developmental education. While state policy seems to take such an approach, administrators in our study demonstrated what is possible through the resourceful use of funds (both public and private) and adherence to institutional mission.

Nonetheless the leaky education pipeline is a concern that must be addressed across the entire system of education. This involves all aspects of education, from teacher and instructional quality, to the most effective diagnostic tools that will ensure that placement of students in developmental or college-level courses is accurate. Equally important are academic and social supports that are holistic in scope and assume a case management approach that accounts for the whole student and not just his or her academic capacity. Finally, Colorado has moved toward a system of standards that may ensure students are college- and career-ready. Yet, until barriers are addressed, whether they be policy limitations, financial burdens by students having to pay out of pocket, or raising the admissions index, Colorado's most vulnerable will be placed at greater risk of underachievement and will delay the state's goal of increasing degree attainment by 2020. We must, as an administrator remarked, acknowledge the role of higher education and hold true to its purpose. As he said:

> Coming up on the 150th anniversary of the land grant university—it's a covenant with the people and something we hold sacred. Wring your hands or someone's else's hands regarding remediation, but it's our problem. We could push them through or we could help them.

7

North Carolina

Of all the five states, North Carolina had the lowest rate of students enrolled in developmental education, and enrollment varied from institution to institution. Indeed, unsuccessful proposals by the state legislature to end developmental education led some institutions to make changes to their course offerings. Despite these changes, the institutions represented in this case study show a strong institutional commitment to serving students who may be underprepared, oftentimes without much consideration of the cost.

State Context

Public institutions in North Carolina are governed by two consolidated governing boards (one for four-year public institutions and one for two-year public institutions), which have broad authority over academic policies and budget decisions. Recently, however, the Board of Governors of four-year institutions diverted much of their authority to the Boards of Trustees of each individual institution.

Unlike other states in this study, North Carolina higher education was less affected by the economic downturn that began in 2008, at least initially. While the state faced approximately US$235 million in total state cuts since 2008, North Carolina increased the proportion of state spending on higher education from 17.8 percent in 2009 to 19.2 percent in 2010. In fact, the General Assembly, North Carolina's legislature fully funded enrollment growth in the state's two higher education systems: the University of North Carolina (UNC) system and the North Carolina Community College System (NCCCS). Thus, North Carolina institutions were able to maintain academic programs and most student support services during the period of this study. Most recently, however, state funding for higher education has been cut by nearly 25 percent between 2008 and 2014.[1]

Still, the state's investment in higher education was critical to their success as North Carolina has the second highest six-year graduation rate (59%) of our five states (second only to Colorado) in 2010. Further, the state had the highest graduation rates for African American (44%) and Latino (61%) students among our five states.[2] Graduation rates in North Carolina were the highest among Asian American and Pacific Islanders (AAPI) where 73.6 percent graduated within six years of enrollment. Graduation rates among white students was 64.6 percent.

Three-year graduation rates at community colleges were more in line with the other four states in this study. The overall three-year graduation rate was 19.7 percent. African American (8.6%) and Latino (12.6%) graduation rates, however, trailed those of whites (17.3%) and AAPI (13.6%) students. If graduation rates remain the same over the next 10 years, 48 percent of the state's adult population between 25 and 64 years of age are projected to have an associate's degree or higher by 2025.[3]

State Priorities and Goals

One of the long-term priorities for North Carolina has been to provide its citizens access to an affordable and quality higher education. Although recent years have shown an increase in tuition, North Carolina's public colleges and universities remain some of the most affordable in the nation. In 2012, average annual in-state tuition and fees in public four-year colleges was below the nation's average at US$6,223.

In line with its goal for college access, the state is home to 110 public and private colleges and universities. Since 1971, all public baccalaureate degree-granting institutions have been a part of the multicampus UNC system. This university system, which includes 16 four-year universities and 1 residential high school for gifted students (the North Carolina School of Science and Mathematics), serves more than 220,000 students. University campuses vary in terms of mission and degrees offered, including baccalaureate, masters, doctoral, and professional degrees. The state also maintains 58 community colleges allowing residents the ability to access a community college within a 30-minute drive radius. With an estimated 840,000 students, the NCCCS is the third largest community college system in the United States. North Carolina also offers its residents 36 private colleges and universities. Most of the state's college students, however, are enrolled in public institutions. In fact, nearly 68 percent of students enrolled in four-year colleges or universities are enrolled in public four-year universities.

Similar to other states, North Carolina is interested in improving workforce development and increasing degree attainment. The state has undertaken a number of initiatives to reach these goals, including increased accountability and collaboration across systems. The UNC General Administration, for example, manages Pathways of North Carolina. Established in 1999 by the state legislature, Pathways seeks to increase college participation in the state by providing residents with resources for college and career planning, information on financial aid, and a process for prospective students to file electronic applications and transcripts to all 110 North Carolina colleges and universities.

Recently, the state attempted to increase accountability for its public colleges and universities, particularly as it pertains to student success and college performance. Success NC, for example, is a collaboration between the NCCCS and the UNC. It is designed to "assist the community colleges in their remedial instruction" and develop programs that can be implemented in two-year institutions that would also help community college students "who might want to then transfer to a UNC institution and get a baccalaureate degree." Thus, this initiative established by the state legislature in 2009 requires the university and community college systems to work together to increase degree completion in the state of North Carolina. It also requires both systems to annually report to the legislature their progress in meeting stated goals.

Other priorities for the UNC system included teacher education. In fact, one system administrator stated that educating teachers was the system's "highest priority." Some UNC administrators viewed teacher education as another way to tackle the problem of developmental education.

State Developmental Education Policies

North Carolina maintained few statewide policies related to developmental education. In fact, at the time of our study, the only statewide policy related specifically to developmental education was enacted in 1995. The policy required all public higher education colleges and universities to communicate information to public high schools. More specifically, public colleges and universities must provide information on the college performance of high school graduates, including (1) the need for developmental coursework and (2) performance in freshman college-level courses. As a result, the UNC General Administration publishes a "Remedial/ Developmental Education Activities Report" each year.[4] The report includes data on the annual enrollment in developmental instruction, the expenses for developmental activities of the previous year (including the percentage funded by the state), as well as retention and graduation rates of students who took developmental education courses.

While this is the only statewide policy that impacted both four- and two-year public institutions, the state did require the community college system to abide by more policies related to developmental education. The state, for example, required all two-year institutions to assess students for placement into developmental education courses. Although community colleges were not required to maintain a specific common cut score, all had to set a minimum placement exam score to determine placement into developmental or college-level courses.

Although many states have moved away from serving students who are considered underprepared by way of developmental education, this is not the case in North Carolina. Developmental courses are still permitted at both two- and four-year institutions in the state. This does not mean, however, that there has been for a lack of trying on the part of some legislators. In fact, there have been repeated attempts by some members of the state's General Assembly to eliminate developmental education from universities and thereby limiting developmental courses to community colleges.

These repeated attempts by the state legislature to purge these courses from the universities' curricula have led some campus administrators to believe that developmental education was "discouraged" by the state. Although campuses maintained permission to offer developmental courses, many institutions decided to remove developmental courses or developed alternatives, measures that led to a 45 percent decrease in developmental education enrollment at UNC institutions between 1991–92 and 2011–12.[5] An executive administrator attempted to explain why this was the case:

> In the early 1990s, there was a decision made that you couldn't spend state money on remedial education or you were, I don't know if it was you couldn't, but you were discouraged from doing [remedial education]...I think there's a sense that students [who] aren't ready for college, generally, they ought to go to the community college. I think that's the prevailing view here in the state.

Consequently, many institutions had to find ways to maintain their institutional missions of serving the people of North Carolina with the realization that offering developmental education courses at four-year institutions was not a priority of the state.

Institutional Responses

The impact of repeated attempts by the state to eliminate developmental education courses seemed to linger at the two universities that we visited in North Carolina.

Information and Accountability

Since the early 1990s, the North Carolina General Assembly has progressively shown a strong interest in increasing accountability. Institutional administrators in North Carolina frequently expressed concern about being understaffed and unable to spend adequate time preparing and analyzing data reports. Some participants, particularly those within the community college state system, attributed the call for more data to a number of factors, including North Carolina's participation in initiatives such as Achieving the Dream, a national community college reform movement initiated in 2004 by the Lumina Foundation and several other funding partners. Administrators in the community college system maintained the sense that state policymakers are not only "data driven" but "data hungry."

In 1998, for instance, the General Assembly directed the State Board of Community Colleges (the state's governing authority for the NCCCS) to review performance measures and define standards to ensure programs and services were of the highest quality. Most recently in 2010, NCCCS president, Scott Ralls, established the Performance Measures Committee that included college presidents and others to develop new performance indicators to measure student success. The measures were approved and adopted by the state's General Assembly in 2012.[6] These measures include student progress in developmental education courses and how well these students excel in college-level math and English courses, and other measures. At the same time, President Ralls appointed another committee, Performance Funding Committee, to develop a performance-funding model. This committee established system-wide benchmarks for each measure.[7] These baselines and goals are scheduled for review and revision in 2016 and are a part of the larger Success NC initiative. Thus, the community college system seemed to welcome the opportunity to provide more data in hopes that increased information may provide evidence for additional financial support.

Despite the recent increasingly significant role information played for community colleges, at the time of our study, North Carolina limited its use of data on developmental education. In fact, the state only collected and reported enrollment and expenditures of developmental education statewide. Each institution of higher education must report to the high schools the percentage of high school graduates who take developmental courses once enrolled in college and the associated costs. Most recently, though, North Carolina has increased its information gathering on developmental education to now include: success rates in gateway college-level courses and graduation rates of students who enrolled in developmental education courses. Still, even with the limited developmental education data reported, there were critical indicators for assessing the role of the high school in college preparation. Moreover, the indicators used in the state reports symbolized to institutions that state lawmakers had growing concerns about the number and costs of developmental education at four-year institutions. Thus, the UNC system and its institutions were involved in strategies designed to assess and address issues related to underpreparation and the need for developmental education.

One such initiative, for example, included the development of a statewide longitudinal student database. A system administrator explained:

> I think one of the key strategies has been first getting our hands around the data and models where we can assess very specifically what the situation is and then aligning our resources and people and initiatives to respond to what the data tells us to be evidence-based. So we spend a lot of time, specifically like in the teacher [education] issues, really getting the data right and understanding the data and then we align initiatives and efforts to respond to what the data tells us we need to do.

As the above comment illustrates, an area where data were becoming increasingly important at the university sector was in the evaluation of teacher's education programs. For UNC General Administration, teacher education was key to reducing developmental education in colleges and universities. This strategy also aligned with the reports to the high school as higher and secondary education played a role in the need to improve college preparation. Another UNC system administrator explained:

> Obviously if we can produce better teachers and motivate students better then we attack the remediation problem from another angle. It's part of the University's responsibility, not totally. The school bears a large responsibility too but to the extent we can have some impact there, we're trying to.

Indeed, some campus administrators and faculty recognize the significance of improving teacher preparation to help improve the college preparation of high school graduates. The following exchange between a university administrator and a faculty member demonstrates this point:

> *Administrator*: I mean, [the] UNC system, our president always talks about, we have to go back to the high schools and see what they're doing, help them do a better job. K-12, K-12, K-12.
> *Faculty*: And then [our president] pointed out that as a university we are training the people to teach in the high schools, so are we doing our job there?

Administrator: Yes, exactly. Training more and better teachers so you won't have students who may have these deficiencies.

While focusing on high schools, and to some extent teacher preparation, takes some pressure off the majority of academic programs in public universities, all institutions were required to report data on their developmental courses and student success. Although developmental education was still permitted at the four-year college, institutional and system-level administrators talked about increasing admissions standards to decrease enrollment in developmental education and/or changing course titles and credits to reduce the number of sections or students enrolled in college developmental courses. Their concerns about rising admissions standards were confirmed when one administrator acknowledged that maintaining minimum admissions standards was one way to reduce developmental education. Although this administrator also recognized other ways to go about reducing the level of developmental education course offerings, he noted that the UNC president wanted to build "projection models to project whether or not based on factors you can know before a student is basically admitted into the university, what is their likelihood of being retained to their sophomore year." The focus on retention rather than graduation was because it was more of an "immediate impact." One system administrator further explained:

> If you say "okay we're going to have a target for six-year graduation rates" and a student comes in now, it's going to be like seven years down the road before we even know how well that's worked and half those chancellors [of the different UNC campuses] will be gone.

While four- and six-year graduation rates remain "on the table," the system primarily focused on retention to help "figure out where's the best place for a student to go." Another system administrator explained:

> The best place for a student to be successful may not always be, if they have certain weaknesses... to come to university and go through remediation. It might be better to do two years of community college and come in at the junior level... so we're spending a lot of time figuring out whether there's a way to make decisions about that for individual students.

A great deal of data appeared to be moving up to the state level, but useful analysis rarely trickled back down to the institutions, leading institutional administrators to question the purpose and meaning of data collection and mandated reports. This lack of understanding around the purpose of data created what one participant identified as "internal panic." Many higher education state or system administrators said institutions were regularly afraid to report data on developmental education because college and university administrators did not want their institutions to "look bad."

With concerns about the use of data and the impact it might have on admissions decisions at the system level, some institutions engaged in behavior that one participant from North Carolina described as "smoke and mirrors." In other words, UNC trend data showed some University of North Carolina institutions with a history of high levels of developmental education courses suddenly reporting no courses, sections, or students in developmental education. One of the institutions we visited served an academically diverse student population but only had one developmental education course in math and offered no English developmental education courses. Campus administrators explained that discouragement from the state General Assembly shaped the way they offered the one developmental education course:

> It's like the math course. It's got a couple of hours of sort of remedial credit and a couple of hours of college level credit so the students might dedicate 4 hours a week to the class, but they're only going to get 2 hours of credit.

Institutional participants speculated that changes in curriculum and developmental course offerings was the result of repeated proposals by the state legislature to end developmental education courses at four-year institutions that subsequently pressured the university system. Clearly, institutional staff and faculty received the message that it is only a matter of time before they will be forced to eliminate these courses altogether.

Despite the fears of institutions about the use of data and the system's disclosure that they are considering ways to "predict student success" at particular institutions, system administrators also raised concerns about maintaining access (perhaps the greatest concern for public colleges and universities as they seek to maintain their institutional missions). One system administrator demonstrated this potential conflict with his own remarks:

> I suppose if you go back ten, twelve years, the great theme was access, but now there's kind of a counter theme. Students really need to graduate and there needs to be student success. Maybe you don't waste your resources on people who don't really have a chance and so what you're beginning to see is an urge toward a greater balance between access and success...and what we're trying to do is basically quantifying access and I think if you set kind of arbitrary cut off points, you may be not giving people a chance

[who] in fact can be successful in certain places with the right kind of support. And so what we're trying to do is say raise the question to successfully provide access, you have to take chances on people.

At the same time, this administrator also questioned how much of a chance to take on students:

> By doing [projection models], we can really say if somebody has a 90 percent chance of being retained and graduating, everybody would take that chance but if it's a 2 percent chance, you might say maybe we ought to think about community college or something. Or if it's 20 percent. But if it's 42 percent, what would you do?

The system administrator's comments suggest that institutional administrators have a reason to be concerned about maintaining their missions of access as they may be, in the future, required to "demonstrate over time their ability to be successful with that student with [a] 42 percent likelihood and if they can be successful that will earn them the right to admit those students." Four-year institutions then may become less welcoming to students considered underprepared.

A university executive administrator described it this way:

> Clearly cost is paramount in terms of [eliminating developmental education courses]. And looking at the preparation of... college students generally, and what is the goal, objective of the university system here? Is it to provide education for people who may not have the skill? Is that the mission, the goal of the system to do that? Or should that be the goal of the community college system to do that? So I think they are making decisions about that now. What are we supposed to be doing? And we have high school, we have community college, we have the UNC system. Okay, what are the roles? And they may be forcing universities to take a look at that, despite what you may say is your tradition, your mission.

Assessment and Placement

Institutions appeared ready to accept the challenge of finding ways to maintain college access while supporting state and system priorities. Since 1993, North Carolina's community colleges were required to determine what tests and cut-off scores to use to place students in various levels of instruction. In 2006, policy became more restrictive as the state required community colleges to use one or more specific tests, including COMPASS and Accuplacer.[8] The state also required minimum passing scores for placing students into college-level courses. Most recently in 2013, the state's Developmental Education Initiative team (formed to redesign developmental curricula and increase course/degree completion in community colleges) helped to establish the North Carolina Diagnostic Assessment and Placement test (NC DAP).[9] Students who do not meet established high school grade-point averages or ACT/SAT scores will be required to take the test.

Four-year colleges and universities had no public policy restrictions on the ways they assessed academic skills or placed students into courses. Four-year colleges may choose, for example, not to assess students at all and place all students into college-level courses. Some four-year universities allowed students multiple opportunities to take placement exams, a practice that began spreading throughout North Carolina's community colleges. Further, one institution that we visited allowed students who placed in a developmental education course to be waived from the course if they did well on an assessment exam given as part of the course on the very first day of class. The students, however, were not informed about this until after taking the exam:

> When I gave the pretest, the comprehension test, I didn't tell them, if they scored 80 percent I would still exempt them from the class. I said, anytime you take any assessment test or evaluation at this institution, take it seriously. Do the very best that you can.

The faculty member who shared this experience also explained that this practice of not informing students was in response to students not taking the exam seriously. Further, the faculty member explained that giving the assessment test in class was essential because "sometimes we realize the condition under which [students] take [placement exams] may not give the true picture, and so we test them again always, in that type of class." Thus, this institution, which is also a minority-serving institution, always gave students enrolled in developmental education courses pre- and post-tests to "double-check."

Instructional Delivery

North Carolina had no public policy restrictions on where developmental education courses can be offered and has no funding limits, but community colleges are clearly the primary providers of developmental education courses. While four-year universities continue to offer developmental courses, state policy also allows them, by statute, to partner with community colleges to offer developmental support and courses to students.[10]

One such program is the Postern Program, a partnership between one community college and a UNC institution. While not a developmental program per se, the Postern Program allows students who were academically denied admission to the four-year university an opportunity to enroll at the local community college. After two successful semesters at the community college, students would become eligible to transfer back to the four-year university. In the program's inaugural year, the university offered this opportunity to 200 students who were denied admission. Only 80 students accepted the offer. At the community college, students were assessed and placed in either college-level or developmental education courses. The goal, however, was that most students would not need developmental education. Rather, they would be able to provide evidence that they are capable of succeeding in college-level work by completing two semesters at the two-year college. The university, however, underestimated how many students who were denied admission to the university would need developmental education when they enrolled at the community college, as

> Over half placed in developmental courses...we thought a fourth would. We were really surprised, because we actually studied what SAT scores that students usually would make that would make them place out of the [developmental education courses].

This was clearly a concern for university administrators as one explained:

> The way we've designed the program it's a two-semester program, and then [students] come here [to the university]. They're not going to get enough transfer hours if they have tons of developmental work. So, we crafted it to where they shouldn't have needed developmental, but maybe a fourth of them would. Over half of them did. And so I don't know what that says yet...but even with our transition program trying to help, we're finding—community colleges need to be thinking about that. And they're much better at it than we are, of course, but I was just, just our particular group I was interested in how that happened...even after we attempted to craft it.

The inaugural year of the Postern Program demonstrates how difficult it is to "project" which students will require developmental courses and further raises questions about what it means to be "underprepared." Moreover, acceptance into the program was limited to a particular group of students that included residency in the same county of the community college and students had to be considered "borderline" for admission. In other words, "it's a certain caliber of denied student" who may participate in the program.

Interestingly, this university, that partnered with the community college for the Postern Program, only offered one designated developmental education course on campus while a second university we visited, a Minority Serving Institution that was also an Historically Black College and University (HBCU), offered many developmental education courses in reading, writing, and math. One of the institution's administrators explained:

> It's something that we don't shy away from. We somewhat embrace [developmental education in English] because our focus here...is on communication skills...So the fact that these students have been identified as needing some help, we are embracing that to bring them up to speed and move them forward in terms of increasing their skills in those areas. So, although it may be considered a type of developmental course, it's something that we have identified, recognized as needed, and we are committed to increasing that level with these students.

To ensure that students in developmental education courses receive the same material, both universities that we visited standardized the curriculum of their developmental education courses. One institution only had one developmental education course (in math) with multiple sections, whereas another had many different courses in math and English. One university administrator emphasized the importance of explaining to students "the benefits of the [developmental] course to other courses that they're gonna take and how it's gonna help them to do better." It was a message that the institution wanted to ensure that every student received.

Conveying consistent messages to the students was a key issue for higher education institutions in North Carolina. In other words, it was important that all faculty expressed high expectations and support to students. Therefore, at both institutions, developmental education was taught by "regular faculty." One academic dean explained:

> We can go all the way from senior [faculty] members to adjuncts. Now, unfortunately, considering the way things work out in general education, in these courses you may have a high number of adjuncts. You may in some areas. But that's not our direction. It's not planned that way. We constantly note every year that these courses should be spread through the entire faculty.

Perhaps more important than who taught developmental education was how it was taught. In other words, as one faculty member explained, "pedagogy is important." She went on to say:

> The university has a very good system of faculty development and faculty take advantage of it. And we look at it. A senior member who's a high-level research faculty member clearly may or may not be the best person to teach a class of 30 freshmen. So it's not that they don't want to. Maybe we don't want to put them there. So, you have that, and you have younger faculty members who are more energetic and relate to the students differently, and are incorporating different types of teaching styles and approaches. Sometimes they embrace that opportunity, so it's a mixture. But there's no real policy that senior level do not teach even so-called developmental courses.

As the above quote suggests, the faculty, whether tenured or pretenured, must be interested in student success. A university administrator explained:

> One of the things the chancellor said to me... [was] to make sure that you have people that's going to work for the goal of student success. That's going be the major thing. He said, "If you have persons in the program now who are not doing that, you don't have to keep them and you certainly don't have to bring in persons who are not on board with that." So that's a part of the conversation with each person that's hired... Student success has to be the number-one goal.

Maintaining a faculty and staff who are "on board" with the idea that they play a key role in students' success was a critical part of instructional delivery. Further, faculty had to be willing and able to maintain a common curriculum with a shared set of principles that serve students whose test scores suggest underpreparation. The developmental education courses at an MSI, for example, required all students to read excerpts from *Narratives of Frederick Douglass* to help remove the negative stigma that sometimes accompanied students enrolled in developmental education courses and to ensure they recognize the significance of the course, as one faculty member explained:

> We read, the very first day, the *Narratives of Frederick Douglass*, Chapter 7, where he's talking about how he learned to read and write. And so, when they read that, to see a slave able to write as well as Frederick Douglass

wrote that narrative, and who was punished if caught reading...then to have them being free to do it, and them not taking it seriously? I think I kind of got them on that because they come in class, they're ready to go. I have not had one complaint.

While the specific method of instructional delivery was not dictated by state policy, many community colleges in North Carolina were moving toward modularized courses that allowed students to complete competencies and/or courses using an online segmented system. These modules allowed students to move through their developmental placement requirements relatively quickly (compared to the traditional two- or three-course sequence) and at a pace individualized to their personal needs. While administrators in the community college system argued that a modularized system has the potential to reduce time and costs associated with developmental education, there was some uncertainty and concern from university leaders around what pedagogical and structural changes are necessary to use this format most effectively.

Instead of modularization, four-year university administrators in North Carolina seemed more focused on blending what would traditionally be called "developmental" courses with "college-level courses." In fact, while one institution appeared to have only one developmental course, there was some disagreement on campus as to whether that course was "developmental or not." The disagreement was primarily because some believed that developmental education courses are generally noncredit courses but the one course in question offers one credit toward graduation.

Regardless of the designation, these blended college-level courses provide "extra support for students who need extra support," as one North Carolina system administrator argued. Indeed, academic support seemed to be one of the highest priorities at our case institutions.

Academic Support

Public universities in North Carolina have a general mission to provide the state's citizens access to a quality education. Part of this mission is to ensure students who matriculate at the various institutions have opportunities for success. One university administrator explained:

> If we admit the students, we have a responsibility to ensure their success, regardless of where they are when they come in. Certainly we would want to have students who are college prepared, who can go into any class and be successful without a lot of development attention. However, we also feel

that even with students who are college prepared, that we know that the competition is very stiff when they leave the institution as graduates, and so we want to prepare them so that they can compete, not only with persons in the U.S., as we know, but persons from around the world.

Accordingly, the institutions that participated in our study demonstrated a strong commitment to students' success as both institutions maintained a large variety of programs and activities designed to provide students with academic and social support. These included supplemental instruction, tutoring (in person and online), learning communities, other programs, and intrusive advising. At one institution in North Carolina, all student support services were centralized. In this way, the institution developed a way for a variety of departments including the writing lab, disability services, and others to meet regularly to discuss students and ways to improve support services. In this case, academic support simply meant to bring more people to the table when making decisions about students and how best to support them.

Faculty and staff at this MSI also indicated that the department of disability services is a key partner in student success. One faculty member who also worked with the writing studio recalled:

> We were just talking how [disability services] did a workshop with [writing studio] tutors last year... And the tutors started having questions of how do we know if it's just a writing issue versus a disability, and they would come to me. And so [disability services] came and did a workshop with us on how we could try to identify some things, and there were times if a tutor comes to me with an issue and I'm not really sure I can just call [disability services].

Indeed, faculty and staff at this institution raised concerns that serving students who may be underprepared means recognizing all that may impact their academic progress.

This MSI therefore took a holistic approach by making academic affairs and student affairs departments partners working in concert towards student success. One faculty member explained what they do in the English developmental education courses:

> What we've done is partnered with the writing studio so that all of the students who are in that class have to come for a visit for at least one assignment, and then if [the writing studio staff] see that they need additional help then sometimes we schedule them for appointments all semester, or that they have to come once a week or twice a week, and so we've been trying to work pretty closely with the coordinator of [the writing studio]

to make sure that we are doing what we can. And so sometimes [the studio] will do one-on-one tutorials and sometimes [they'll] do small-group sessions, depending on what the teacher suggests, or sometimes [they] do classroom workshops too.

This type of intrusive support can also be found with the advising practices of the two institutions that participated in this study. As one university administrator explained, students enter the MSI knowing that there will be at least one person who will be committed to their success.

> [Students] know who their advisors are from day one. They are instructed and sign a contract to meet with those academic advisors [at] the beginning of the semester...at least once a week for the first four weeks to try to—before they get too far along on the wrong track, that somebody is checking and monitoring that progress. For students who are placing into two or more of the developmental courses...those students are restricted to taking only 12 credit hours per semester, whereas otherwise they could take a minimum of 15. And we do that so that we can try to help them to establish a strong GPA in the beginning so they don't have to be wrestling with catching up for the rest of the time that they are in school.

As academic advising and other supports were available, students knew the institution took intentional steps to help them succeed. Indeed, administrators and faculty in North Carolina stressed the need to meet "students where they are."

Social Support

The focus for most four-year colleges seemed to be on strengthening instructional delivery in the traditional classroom and/or providing myriad intensive support services that address the complexity of student needs. Perhaps due to economic downturns and perceptions of state policy priorities, some institutions, as indicated, had many developmental courses but very few additional student support services while some others had very few developmental courses and many student support services. Whether the institution had one developmental course or many, both institutions in this study maintained a plethora of academic, social, and personal supports in place. With so much academic and social support available to students, one university administrator questioned:

Would these students do just as well if they were not in developmental [courses], going right into [college level courses]? And...we did do an experiment with that, with a group of students one year. And some of them did very well going right into the regular courses.

Despite the questions, neither of the institutions we visited considered whether to eliminate their developmental education courses, although other institutions in North Carolina did.

One of our case study institutions, however, went as far as supporting a living-learning community specific to students needing academic support. One campus leader explained why they provide so much support for students, particularly the need for a learning community specific to students whose test scores suggest underpreparation:

> I definitely believe strongly in the...engagement phenomenon about students being engaged academically and socially and learning communities provide that. So if you are underprepared...you are in a community that brings together the academics and the co-curricular in one setting, provides extra support be it a faculty member who is showing care and concern, [or] whether its increased academic advising as a result of being in the learning community.

Another campus leader attributed their success to moving toward parity across racial and ethnic groups in terms of academic achievement to the variety of supports available to students:

> We have eliminated racial disparities...in graduation rates and that's something that I think a lot of these [support] programs have helped with. We were just recognized last week by a national organization and they pointed out that certain institutions that had very high rates of disparity between racial groupings and institutions that had very low and in some cases actually graduated African American students at a higher rate than their white students. Ours was exactly zero. I mean zero disparity, which was good, and when we look at specific programs like our summer transition program, you can see quite a bit of difference in terms of [students of color] graduation rates compared to students who didn't participate in the program.

Reaching parity in terms of graduation rates across racial and ethnic groups, in a state, where African Americans' statewide graduation rate is 44 percent compared to 64.6 percent of whites is an important milestone, although faculty and staff shared that there was still much work to do to improve success among students of color.

Despite the apparent success of academic and social supports, some at the UNC system administration expressed concern about the cost and scalability of such programs:

> Look at the various interventions that the campus might have in place and so what is it that this one institution is doing that allows them to be successful with students with these characteristics or that fall into this range. And is it replicable? What is the best practice there that we might want to talk with others about? There's no silver bullets. Everything moves the clock a little bit and the question is "Is that enough to justify what it costs to do those kind of things?"

While the university system raised concerns about the cost of student supports, for one campus executive, cost was secondary to fulfilling the mission of its institution; that is to ensure students who enter are successful:

> We're still founded as an undergraduate teaching institution and it's a real big part of our culture here so I don't really worry about it too much. There are people who wring their hands over it all the time, but I think when you see [the variety of supports]...I don't know how many FTE are tied up in all that, but it's not trivial by any means.

He went on to say,

> I don't think we've ever added up how much money we're spending on these programs and I'm pretty sure we've never determined whether any one of them is cost effective, however you might define that...we're having some discussion about because things have gotten tighter here. You just got to try to determine well, "Is this worth anything you can throw at it?" or "Do we maybe need to raise our admission requirements, send more students to the community colleges. I've always been one who thinks that if you've got a student who's ready for college, if you can give them a four-year experience, that's a good thing.

Fiscal Strategies

As institutional faculty and staff stressed a commitment to serving students needing developmental education or students who may enter the institution underprepared, they also expressed concern that state policy leaders' commitment to education did not always match that of the institutions. While North Carolina state policies did not limit funding or services for developmental education, institutional leaders consistently expressed concern about the impact a fiscal exigency may have on

resources that may already be inadequate. As one administrator stated, "in these tight-budget times, you can see, [policymakers are] questioning most things."
Another university administrator expounded:

> We're being asked to do more in tracking all of the innovations that were put in terms of the courses, in particular our developmental courses. The state is demanding that we either provide evidence that these have helped students to be successful at upper levels or not, and they're saying to us, if they have not helped, we need to look at another way of doing this.

Campus leaders, however, argued that supporting students to be successful, albeit costly, brought financial gains to the institution, as one university executive administrator explained:

> I would say it's expensive but one of the things we've done is...analysis. If we can improve our retention and graduation rates by this percent, what revenue does that mean to us? And so we talk in those terms. The revenues that come through, if we can improve retention and graduation rates, it offsets the cost of doing anything on the other side. So we believe in student success. We're for putting money towards that.

One of the challenges in making fiscal decisions about developmental education is what counts as developmental and how to calculate the associated expenses. The one developmental math course at one institution, for instance, was considered less expensive than a traditional developmental education course because only part of the course was considered "remedial." One campus leader explained:

> [The math] course...is not officially on the list of remedial courses, because there is...one credit hour that counts towards the degree. It's a three contact hour course, so when we calculate, we take the instructor's salary for that course, and multiply it by two-thirds, and add that to the remedial costs. I don't know if that's the best way to do it, but that's the way we've done it.

Questions also arose about whether, student support programs should be considered in developmental education costs. One of the more expensive student support programs, which shed light on the fiscal issue, is the summer bridge program. These programs prepare admitted students for the rigors of college academic life by bringing them on to campus during the summer. Campus and system-level administrators stated that they encountered success with these programs but none were fully supported by institutional or state appropriations. Instead, most relied on grants from private foundations or the US Department of Education.

More specifically, university administrators felt particularly challenged to fund these programs because the state did not permit public funding for summer programs, despite their success. Instead, the UNC system developed a grant to fund summer bridge programs at public institutions. It was not clear, however, how long the system administration would continue to fund these programs. Although administrators at the system level seemed to be satisfied with the effectiveness of summer bridge programs, it was uncertain how they would be sustained or brought to scale.

Regardless of the program or course, institutional administrators have been left with the idea that "we are primarily supposed to be teaching college level credit courses...we are asked every year to report exactly how many students are in what did you teach that was remedial? How many students? How many sections?" Indeed institutions recognize that the UNC system and the state are "watching [developmental education very closely." Developmental course offerings and expenditures, thus, vary across campus:

> There certainly are [institutions] where more [developmental education] is taught than others. And I was looking at the last [developmental activities report] that was available, and ours is math, and at [another institution] you'll see a little bit of math, not anything else. At other institution[s] you'll see maybe there's something in English and math, or no math—it kind of somewhat depends on the institution, and then there are a few that, "Absolutely no; we teach no remedial." There's zero in every single column.

Similar to concerns about data collection, reporting funding also led institutions to change their strategies around serving students who are underprepared.

Conclusion

North Carolina is a state that finds itself in the center of the futile access versus success debate. While the state has pushed institutions to be held more accountable for students' success and has discouraged four-year institutions from offering developmental education courses, institutional leaders have scrambled to continue to admit students within the geographic region they are committed to serving and to ensure their success. Thus, institutions have focused not only on improving developmental education courses but also in developing and improving adequate academic and social support for students.

While meaningful data and information could be quite useful to institutional leaders in their endeavors to better serve students, particularly those who are underprepared, fear of how the data are being used by state policymakers may cause those on campuses to take developmental education courses and academic or social supports undercover. Indeed, the legislature's ongoing attempt to remove developmental education confirmed some institutional leaders' fears. Still, university administrators and faculty from the executive level to the academic departments remained committed to putting financial and human resources in the areas where students needed them most.

North Carolina also raises questions about the best way to serve students with academic profiles that suggest a need for developmental education. Community colleges in North Carolina are introducing more online modular courses in part to cut costs and make inroads with the legislature. Administrators at the HBCU we visited maintained they only had one level of developmental education but courses were available in reading, writing, and math. The other four-year university had not only one level of developmental education but also one course in one subject area: math. Both four-year institutions demonstrated success with students who were academically underprepared, in terms of course and degree completion. Therefore, the question about which strategy is best arises. Perhaps the answer can also be found in North Carolina where institutions seem to focus on their institutional missions and are doing everything they can to get to know their students to fit services and support that are best for their student populations.

8

Kentucky

Of the five case study states, Kentucky has the highest rates of enrollment in developmental education courses. With 32 percent of first-time freshman in four-year institutions enrolled in developmental education Kentucky also used one of the most innovative approaches to tackle this issue. While other states talked about the need to coordinate efforts between K–12, community colleges, and four-year colleges and universities, Kentucky took steps, by statute, to make these efforts a reality. This chapter includes more input from the community college system as they were a central part of the work that occurred across the state.

State Context

The Commonwealth of Kentucky, with 4.3 million people, is the 26th most populous state in the nation.[1] Approximately 86 percent of the population is white, 8 percent is African American, 3 percent is Latino, and 1 percent is Asian American.[2] Similar to many states in the nation, including the states we studied, Kentucky is facing harsh economic realities. In 2011, Kentucky's seasonally adjusted unemployment rate hovered around 9.5 percent. This compares with a national average of 8.9 percent in 2011.[3]

Historically known for its agricultural production, manufacturing is now a key component of the state's economy. To compete with neighboring states, the workforce needs in Kentucky have shifted considerably in recent times and have led to increased demand for a more highly educated population. As one university executive administrator declared, "Kentucky's economy is...determined by the educated level of its workforce. And we can no longer exist with the workforce that is dominated by high school graduates or high school dropouts." Accordingly, state leaders in Kentucky view higher education as central to achieving state economic and workforce development goals. State higher education appropriations reflect this priority. At US$279.71 per capita, higher education appropriations ranked 15th in the nation and exceeded the national average of US$242.45 in 2011.[4]

Despite the need for a highly educated population, only 21.8 percent of Kentucky's adult population over the age of 25 held a postsecondary degree according to the 2012 American Community Survey, compared to 29.1 of the adult population nationwide.[5] The state also struggled with college-readiness as approximately 50 percent of all entering students in Kentucky's public colleges and universities required developmental instruction in one or more subjects over the past decade.[6] Developmental education course-taking, however, varied significantly by race as 76 percent of African American students took such courses, compared to 45 percent of white students in the 2006 entering cohort.[7] In the 2008–9 academic year, the four-year public colleges offered nearly 900 sections of developmental courses serving 17,793 students. The two-year public colleges offered more than 3,000 developmental class sections serving 55,985 students.[8]

Among full-time entering students seeking a bachelor's degree in the fall of 2003, approximately 48 percent graduated in six years. Graduation rates varied significantly by college-readiness (see table 8.1) and by race/ethnicity (see table 8.2).

Governance of Kentucky's higher education institutions is quite decentralized. The state is home to eight governing boards for public four-year institutions and one governing board, the Kentucky Community and Technical College system (KCTCS), for the state's two-year institutions. The KCTCS includes 13 community colleges and 15 vocational-technical postsecondary institutions. The University of Kentucky though maintains two institutions: the main university campus and the Lexington Community College. The remaining four-year universities maintain their own governing boards. All campuses are coordinated by the Kentucky Council for Postsecondary Education (KCPE) whose regulatory powers were strengthened by the legislature in the late 1990s. KCPE now has statutory authority to determine tuition, set accountability measures,

Table 8.1 Graduation rates of 2003 cohort by college-readiness

	College-ready (%)	Not college-ready (%)	Total (%)
4-year graduation rate	25	5	18
5-year graduation rate	50	23	40
6-year graduation rate	61	34	51

Note: Kentucky Council on Postsecondary Education, "Number of Developmental Courses by Subject and Institution," December 30, 2009, http://cpe.ky.gov/NR/rdonlyres/9E26D448-EF95–4910-B3CA-4774C2FF363C/0/Dev_Courses_by_Sector_20091230.pdf.

Table 8.2 Six-year graduation rate for full-time, degree-seeking freshmen entering four-year universities in fall 2002

Race/ethnicity	Graduation rate (%)
White	46.8
Asian American or Pacific Islander	46.2
Latino	38.7
African American	32.6
American Indian or Alaskan Native	14.7
Total	45.4

Note: Kentucky Council on Postsecondary Education "Graduation Rates of 2003 Entering Students by College Readiness," http://cpe.ky.gov/info/retention/.

and to establish admissions standards for public colleges and universities. KCPE's new level of authority was a key ingredient in the way Kentucky approached developmental education.

Developmental Education as a State Priority

Given Kentucky's economic challenges, the belief among state leaders that education is central to facilitating economic development, and the high number of students in need of developmental education, it is not surprising that the question of what to do about developmental education is being urgently addressed in Kentucky. University presidents, state political leaders, public higher education system leaders, and provosts consistently spoke of the high priority developmental education has within Kentucky and at their respective institutions. Similarly, a university president suggested that developmental education, "gives a second opportunity for the Commonwealth of Kentucky to make sure that these students become contributing citizens... to drive industry and to drive economic development in the state." Another university president explained, "Given the extraordinarily high percentage of Kentucky high school graduates requiring remediation, we cannot throw away a generation of young Kentuckians without trying very hard to make them successful in college... It is one of those things for which we have a moral obligation... If we are to be successful in meeting our goals for student success, developmental education is essential." System leaders similarly concurred. An administrator within the KCTCS, for example, declared, "Everyone pretty much agrees this is an issue we all have to tackle." Even Governor Steve Beshear proclaimed the importance of academic success to the state of Kentucky when he designated September 2010 as "College and Career Readiness Month."[9]

State Developmental Education Policies

The central role of developmental education in achieving state educational goals is apparent in the significant amount of legislation aimed at improving college-readiness and success in developmental education courses. The extensiveness of this legislation has been aided by a political culture that promotes innovative educational policy development. A KCTCS administrator proclaimed, "There are a lot of people in the legislature that are very interested in education reform... It's not terribly difficult for us to do positive change with policy... they've [the state legislature] been fairly intimately involved in education, and education reform in Kentucky is bread and butter." One institutional administrator explained how the state's willingness to pursue educational innovation is an outgrowth of the state's frontier history and said, "the council [of postsecondary education] here is truly very forward looking."

Kentucky has a recent, but extensive history of state policies related to developmental education and/or college-readiness. Though Kentucky maintains multiple state policies related to developmental education, they are less restrictive than those in a state like South Carolina. In 2000, for example, the General Assembly implemented the Kentucky Early Mathematics Testing Program, which offered voluntary online math testing. A year later, Kentucky passed a placement policy that mandated students be placed in developmental coursework or receive academic assistance when earning a score of 17 or below in ACT math, reading, or English. In 2004, the state implemented a statewide placement policy, guaranteeing placement into credit-bearing coursework with ACT scores of 18 or higher in English and 19 or higher in math.

In 2006, Senate Bill 130 required all tenth graders to take the PLAN standardized test in English reading, math, and science and all eleventh graders to take the ACT to determine college-readiness. In collaboration with public colleges and universities, high schools were then expected to offer additional academic support to students whose test scores did not demonstrate college-readiness.

Kentucky also made changes to its admissions policies for public colleges and universities in recent years. Admissions guidelines were modified in 2009 and amended in 2011 to establish institutional responsibility for mandatory assessment and placement of students considered underprepared.[10] Institutions were required to administer placement exams to students who did not meet admissions guidelines. Moreover, institutions became responsible for determining "the remediation required" for students who did not meet ACT cut-off scores.

In 2009, Senate Bill One (SB1) further strengthened Kentucky's strategies to improve college- and career-readiness throughout the state. In relation to developmental education, the bill included the following policies:

- A high school student below ACT standards for college-readiness must be provided an opportunity for accelerated learning to address his or her academic needs prior to high school graduation. A student is eligible to retake the ACT at state expense after completing the accelerated course.
- KCPE and the Kentucky Department of Education (KDE) must provide technical assistance to schools and districts.
- Secondary institutions are required to reduce the need for developmental education by 50 percent from 2010 to 2014. Postsecondary institutions are required to increase graduation rates among developmental education students by 3 percent annually from 2009 to 2014.
- Students are required to take developmental education courses in the first two semesters of college.
- KCPE is required to lead work with KDE, the Kentucky Board of Education (KBE), and the postsecondary education institutions in the alignment of high school academic content standards with the academic content requests for successful entry into postsecondary education.
- A technically sound longitudinal comparison of the assessment results for the same student will be developed.
- A unified plan from KCPE, KBE, and KDE will be developed to reduce developmental education and increase graduation rates.[11]

This unified plan across educational sectors was developed in 2010 and included strategies to increase accelerated learning opportunities in high schools, provide targeted interventions for all students who are not college- and career-ready, increase access to and quality of college and career-readiness advising, and increase the college completion rates of students entering with one or more developmental or supplemental course needs. Also in 2010, the KBE, KCPE, and the Education Professional Standards Board adopted the Kentucky Core Academic Content Standards for English/language arts and mathematics to reflect a rigorous set of standards that meet college and workplace-readiness expectations.

Assessment, Placement, and Instructional Delivery

In the past decade, state policies have increased the minimum ACT scores required to place into college-level coursework in Kentucky public higher education institutions. Indeed, Kentucky legislators have demonstrated a willingness to revise and increase placement scores over time to reflect what they believe is the most accurate measure of college-readiness. Most recently in conjunction with a senate bill (SB1), KCPE raised the minimum ACT requirements from 18 in math, English, and reading to 19 in math and 20 in reading. English remained the same at 18. The state also reduced institutional discretion in determining the placement of students into developmental education courses by mandating all students whose scores fall below the cut scores to take developmental coursework within their first two semesters of college.

In terms of delivery, a state-level administrator revealed that there had been discussions in the legislature about shifting all developmental education courses to the community and technical colleges. He recalled that four-year colleges opposed the measure because the institution's administration realized, "that developmental education makes money for campuses." Thus, the question "about developmental education being expensive kind of went away because several universities realized they couldn't really afford for it to go away."

The increased collaboration between postsecondary and secondary systems required by SB1 has also resulted in better alignment between high school and college-level courses, which further enables "delivery" of developmental education course material to begin at the secondary level.

Information and Accountability

Data collection and reporting related to developmental education increased in the state in recent years with extensive data on college-readiness made available through the KDE and KCPE web sites. In crafting legislation, data were used to build a sense of urgency that eventually led to the state's current policies. Through a high school feedback report, efforts are also being made to track the academic progress of individual students from specific high schools throughout their postsecondary endeavors.

SB1 holds secondary institutions accountable for reducing the need for developmental education and postsecondary institutions accountable for increasing the graduation rates of students taking developmental courses. The goals outlined in the legislation, however, are rather lofty, and include a stated goal of reducing the need for developmental education by 50 percent in two years and increasing graduation rates among developmental education students by 3 percent annually. Furthermore, none of the higher education leaders we spoke to could name tangible ways in which these accountability measures would be enforced beyond the potential for public embarrassment. Kentucky, therefore, has not yet fully capitalized on the use of accountability as a potential policy lever.

Fiscal Strategies

Funding has been minimally used as a policy lever in Kentucky. In 2006, the Regional Stewardship Program provided incentive for universities to engage with community needs. Some institutions use these funds in efforts to improve college-readiness among high school students. Funding decisions also reflect the high priority of developmental education in the state as even in a time of budget cuts, the state budget included moderate increases to implement SB1. The state also provided funds to pay for all high school students to take the ACT and PLAN assessments to assess college-readiness before students enrolled in college.

The postsecondary funding strategy in Kentucky allocated funds based upon enrollment growth that is not differentiated by student academic needs. According to one KCPE administrator, there has been no "public conversation and discussion" about whether funding should be differentiated in a manner that offers additional financial support to those institutions enrolling higher numbers of students requiring developmental education.

State Policy Development

At the time of our study, SB1 was well received throughout the state and this likely relates to the process by which this legislation was created. First, state leaders set a tone that effectively prioritized developmental education and demonstrated a need for all educational sectors to work collaboratively toward achieving developmental education goals. As the policy was being created, broad-based input and support from all sectors enabled the policy to be developed in a manner that made sense at the ground level. Finally, policymakers' decisions were based on extensive data and information.

The Importance of Leadership

When statewide dialogues about developmental education initially began, they were primarily focused on the cost of developmental education to the student and the state. Through relentless efforts led by one developmental education leader in particular, the conversation shifted to focus on the role developmental education can play in creating a foundation to improve college-readiness. Thus, many throughout the state began to view developmental education as a potential solution rather than a problem.

A state legislator, who also happened to have ground level experience with developmental education, helped to write SB1. His dual role as an administrator and a legislator enabled him to see the importance of writing policy that facilitated collaboration between secondary and postsecondary educators. He and other legislators were praised by numerous individuals for their interest and involvement in developmental education, as well as their willingness to be advised by educational practitioners during policy development.

Although they both arrived in Kentucky after SB1 legislation was written, the commissioner of KDE and the president of KCPE have been widely praised for prioritizing the goals of the bill and for working collaboratively to help ensure effective implementation. One state legislator noted, "We have now a commissioner [of education] and a president of our postsecondary council...that are very much into alignment and collaboration, so they have embraced [the SB1 policy]." Administrators within both the Department of Education and the Council for Postsecondary Education also confirmed these leaders have helped to make developmental education a state priority in Kentucky.

Broad-Based Input

Before SB1 was written, a task force on developmental education was created that included members from each of the four-year postsecondary institutions, state legislators, the commissioner of KDE, the president of KCPE, the chancellor of KCTCS, and the vice president of Kentucky Adult Education. In February 2007, the Task Force submitted a report written to improve college-readiness and success. A KCPE administrator explained, "I really believe that this document laid the groundwork for the legislature to write Senate Bill One." Similarly, a university administrator responded this way when asked whether insights from her university made it into the final policy, "Oh, definitely, because of the way the discussions were going on. Everybody was at the table; people presented what was happening on their campuses." One task force member spoke of the importance of having legislators involved in the task force, as it was "an education process for them." This collaborative approach, according to one higher education administrator, worked effectively as SB1 was greeted with "unanimous legislative support and top-level support."

As the unified implementation plan was developed, there were also significant opportunities for broad-based input as KDE, KCPE, and the KBE were involved in its development. A KDE administrator described that the drafts of the unified plan were reviewed and edited:

> Over and over again because we knew with this type of unified plan we needed to be able to say it has been before almost every role group, every program that has a part of this in order to say we've got buy in.

Utilizing Information to Inform Policy Development

Data and research played a large role in helping state policymakers to initially focus on prioritizing developmental education and think about forming effective developmental education policies. KCTCS' involvement in the Achieving the Dream initiative caused Kentucky higher education leaders to look more closely at state data; they found that educational outcomes among Kentucky's developmental education population were "getting worse instead of better and that it was something that we needed to pay some attention to."

The work of educational researchers and national professional organizations also had a large influence in the state. The 2007 Developmental Education Task Force Report that later became the groundwork for SB1 concluded with a resource list referencing ten works by higher education scholars who studied college developmental education as well as links to the Kentucky Association for Developmental Education, National Association for Developmental Education, and the National Center for Developmental Education.[12] One task force member declared, "If we don't have the research to back what it is we are doing, we are nowhere. But everything that we have in the strategic plan at this point is research based."

The Impact of Policy

From Finger Pointing to Collaboration

The way in which state policies were developed collaboratively prompted different educational levels to stop blaming one another for the existence of developmental education and, instead, to begin collaborating with one another to find solutions to state developmental education rates. A staff member at the Department of Education shared, "The postsecondary community and the K–12 community providers aren't known for getting together to work on projects... our agencies traditionally have just worked on their own issues." Numerous participants specifically mentioned the history of "finger pointing" within the state. It was explained that the postsecondary sector would point a finger toward secondary schools and blame them for not sending along students who are prepared for college, and secondary schools would blame postsecondary institutions for not adequately preparing teachers to teach in K–12. One KCPE administrator described this a "vicious circle of blame." A state legislator argued:

> In the past, I think it's been clearly the attitude of much of higher education or postsecondary that we can't help it if they're sending us these kids that don't meet our standards. And that's not our fault and it's not our responsibility to do anything about it.

The intentional efforts of state legislators to promote increased collaboration through SB1 have effectively been translated into action based upon the words of those we interviewed. One KCPE administrator affirmed, "we made a commitment very early on that we weren't going to do that [blaming], that this was Kentucky's problem; this was our problem...everybody was in this together." Similarly, a KCTCS administrator stated, "I think we're beyond the finger pointing and we realize that doesn't do us any good. We must move forward." Another KCTCS executive argued, "Senate Bill One said, 'Thou shall play together'...here's how we have to make this one seamless curriculum...That was a major shift in philosophy."

Two public proclamations made in September 2010 suggested the urgency of making a successful shift in philosophy. First, the presidents from Kentucky's public colleges and universities signed on to a "Commonwealth Commitment" in which they pledged to implement the expectations of SB1 by working collaboratively with the KDE to improve college- and career-readiness.[13] The second proclamation came from the governor of Kentucky as he stated that SB1 requires educational partners to engage in an "unprecedented and historic collaboration for the betterment of students and the future prosperity" of the Commonwealth.[14] A press release from the Kentucky Council on Postsecondary Education confirmed, "Senate Bill One has re-energized our efforts at the highest levels on our campuses" and that the "level and depth of cooperation and collaboration" was rare in state educational systems.[15]

The joint work that began as a result of SB1 led to many other collaborative efforts beyond the initial expectations. KDE and KCPE invited one another to be involved in their respective strategic planning processes. A Kentucky Council on Postsecondary Education administrator explained how an upcoming meeting to examine ways postsecondary education can assist secondary schools with professional development would have never happened five or ten years ago. A new database is being created to track the academic success of individual students longitudinally. Universities are redesigning their principal and teacher preparation programs, "and it really is all coming together around Senate Bill One," explained one KDE administrator.

Another outgrowth of increased collaboration in the state has been the development of the Kentucky College and Career Readiness High School Feedback Report. This report, which is jointly produced by a number of education agencies across the state, provides public access data for each high school including graduation rates, average ACT scores, AP test results, college-going rate by sector, percentage of high school graduates with developmental needs in college by subject and sector, and a comparison of a school's average ACT scores with district, state, and national ACT scores.

Building upon Prior Legislation

SB1 also provided a means for prior legislation to be more effectively utilized and implemented. Through the use of mandatory ACT and PLAN testing, Senate Bill 130 gave parents, teachers, and schools an assessment of college-readiness. Senate Bill 130 intended that this assessment would be followed by accelerated learning opportunities to help support students whose scores were not showing potential for college-readiness. A state legislator, however, pointed out, "That requirement was not really being met." He believed that SB1, "will help implement Senate Bill 130," as he reported, "universities are helping school districts with that requirement."

While legislation prior to SB1 did mandate the use of assessment and placement scores to determine developmental education needs, the policy was not rigid in requiring students to take developmental coursework immediately after entering college. As a result, SB1 includes a requirement that students must take developmental education courses within the first two semesters of enrollment. Under the former legislation, one KCPE administrator explained, "Developmental education students were not taking their... credit-bearing course right after they took their developmental education course, which was dramatically... impacting their success rates moving into their second year of college."

As previously mentioned, Kentucky heavily relied on research and data to inform state policy making prior to the implementation of SB1. One of the goals of this new legislation is to bring even greater attention to statewide and institutional data. A state-level administrator expressed the belief that the public reporting of the developmental education performance data will cause institutions to feel pressure to make progress and "feel negative consequences" if they cannot show progress. He explained, "the pressure to perform is probably higher than it's ever been."

Institutional Responses

While state- and system-level responses to developmental education policies were generally positive, institutional level reactions to policies were more mixed. Although faculty and administrators were generally enthusiastic about the possibility of having better prepared students in the classroom, many study participants, however, expressed concern that state policies had unrealistic goals, particularly given the lack of funds available to support achievement of these goals. Further, institutional leaders reported that students are frustrated with the need to enroll in noncredit developmental classes before entering credit-bearing courses.

Still, most postsecondary administrators expressed hopefulness about the effect that state policies could have on the academic preparation and success of students. One four-year college math professor explained, "I think the hope is that our students will come in better prepared and less developmental courses will be needed." Many faculty and staff spoke of the historic need for curricular alignment and their optimism that this legislation could finally have a significant impact on alignment. Faculty were also pleased about the heightened rigor in high school graduation requirements. A math professor at a four-year college expressed her belief that the prior absence of senior year math caused students to be shocked by the work when they arrived in a college-level math course, subsequently impacting their academic success. She and her math colleagues were "very optimistic that [the graduation requirement] is going to be a great impact, not only with our program, but throughout the state, as well."

Fiscal Strategies

SB1 provided additional financial support for some of the developmental education work already being done on campuses. An administrator at a university observed, "When it comes to trying to get money in difficult economic times, it helps to have the law behind you." A top KCTCS leader agreed that this law would cause a reprioritization of funding. He believed having the campus presidents state that they are going to put more money into developmental education will, "make a big difference too." One university executive administrator explained that SB1 would cause more funds to be allocated toward developmental education for at least a few years. He further argued that "since we're not getting any new state money and since our tuition increases have been limited" by the Kentucky Council on Postsecondary Education, efforts to increase developmental education spending can only be achieved by reallocating funds from other areas.

Assessment and Placement

Several participants argued that raising the ACT cut-off scores for placement exams resulted in larger numbers of students who placed into developmental education courses. A university math faculty member believed this has resulted in students who are better prepared when they enroll in credit-bearing math classes. She reported that in the past, students who might have barely made it into a college-level course (based upon ACT scores), were unsuccessful. She believed that the higher cut scores give students an opportunity for "additional time to work on their mathematics" before facing a credit-bearing course.

Many college administrators, however, were uneasy about changes in assessment and placement. One college president, for example, argued that changing placement scores meant more students are placed in developmental education without any additional resources. A KCTCS administrator articulated concern about the legislation's goals, "In five years, a 15 percent increase in graduation rates is almost unheard of…it's going to be—it's going to be really tough." A developmental education practitioner similarly argued, "When you say you're going to cut the number of students needing developmental education by 50 percent in five years, how realistic is that?"

Numerous study participants in Kentucky also described how surprised students are when they discover they do not yet qualify for credit-bearing courses. A KCTCS administrator explained how the change in placement scores after SB1 has added to the confusion. A director of a developmental education program observed:

> I think there's a frustration…many of our students arrive, and they don't realize that they're not college ready…they don't realize they need as much developmental education as they do…there is a sort of disappointment that goes on when they first discover that they're not going to be taking college-level work yet.

An academic advisor similarly noted:

> It's very difficult to explain to the students, that the developmental courses do not go towards graduation...And the students are always looking to get out of the developmental courses, and actually the parents are kind of the same way.

The advisor went on to say that this discovery was particularly disappointing for out-of-state students who pay higher tuition rates.

Instructional Delivery

Though no written policy in Kentucky mandates where developmental education courses can be offered, some institutional leaders expressed concern that SB1 may result in a de facto policy that shifts developmental education away from four-year universities and toward community and technical colleges. As four-year universities are increasingly held accountable for raising admissions standards and reducing developmental education rates, a greater proportion of developmental education courses may shift to the community and technical colleges. A university leader was concerned about the effect that increasing admissions standards might have throughout the state, as she believed that pushing the majority of students who are considered underprepared toward community colleges will effectively result in the "unintentional re-segregation of higher education." The state's disparities between African American and white students in terms of enrollment in developmental education illustrate this point as three-quarters of African Americans and less than half of whites enroll in at least one developmental course.

Still the state policy focus on developmental education and accountability measures has contributed to innovation in delivery methods. The community and technical colleges, for example, shifted toward the use of online modulars to deliver developmental education to lower costs. The collaborative work between postsecondary and secondary education institutions led to the spread of transitional courses that high school students can take to better prepare for college-level work and, hopefully, reduce their chances of enrolling in developmental education. Intensive summer bridge programs and first-year support programs were also offered at colleges and universities to provide academic support to students prior to or upon enrollment.

Online Modular Courses

KCTCS developed an online modular system through which students can complete courses and/or competencies. These modules allow students to move through their developmental requirements at a pace that works for their learning needs. KCTCS, for example, offered an online pre-algebra course that is broken into six different modules from "Whole Numbers" to "Tables and Graphs." Thus, a student can quickly move through areas of competence and take more time to learn other aspects of pre-algebra. Each module is taken separately and assigned an accompanying credit hour value and a corresponding tuition ranging from US$39 to US$91 per module.

A KCTCS executive administrator argued that to address individual needs, "You must use technology because there's not a way that you can have enough resources to provide individual attention unless you have some way to deliver through a technology enhanced environment." He also believes the KCTCS online model is different from those offered at other institutions because "it goes through an approval process. So the course is developed by a team of experts of our faculty." He further reported that KCTCS is also considering 24/7 online tutoring services to supplement the teaching by the facilitator of the course. Interestingly, while online modular courses were a big push at Kentucky's community colleges, it was not raised as an interest by four-year college administrators or faculty.

Curricular Alignment and High School Transitional Courses
One outgrowth of SB1 that has received unanimous praise is the way in which it has caused postsecondary and secondary educators to improve curricular alignment and develop high school transitional courses. One KCTCS administrator stated:

> I think the biggest strength and what I'm most thrilled about is that it is bringing the [postsecondary] faculty and KDE instructional staff together to align that curriculum. Because even with the best supports in the world if the curriculum is as out of line as it has been in our state, there's still going to be that gulf in terms of college readiness... I've been engaged for a lot of years in trying to pick up the pieces as a result of that not being a really well developed curriculum alignment.

Many successful partnerships have developed between school districts and four-year universities as a result. In one particular partnership, the math department at a four-year university worked with secondary educators for two years to develop high school senior year transitional courses designed to prevent the need for developmental education. The university math department also developed an initiative for kindergarten through ninth graders that works with students to improve automaticity in math (quick recall of multiplication, addition, division, and subtraction facts through repetition and practice). The initiative began with four or five schools and has now grown to 14 school districts. The success of these efforts led the English department to engage in a similar initiative. Participants explained this work has been effective because it opened up the conversation between colleges and high schools about expectations for college-level work in math and it has enabled "a strong bridge of relationships" to be built between the two educational sectors.

One of the faculty members involved in the initiative explained that the program works in three phases. In the first phase, university faculty meet with teachers, administration, counselors, guidance counselors, and any other stakeholder in a particular school or district to discuss the program and engage interest. In the second phase, the university faculty provide materials and consult with teachers in the schools. High school teachers subsequently complete implementation of the program. In the third phase, the university faculty analyze data and results for students who participated in the program. University and high school faculty then work together to consider the next few steps for their particular students.

Responses from school districts, teachers, students, and parents have been quite favorable. University faculty members explained how teachers worked very hard to effectively implement the program and how the schools have done a great job of explaining the implications of college underpreparedness to parents and students. A faculty member argued that these efforts led to high levels of motivation among students: "We have had just tremendous success with our program, great teacher buy-in, and really a lot of student buy-in, which we did not expect." In the initial pilot year, she reported that, "of 185 students who would have been developmental in [our] county, 150 to160 are now in a credit-bearing math class entering college." She believed that this success is due to the hard work of teachers and students as well as the fact that all of the postsecondary faculty members involved in the project had previously been high school teachers. This led to deep respect for high school teachers because of "having been in their shoes."

The Kentucky Department of Education has also consulted with postsecondary and secondary educators to develop similar transitional courses that can be utilized by high school students and teachers throughout the state. The transitional courses target students who scored one to three points below the college-readiness standard on the ACT. These courses can then be adapted to meet the specific needs of each high school and designed to offer flexible entry and exit based on preassessment scores.

Academic and Social Support

Some universities in Kentucky have chosen to address developmental education through intensive academic and personal support programs. Such a model exists at one of the state's Historically Black Colleges and Universities. This program began as a summer bridge experience and continued through the fall semester of participating students' sophomore year. A program administrator explained:

> The idea was to provide the support not only for the developmental course work, but for the gateway courses as well... [Students] needed solid structure that sort of loosens up as they go along so we're not just throwing them out there, but we're developing something and there's a decent transition.

Among the 2008 program cohort, more than 93 percent passed introductory English compared to 68 percent of students in the control group. In math, 73.2 percent of program students passed, while 51.3 percent passed within the control group.

Program participants focused on developmental education requirements in the summer before entering college as they took courses in English, reading, and university skills with a cohort of 15. Title III federal funds were used to provide free tuition, housing, and meals for participating students. Students lived together in the same residence hall where living-learning assistants coordinated activities and mandated evening study. They were also provided access to a software-based math workshop twice a week so they could work on specific topics in which they needed math assistance.

The program provided intensive personal support as university administrators believe that significant personal needs often hinder the potential success of students. An administrator remarked:

> All of our students come with baggage, but looking at the kids whose parents have kicked them out of the house, or the kids who are worried about the little brothers back home who are on drugs, and the kid who just this fall watched his brother being shot down at the corner while he was standing there. And then he comes back to school, and he gets grief about not getting his essay turned in on time.

In addition to the personal support available through the living-learning communities and cohort models, the university offered program participants mentoring groups. One program administrator elaborated:

> We have some kids carrying around some really serious baggage and so the mentoring has been wonderful and we've had students who have come to individuals and say "I think I'm ready for some counseling. I think I'd like to talk more with you about..." Some students who have opened up and written things and said things that they've been carrying around for years and when they're hauling that stuff around, they're not going to get to the reading.

Through relationships built with students and one another, faculty and staff hoped they could recognize early warning signs to prevent a student from academically failing. The faculty leaders and supplemental instructors "meet regularly to talk about how the students are doing in class, and to also talk about where we are in [the] syllabus, and what kind of activities would best support what's going on at that time." Faculty conduct early interventions with program students at the two-, four-, six-week and mid-term point of the semester.

In order to provide these additional supports, faculty and staff inevitably had to go above and beyond their job responsibilities. One faculty member pointed out how the faculty teaching developmental courses are typically paid much less than other faculty and are expected to work much more to offer the additional supports needed by students.

Unintended Consequences

The perception that there will be accountability for failing to achieve the goals of SB1 in combination with the belief that the goals are unattainable may lead to unintended consequences around admission standards and data collection, although it was too early to know at the time of our study. A postsecondary administrator explained that he has seen a lot of higher education institutions questioning, "how many of those developmental education students they want to be held responsible for now that they're being asked for some accountability on their success rates with them." One institutional administrator reported that this legislation does inadvertently put pressure on the four-year institutions to not accept people who might not graduate. He said, "universities are going to be looking for ways to increase their graduation rates, which means that they will, in effect, become more selective on the students they take chances on." A university leader confirmed, "Something I wanted to do a long time ago was to increase our admissions policies." He stated that he used SB1 to justify doing so.

Some universities have dealt with this by altering who gets counted toward achieving the goals of SB1. A state-level administrator argued:

> There are a lot of games played with these students... different institutions shuffle them different places; they admit them in different ways... Some schools have... chosen to deal with this by putting the students that would need developmental remediation into their community college. So they have almost a double system in the sense that they can count those students in their overall head count, so they're meeting overall enrollment goals, but they don't have to count them in graduation and retention rates... And sometimes they'll admit students in the spring, rather than in the fall, because of the IPEDS cohort is when we count it. In other words, institutions limit their risk of lowering retention and graduation rates when students who may need developmental education are admitted in the spring semester rather than the fall.

Conclusion

Kentucky is a state where leaders view developmental education as a strategy that can be utilized to increase educational attainment and thereby improve economic development. This positive view of developmental education has resulted from state educational and political leaders who have worked hard to steer the public dialogue in this manner. Leaders have successfully integrated data and research into discussions in order to develop policy that is informed by a larger picture. The successful implementation of policies has occurred because of a collaborative approach to policy development that enabled many opportunities for input from practitioners at the ground level.

Perhaps the most promising model offered by Kentucky is the way in which policy served as an incentive for postsecondary and secondary educators to stop blaming one another and begin to work together to create solutions. These innovative "solutions" of early college-readiness assessment, high school transitional courses, consistency in assessment/ placement policies, better course alignment between secondary and postsecondary classes, summer bridge programs, and online modular community college courses offer much promise of increasing educational attainment among Kentucky's citizens. Early indicators suggest Kentucky is moving successfully toward their goal as ACT scores have increased and although racial/ethnic disparities remain, Blacks and Latinos made the greatest gains in scores. Students reaching college-ready benchmarks are also on the rise allowing more students to avoid developmental education courses and directly enroll in college-level courses.[16] Extensive data collection and subsequent reporting in Kentucky, if fully executed, will make it possible for the rest of the nation to observe whether this promise is able to become a reality and whether the Kentucky model is worth replicating elsewhere.

9

Rethinking Developmental Education Policy and Practice

Due to longstanding social and educational inequities across the United States, scores of students entering postsecondary education systems are identified as "underprepared" and thus required to enroll in developmental education courses. These courses are often noncredit and aim to prepare students for college-level academic work. A constant on college and university campuses, developmental education is alternately upheld and reviled by an educational system that is charged with the task of balancing opportunity with excellence, and to do so with dwindling state resources and often confounding education policies.

The challenge embodied by students considered academically underprepared has led state legislatures and higher education institutions to position themselves on the defensive of an "ideological battleground...on which the larger issues of meritocracy, educational access, individual responsibility, and the quality of public schools are being debated."[1] In an age of high standards and debated definitions of "quality education," developmental education has assumed a decidedly negative connotation, leading some to assume that students taking developmental courses are academically deficient and incapable of learning. Instead of critically examining the norms we use to define "excellence" or the inequities fostered by an educational system that frequently fails the people it is supposed to serve, students are too often left to blame for their academic performance.

Developmental education policy thus represents a central paradox. On one hand, access to higher education is the means to greater social and economic opportunity for American citizens. All high school graduates are expected to be "college- and career-ready." Developmental education, one may argue, adheres to these democratic principles as it enables students an opportunity to access and succeed in postsecondary environments.

On the other hand, a commitment to standardized tests and a desire for institutional prestige through selective admissions suggests that some of those very same citizens may have their opportunities curtailed because of restrictive education policies that place access and success far beyond reach. Standards and benchmarks differentiate between "college-level" and "developmental" education. Placement tests are used to reveal competence and sort students accordingly, assigning students a label that is indicative of each student's presumed abilities. Yet, as research shows, the need for developmental education is arbitrary and subjective.[2] Students with similar academic preparation and credentials can be enrolled in colleges within a 20-mile radius of each other and may need developmental instruction in one institution but not the other.

As the nation grapples with accountability and academic standards in the quest for global competitiveness, developmental education and its continued role in higher education has focused prominently in recent national debates. The questions raised around developmental education have shifted from what it takes to successfully serve students to what it takes to make developmental education programs most efficient. This is a subtle yet significant difference in approach as the former focuses on student success and the latter on success of the institution. The discourse around developmental education is thus reduced to one of function and utility, leading to an alarming disconnect between policy and practice where the question of how to move students through developmental education quickly and in the most cost-effective way is one whose answers are often fervently desired by higher education leaders and policymakers.

Numerous policy perspectives exist, from a push to "mainstream" those considered underprepared, as was the case in North Carolina, to the outright elimination of developmental instruction by state policy chambers, as in South Carolina. Perhaps what is most disturbing about this debate and ensuing state education policy is that the common denominator for all is the financial bottom line rather than what is in the best interest of students. Indeed, developmental education policy engineered in many states over the past three decades has restricted students needing developmental coursework to the community college sector, a sector already disadvantaged by limited resources. In the implementation of these policies, equitable opportunity to college access and success for countless underrepresented and underserved students who have already been shortchanged by the system of schooling is denied.

Colleges and universities across the country are caught in a quandary as they struggle to simultaneously maintain access for the communities they serve and be accountable to state demands for rigor and increased graduation rates. Indeed, at different times throughout the history of higher education, policymakers and higher education leaders have identified developmental education as a threat to academic excellence.[3] Despite its presence on college campuses since the opening days of America's first college in 1636, questions concerning the appropriateness of developmental education courses in higher education have spawned a chronic debate that unnecessarily pits student access and postsecondary quality against one another as if they are two mutually exclusive educational goals. Consequently, this intricate balancing act between access and excellence is too often construed as a policy "problem" that threatens degree completion. Given the current national focus on college completion, the increasing racial and ethnic diversity of the student population, and the disproportionate placement of students of color in developmental education courses, it is time to critically examine the implications of public investments in or divestments from developmental education if higher education is to successfully meet state and national goals of access and degree completion.[4]

To begin, it is important to understand the ways institutions implement and respond to state policies related to developmental education. In other words, it is the people within higher education institutions who ultimately have the responsibility for determining the extent to which they will serve students considered underprepared within—or outside— the boundaries of state policy. With institutional missions, priorities, and practices in mind, higher education leaders have the capacity to develop institution-wide policies with the potential to positively influence behaviors that may ultimately improve educational outcomes for all students, including those needing developmental instruction and support.

Using our conceptual framework as a lens to understand the way state policy shaped institutional behaviors related to developmental education, it is apparent that state policies influenced the practices of system and institutional leaders, but perhaps not in the way intended or in a way that effectively meets the needs of academically underprepared students. In some instances, increased cut scores on placement exams meant that students who would have previously entered higher education college-ready are now deemed in need of developmental instruction, as was the case in Kentucky. In places where early assessment identified high school students who are most likely to need developmental education, the lack of coordination between K–12 and higher education and/or support services for those students may not be available to make a difference at the time of college entry. The continual demand for data reporting on placement and success rates in developmental courses will make very little difference to outcomes without the sophisticated analyses that will yield changes to curriculum, pedagogy, and instruction.

So while the framework suggests these policies can be used to improve developmental education and subsequently degree completion, and there is evidence across the five states of this study that these policy levers are in existence, there continues to be a lack of consistent application, alignment, and coordination between the systems to improve developmental education presently and eliminate its need in the long term. For certain, as the history of developmental education and the states and institutions highlighted in this book indicate, students with varying academic skills and backgrounds will always challenge higher education. Eliminating the developmental education courses does not eliminate the need and moreover, there are some institutions, such as the four-year colleges and universities we visited, that rely on students with varying backgrounds to maintain enrollment and fulfill their institutional missions. While institutions recognized these realities, only Kentucky seemed to recognize this at a state level.

Further, removing state funding from higher education institutions that offer developmental education will only require institutions to find ways around such a policy. Restrictive funding policies associated with developmental education forced four-year institutions to take less-than-desirable approaches to how they will serve their students who enter underprepared. These institutional responses, including the necessity to "shift" resources, or to make students pay out-of-pocket for their arbitrary designation as academically underprepared, all have indelible consequences on the wide institutional context, culture, and behaviors. Even when colleges and universities chose to mainstream students or create "enriched" courses that offered college-level credit and supplemental support, institutions were forced to "hide" students. Because of this concealment, the number of students who take advantage of these courses and the ability to access adequate funding may be limited.

Thus, the question remains—did the policies enacted attain their stated purpose? At the institutional level, there was great variation in what study participants believed the policies were intended to do. Some institutional leaders suggested that state policymakers used policy primarily to cut costs, rather than reduce the need for developmental education. Others noted that institutional prestige and greater selectivity may have been at the root of enacted policies. Policy language in each of the five states suggests that these policies were enacted with the intent to improve student outcomes. This lack of clarity in conjunction with some very restrictive mandates is what we see as contributing to a host of policy interpretations across institutions, all of which lead to varying strategies and approaches to the delivery of developmental education even within the same state.

The following discussion on data collection and analysis, collaborative efforts, delivery, and funding offers recommendations for how states can more effectively use higher education policy to improve institutional practice and services for students who are underprepared and/or enrolled in developmental education courses.

Collect and Report Data for a Clear Purpose

Institutions across our five states argued that the need for more and better information on developmental education was required. Some leaders at the state and community college levels credited Achieving the Dream, a Lumina Foundation for Education initiative designed to improve degree completion at two-year institutions, with highlighting the value of data. Indeed, Achieving the Dream helped some higher education systems and community colleges, such as those in North Carolina, to better understand what was happening on their campuses as it related to developmental education. The four-year colleges and universities, however, did not participate in any initiatives like Achieving the Dream and perhaps as a result institutional leaders did not often recognize the need for collecting and reporting data on developmental education courses.

The implications for policy are therefore clear. If states are serious about the reform of developmental education, they must gather, analyze, and report meaningful data on the success of all students in developmental education for the purpose of improving policy and practice. As recently demonstrated in Kentucky and to some extent in Colorado, doing so can create a sense of urgency that can facilitate innovative change. While states highlighted in this book already have data collection and reporting policies on record as in South Carolina, institutional administrators indicated that the purposes for data collection were unclear and that this lack of clarity led to panic and a desire to "hide" unfavorable data. Furthermore, the time it takes to conduct data analysis is problematic as it diverts faculty and staff from other job-related responsibilities.

University systems and institutions need to become partners in the analysis of data, and the ways data are to be used; at the state level, unambiguously articulating the purpose of data and analysis is necessary to reduce fear and incentives to "play games" with numbers. The collection of data should be limited to that which can be used in meaningful and practical ways to support institutional efforts at improving practice rather than creating unnecessary work for busy front-line administrators. States, systems, and institutions must engage in efforts for continuous improvement, not only of outcomes but also of processes. It is, therefore, crucial that communication pertaining to data not be solely a top-down strategy but must be one tha consistently moves back and forth between institutions, states and higher education systems. Moreover, there ought to be recognition that some information cannot be captured by quantitative measures alone and increased collaboration with administrators at the ground level will help provide the qualitative context to complement the analysis of quantitative performance indicators.

Similarly, we noted that no state in our study—and according to the Getting Past Go developmental education policy database, no state in the nation—disaggregated comprehensive developmental education data. Oklahoma's policies stated that data would be reported by race and ethnicity but we found no indication that it was ever reported to the state or general public. The failure of states to review data and information without such disaggregation may limit the success of various interventions and inaccurately state the success of others. What may work for one group of students, for instance, may not work for another. Again, quantitative and qualitative data will help states and institutions understand if students of color, as well as low-income and first-generation college students, are having similar experiences and educational outcomes in developmental education courses or interventions as their white, higher income, second-generation peers.

As demonstrated by developmental education rates, the inconsistency in data across time, institutions, systems, and states also limits the usefulness of data to inform policy and practice. Deriving specific, nationally utilized indicators pertaining to which students get counted in data analysis (e.g., race/ethnicity, full-time, part-time, degree-seeking, etc.), what assessment scores lead to placement in developmental education courses, and what counts as success in developmental education efforts (e.g., passing a developmental education course, enrollment in a credit-bearing course, graduation, etc.) would enable large-scale analysis of policies and practices.

Collaborative Efforts

A consistent theme in the five states we visited was the necessity of collaboration across educational sectors. Collaborative efforts cannot begin, however, until finger pointing ends. Study participants in Kentucky, Oklahoma, and Colorado described the tendency to "point fingers" and place blame on another educational sector for the existence of developmental education. While abdicating responsibility by placing it on others (e.g., community colleges or high schools) may seem easier in the short term, it is an ineffective way of making forward progress on college readiness in the long term. The busy lives of educators may also prevent collaborative work from occurring naturally, but this study demonstrates that policy can positively impact the assessment of college readiness, placement of students, and delivery of developmental education through the facilitation of collaborative efforts and curricular alignment between educational sectors. These increased efforts can lead to a more comprehensive approach to addressing college-readiness and developmental education.

Kentucky was able to end the finger pointing and move toward collaboration because educational and policy leaders recognized the urgency of the situation and because Senate Bill One mandated them to do so. Study participants described this transition as significant and difficult, but Kentucky demonstrated the value of pushing through this difficulty. Early assessment of college-readiness, access to courses in high school with a focus on transitioning students to college-level work, and free, online math placement tests for high school students, have had an impact. According to a recent press release from the Kentucky Department of Education, the results of collaborative efforts around Senate Bill One are beginning to show. While ACT scores across the nation have remained flat between 2010 and 2014, the composite ACT scores of public high school graduates in Kentucky have increased by nearly one full point. As a result, the number of Kentucky public high school graduates required to take developmental education courses has decreased. Education Commissioner Terry Holliday described this as "validation that we are on the right track and that Senate Bill One is accomplishing what was intended."[5]

Instructional Delivery and Support Are Equally Important

The states presented in this book revealed a variety of attempts to improve developmental instruction. While community colleges focused on online and modular courses, four-year institutions were more interested in improving pedagogy and curriculum. Some, as was the case in North Carolina, standardized developmental education courses so that all sections received the same curriculum and positive messages from faculty. Other institutions, like those in South Carolina, focused on enriching college-level courses with academic supports. Finally, some institutions like those in Kentucky emphasized summer bridge programs. While these new approaches appear promising, it is unclear whether they will work for different groups of students at different institutions. In other words, what works for some, may not work for all. State policymakers should take this into consideration when advocating for and/or funding strategies for instructional delivery of developmental education. It is clear, however, that four-year colleges and universities have used innovative strategies in preparing students while enrolled in college.

What seems to be most apparent is that courses are only one piece to the developmental education puzzle. According to institutional leaders, the integration of courses with adequate student support services is most critical. While a modularized curriculum or other so-called innovations may decrease the course sequences of developmental education, they may be inadequate for students who face challenges that extend beyond basic academic skills. This complements research by Jenkins and Cho that found institutions should support students throughout their college experiences to progress to college-level courses and a specific program of study.[6] Our recommendation for increased student supports also aligns with recommendations from Complete College America that argue for "co-requisite" supports in college-level courses.[7] Further, we argue that it is also necessary to provide adequate support to address barriers in students' personal lives that may impact their potential for achieving academic success but are not necessarily academically related. Without social and personal support for students, no curriculum will reach maximum success.

Finally, it is also important to note that some institutions, particularly those in North Carolina, South Carolina, and Kentucky, talked about the investment they are making by providing academic and social support for students. In other words, retaining students who may have been admitted underprepared for college provides revenue for institutions. Helping students who need academic support also helps the institution. While some state leaders bemoan that they cannot afford developmental education, some institutional leaders argue they cannot afford not to. Investing in students by providing adequate and appropriate academic and social support will likely see high returns for the state and its higher education institutions.

State's Priorities Should be Reflected in Funding for Developmental Education

While funding has the potential to serve as an incentive for innovation in developmental education, the message campuses received often served as a disincentive to innovation and implementation of effective practices. Study participants shared numerous institutional innovations that are aimed at improving developmental education practices including modular courses, online delivery of developmental education, summer bridge programs, outreach by postsecondary educators to K–12 educators, and efforts to support the personal needs of students. The ability to bring these innovations to scale, however, was hindered by lack of funding or fear of change. Furthermore, adequate financial support is necessary to enable time for staff to appropriately evaluate the effectiveness of innovations. Innovation along these lines may be more likely to occur if states were explicit about their interest in innovative change and success as demonstrated through funding incentives. While new funding may not be realistic, it may be more important to reconsider how current funding is allocated.

States must consider how funding impacts the delivery of developmental education and whether funding models provide an economic disincentive to pursue approaches that increase the likelihood students will complete their coursework. In other words, it is important to understand the ways funding decisions may result in unintended consequences. As legislators express concerns about the cost of developmental education and consider linking funding to performance in these courses, many institutions may choose to simply report they do not offer developmental instruction and find other ways to serve students who are underprepared. If achieving academic success among all students is truly a state's priority, then funding policies should reflect this. State lawmakers who constantly threaten to end developmental education and/or its funding, however, hamper innovation and send a message to institutions that high rates of enrollment in developmental education are an indicator of their institutional failure. Enrolling students who need academic support and/or developmental education should not be viewed as institutional failure. Rather such need represents an opportunity for systems and institutions of higher education to show how well they can educate the seemingly underprepared. Two of our case study states provide examples:

- In Oklahoma, students who enrolled in developmental math not only increased their chances of success in college algebra, but also performed at a rate that was only 3–6 percentage points less than students who never enrolled in developmental courses. Additional state support may even improve these outcomes.
- Some Kentucky policymakers have considered allocating more funding to institutions with large numbers of students who are academically underprepared to better support institutions that face these challenges. Although higher education system administrators in Kentucky are doubtful that this possibility will become a reality, such an approach is worth consideration if policy and funding are to be consistent with state goals.

Given the increasing diversity of higher education and that students of color are disproportionately enrolled in developmental courses, improving developmental education (with adequate funding) allows states a means to directly and positively impact racial and ethnic equity goals. This is particularly important for our case study states that have significant populations of blacks and Latinos who are the most likely to require developmental education. Failing to recognize this as an opportunity is what threatens our societal goal of having a more educated, better-prepared citizenry that will contribute to the further development of this country. Future studies must, therefore, focus on the effectiveness of policies and practices contributing to the success of students in developmental education courses and the extent to which these models can thrive at four-year institutions.

Leadership, Collaboration, and Coordination

It has been noted throughout this book that institutional faculty and staff recognized a disconnect between the mandates of policy and the reality of student academic needs. As the data show, significant populations of students graduate from high school needing some level of developmental instruction. The diversity of this student population makes clear that this is a problem that spans demographics, from ethnicity to income to academic background. As such, policy that takes a singular approach to the issue (i.e., deny funding, limit time to complete coursework, restrict courses to community colleges, etc.) fails to understand the complexities of student academic preparation.

The need for leadership, therefore, is great, and a more nuanced perspective on the issue cannot surface without the collaboration of those who are on the front lines. Thus, initiatives such as Senate Bill One in Kentucky, if continually successful, may be held as a standard for replication as this effort catapulted a statewide discussion that crossed sectors. A noteworthy component of Senate Bill One policy development was the broad-based input sought before policy was written. A Developmental Education Task Force was created that included members from each of the four-year postsecondary institutions, the commissioner of the KDE, the president of the KCPE, the chancellor of the KCTCS, the vice president of Kentucky Adult Education, and state legislators. This collaborative approach worked effectively as SB1 was greeted with, "unanimous legislative support and top-level support," according to one higher education administrator.

Conclusion

In a speech to the students of the University of Texas, Austin, President Obama acknowledged the challenge of both granting access and assuring success for all college students. He said:

> Over a third of America's college students and over half of our minority students don't earn a degree, even after six years. So we don't just need to open the doors of college to more Americans, we need to make sure they stick with it through graduation. This is critical.[8]

The fact that developmental education impacts students from all walks of life, regardless of socioeconomic status, race, ethnicity, and residence (urban/suburban/rural), suggests that no state can afford to ignore the policy questions surrounding developmental education. Noteworthy to the topic presented in this book is the recognition by a significant percentage of institutional actors as to the need for developmental instruction on their campuses. On very few occasions did we hear that these courses were unwanted on their campuses, but rather we heard more of a general feeling of wondering, "what more can [they] do" to make their students successful. At the same time, these perspectives were frequently tempered by policies that, at times, seemingly forced them to mask the instruction and services they needed to provide to meet the needs of students considered underprepared for college-level work. In other words, state policies, whether restrictive or more guiding, did not change the fact that many admitted students were still in need of academic support to succeed in college.

Kentucky seemed to be the exception as recent state policies (SB1) clearly suggest that state legislators recognized the potential for developmental education to be a strategy enabling academic success for students who are underprepared. One university president suggested that developmental education "gives a second opportunity for the Commonwealth of Kentucky to make sure that these students become contributing citizens... to drive industry and to drive economic development in the state." Thus, reforming and improving developmental education in Kentucky was not only viewed as important for institutional purposes, but also for meeting state priorities and goals related to college degree attainment, economic development, and productivity. This president further argued, "It costs more money to put those students into jail than to prepare them for a college education." Indeed, what a state chooses to do about developmental education is an indication of its priorities.

Given the demands of our global economy and the call to action by our president to increase this country's college degree attainment rates, policymakers and institutional leaders need to critically ask themselves what it will take to develop and see through more effective developmental education policy. As demonstrated in the findings presented here, Kentucky's SB1 and the promising start of Colorado's CAP4K initiatives build on a foundation that frames developmental education as a strategy to be used in promoting academic success, degree attainment, and workforce development. In doing so, postsecondary institutions are empowered to pilot, implement, and bring to scale effective practices that prioritize long-term goals related to the common good over short-term financial decisions and the pursuit of individual institutional prestige.

While some state leaders may argue that financial instability and economic imperatives require higher education to eliminate developmental education in some contexts (due to what some narrowly view as ineffective or inefficient programs), we see a moral imperative for students who are so-called developmental or underprepared to not only have access to four-year institutions (if they choose), but also maintain the full commitment of their institutions to support their success. We believe, like so many of those we interviewed, that four-year colleges and universities with missions to serve their regional communities and beyond must not only admit but also educate the students who knock at their doors. To meet this moral imperative, policymakers and institutional leaders must be committed to serving all students, not just those whose test scores are high. Our research attests that four-year colleges and universities play a critical role in developmental education. Most of the faculty, staff, and administrators who work within the institutions we visited seem to understand this. The key is to move more policymakers to understand this as well so they may develop more thoughtful and contextually appropriate policies that support institutions in their efforts. We live in an age where a college education is not a luxury but a necessity. Our nation can ill afford to pick and choose who has access and still expect to become the most educated citizenry in the world.

Notes

1 Introduction—The State of Developmental Education

1. David R. Arendale, "A Glossary of Developmental Education and Learning Assistance Terms." *Journal of College Reading and Learning* 38, no. 1 (2007): 10–34.
2. Ibid.
3. David R. Arendale, "Special Issue: Access at the Crossroads—Learning Assistance in Higher Education." *ASHE Higher Education Report* 35, no. 6 (2010): 1–145.
4. Tara L. Parker, "The Role of Minority-Serving Institutions in Redefining and Improving Developmental Education," *Southern Education Foundation* (2012), 3–21. These states include Arkansas, Colorado, Florida, Georgia, Louisiana, Missouri, Montana, Nebraska, Nevada, Ohio, Oklahoma, South Carolina, Tennessee, and Utah.
5. P. Attewell, D. Lavin, T. Domina, and T. Levey, "New Evidence on College Remediation." *Journal of Higher Education* 77, no. 5 (2006), 886–924.
6. J. Immerwahr, *Public Attitudes on Higher Education: A Trend Analysis: 1993 to 2003* (San Jose, CA: National Center for Public Policy and Higher Education, 2004).
7. Attewell et al., "New Evidence on Remediation," 903.
8. Complete College America, *Remediation: Higher Education's Bridge to Nowhere* (Washington, DC: Author, 2012).
9. Attewell et al., "New Evidence on Remediation," 888.
10. Arendale, "Access at the Crossroads," 3.
11. C. A. Kozeracki, "ERIC Review: Issues in Developmental Education." *Community College Review* 29, no. 4 (2002): 83–100; B. T. Long, "The Remediation Debate: Are We Serving the Needs of Underprepared College Students?" *National Crosstalk* 13, no. 4 (2005), http:www.highereducation.org/crosstalk/ct0405/voices0405-long.shtml
12. David W. Breneman and William N. Haarlow, "Remediation in Higher Education. A Symposium Featuring 'Developmental Education: Costs and Consequences,'" *Fordham Report* 2, no. 9 (1998); Strong American Schools, *Diploma to Nowhere* (Washington, DC: Author, 2008).
13. See, e.g., Jay P. Greene, "The Cost of Developmental Education: How Much Michigan Pays When Students Fail to Learn Basic Skills. Estimates

of the Annual Economic Cost to Businesses, Colleges, and Universities to Counteract Employees' and Students' Lack of Basic Reading, Writing, and Arithmetic Skills" (Midland, MI: Mackinac Center for Public Policy, 2000).
14. Breneman and Haarlow, "Remediation in Higher Education."
15. Strong American Schools, *Diploma to Nowhere*.
16. Alliance for Excellent Education, *Paying Double: Inadequate High Schools and Community College Remediation* (Washington, DC: Author, 2008).
17. Alicia C. Dowd and Laura M. Ventimiglia, "a Cost Estimate of Standards-Based Remediation in a Community College Developmental Education Program." Unpublished manuscript (2008).
18. R. Phipps, *College Remediation: What It Is, What It Costs, What's at Stake* (Washington, DC: Institute for Higher Education Policy, 1998).
19. Ibid., vii.
20. Merisotis and R. A. Phipps, "Developmental Education in Colleges and Universities: What's Really Going on?" *The Review of Higher Education* 24, no. 1 (2000): 67–85.
21. Ibid., 78.
22. The College Board, *Trends in College Pricing* (Washington: Author, 2013).
23. Dowd and Ventimiglia, "Cost Estimate of Remediation," 3–41.
24. Tatiana Melguizo, Linda S. Hagedorn, and Scott Cypers. "Remedial/Developmental Education and the Cost of Community College Transfer: A Los Angeles County Sample." *Review of Higher Education* 31, no. 4 (2008): 401–31.
25. Watson S. Swail, with Kenneth E. Redd and Laura W. Perna, "Retaining Minority Students in Higher Education: A Framework for Success." *ASHE-ERIC Higher Education Report* (San Francisco, CA: Jossey-Bass Higher and Adult Education Series, 2003).
26. Eric Bettinger and Bridget T. Long, "Addressing the Needs of Under-Prepared Students in Higher Education: Does College Remediation Work?" Working Paper 11325 (Cambridge MA: National Bureau of Economic Research, 2009).
27. Mark Schneider and Lu M. Win, "Completion Matters: The High Cost of Low Community College Graduation Rates," *American Enterprise Institute for Public Policy Research*, no. 2 (Washington, DC, April 2012).
28. Georges Vernez, Richard A. Krop, and C. Peter Rydell, "Closing the Education Gap: Benefits and Costs." Center for Research on Immigration Policy (Washington, DC: RAND Education, 1999).
29. Alliance for Excellent Education, *Paying Double*, http://all4ed.org/wp-content/uploads/remediation.pdf
30. CUNY Board of Trustees voted in May 1998 to phase out developmental education courses in its four-year colleges.
31. Mariana Alfonso, "The Impact of Community College Attendance on Baccalaureate Attainment." *Research in Higher Education* 47, no. 8 (2006): 873–903; Alison Bernstein and J. S. Eaton. "The Transfer Function: Building Curricular Roadways Across and Among Higher Education Institutions," in M. J. Justiz, R. Wilson, and L. G. Bork (eds.) *Minorities in Higher Education*

(Phoenix: American Council on Education, 1994): 215–60; Kevin J. Dougherty, "Community Colleges and Baccalaureate Attainment." *Journal of Higher Education* 63, no, 2 (1992): 188–214.
32. "Obama Administration Launches College Scorecard," http://www.whitehouse.gov/blog/2013/02/13/obama-administration-launches-college-scorecard
33. A. Russell, *Enhancing College Student Success through Developmental Education* (Washington, DC: American Association of State Colleges and Universities, 2008), 5.
34. Attewell et al., "New Evidence on Remediation," *The Journal of Higher Education*, 77, no. 5 (September/October 2006): 886–924, 916.
35. Melguizo et al., "Remedial/Developmental Education," 420.
36. Ibid., 425.
37. M. K. Callahan and D. Chumney, "'Write Like College': How Developmental Writing Courses at a Community College and a Research University Position 'At-Risk' Students in the Field of Higher Education." *Teacher's College Record* 111, no. 7 (2009): 1619–64.
38. Ibid.
39. Ibid., 1661.
40. J. S. Brubacher and W. Rudy, *Higher Education in Transition*, 3rd ed. (New York: Harper & Row, 1976), 109.
41. D. McGrath and M. B. Spear, *The Academic Crisis of the Community College* (New York: State University of New York Press, 1991), 46.
42. Christopher Jencks and David Riesman, "The Academic Revolution." (1968), quoted in McGrath and Spear, *The Academic Crisis*, 491–92.
43. William G. Tierney and Lisa D. Garcia, "Preparing Underprepared Students for College: Remedial Education and Early Assessment Programs." *Journal of At-Risk Issues* 14 no. 2 (2008), 1–7.
44. Bettinger and Long, "Addressing the Needs."
45. Attewell et al., "New Evidence on Remediation"; Alexander McCormick, Paula R. Knepper, and Laura Horn, *A Descriptive Summary of 1992–93 Bachelor's Degree Recipients 1 Year Later: With an Essay on Time to Degree* (Darby, PA: Diane, 1996); Clifford Adelman, "Answers in the Tool Box: Academic Intensity, Attendance Patterns, and Bachelor's Degree Attainment" (Washington, DC: US Department of Education, 1999); Clifford Adelman, "The Toolbox Revisited: Paths to Degree Completion from High School through College" (Washington, DC: US Department of Education, 2006).
46. Adelman, "The Toolbox Revisited."
47. Adelman, "Answers in the Toolbox."
48. Eric P. Bettinger and Bridget T. Long, "Remediation at the Community College: Student Participation and Outcomes." *New Directions for Community Colleges*, no. 129 (2005): 17–26.
49. Two-year college students were included in the sample only if they indicated intent to transfer on their community college application; Bettinger and Long, "Addressing the Needs."
50. Ibid.

51. Bettinger and Long, "Remediation at Community College"; Bettinger and Long, "Addressing the Needs."
52. Juan Carlos Calcagno, Peter Crosta, Thomas Bailey, and Davis Jenkins, "Does Age of Entrance Affect Community College Completion Probabilities? Evidence from a Discrete Time Hazard Model." *Educational Evaluation and Policy Analysis* 29, no. 3 (2007): 218–35.
53. Bettinger and Long, "Addressing the Needs"; Attewell et al., "New Evidence on Remediation."
54. Attewell et al., "New Evidence on Remediation," 912.
55. Ibid.
56. J. M. Ignash, "Who Should Provide Postsecondary Developmental/Developmental Education?" in J. M. Ignash (ed.), *Implementing Effective Policies for Developmental and Developmental Education, New Directions for Community Colleges*, no. 100 (San Francisco: Jossey-Bass, 1997); The National Center for Education Statistics (NCES), US Department of Education, "Developmental Education at Degree-Granting Postsecondary Institutions in Fall 2000" (NCES 2004–10). Accessed May 30, 2014, http://nces.ed.gov/surveys/peqis/publications/2004010/; Merisotis and Phipps, "Developmental Education," 69.
57. Attewell et al., "New Evidence on Remediation," 898.
58. Ibid.
59. Ibid., 908.
60. Thomas Bailey, Dong Wook Jeong, and Sung-Woo Cho, "Referral, Enrollment, and Completion in Developmental Education Sequences in Community Colleges." *Economics of Education Review* 29, no. 2 (2010): 255–70.
61. Thomas Bailey, "Rethinking Developmental Education in Community College: CCRC Brief No. 40," Community College Research Center (Columbia University, 2009), 2.
62. Anne Schneider and Helen Ingram, "Social Construction of Target Populations: Implications for Politics and Policy." *American Political Science Review* 87, no. 2 (1993): 334–47, 334.

2   A History of Developmental Education

1. Alexander W. Astin, "Rethinking Academic Excellence." *Liberal Education* 85, no. 2 (1999): 8–18; J. P. Merisotis and R. A. Phipps, "Remedial Education in Colleges and Universities: What's Really Going on?" *Review of Higher Education* 24, no. 1 (2000): 67–85.
2. The National Center for Education Statistics (NCES), US Department of Education, "Remedial Education at Degree-Granting Postsecondary Institutions in Fall 2000" (NCES 2004–10). Accessed May 30, 2014, http://nces.ed.gov/surveys/peqis/publications/2004010/; Merisotis and Phipps, "Remedial Education," 67–85.
3. Merisotis and Phipps, "Remedial Education," 69.

4. M. E. Casazza and S. L. Silverman, *Learning Assistance and Developmental Education* (San Francisco: Jossey-Bass, 1996).
5. J. S. Brubacher and W. Rudy, *Higher Education in Transition*, 3rd ed. (New York: Harper & Row, 1976), 109.
6. Ibid., 268.
7. Casazza and Silverman, *Learning Assistance*, 4.
8. F. Rudolph, *The American College and University: a History* (Athens, GA: University of Georgia Press, 1990), 6.
9. Brubacher and Rudy, *Higher Education*, 3–5; Rudolph, *The American College*, 3–22.
10. Brubacher and Rudy, *Higher Education*, 10.
11. Ibid.
12. W. H. Jeynes, *American Educational History: School, Society and the Common Good* (Thousand Oaks, CA: Sage, 2007).
13. D. A. Clowes, "Remediation in American Higher Education," in J. Smart (ed.), *Higher Education: Handbook of Theory and Research*, Vol. 8, 460–93 (New York: Agathon Press, 1980); Brubacher and Rudy, *Higher Education*, 100–119.
14. B. T. Long, "The Remediation Debate: Are We Serving the Needs of Underprepared College Students?" *National Crosstalk* 13, no. 4 (2005), http:www.highereducation.org/crosstalk/ct0405/voices0405-long.shtml
15. Rudolph, *The American College*, 63.
16. Brubacher and Rudy, *Higher Education*, 107.
17. A. M. Cohen, *The Shaping of American Higher Education: Emergence and Growth of the Contemporary System* (San Francisco: Jossey-Bass, 1998); Rudolph, *The American College*, 21–22.
18. Brubacher and Rudy, *Higher Education*, 11–12; Rudolph, *The American College*, 21–22.
19. Casazza and Silverman, *Learning Assistance*, 8.
20. Brubacher and Rudy, *Higher Education*, 11–12.
21. Ibid., 244.
22. Rudolph, *The American College*, 47; Cohen, *Shaping American Higher Education*, 65.
23. H. R. Boylan and W. G. White, "Educating All the Nation's People: The Historical Roots of Developmental Education, Part 1." *Review of Research in Developmental Education* 4, no. 4 (1987): 1–4.
24. M. E. Casazza, "Who Are We and Where Did We Come From?" *Journal of Developmental Education* 23, no. 1 (1999): 2–7.
25. Ellen Brier, "Bridging the Academic Preparation Gap: An Historical View." *Journal of Developmental and Remedial Education* 8, no. 1 (1984): 2–5, quoted in Casazza and Silverman, *Learning Assistance*, 8.
26. Casazza and Silverman, *Learning Assistance*, 10.
27. Boylan and White, "Educating the Nation's People." 1–4.
28. D. Arendale, *Then and Now: The Early Years of Developmental Education* (Kansas City, MO: University of Missouri–Kansas City, n.d.); E. Boyer,

College: The Undergraduate Experience in America (New York: Harper & Row, 1987).
29. D. Arendale, *History of Developmental Education: 19th Century Preparatory Academies* (Twin Cities, MN: University of Minnesota, n.d.).
30. Clarence Shedd, "Higher Education in the United States," in *The University in a Changing World: a Symposium* (1932): 125–62, quoted in Casazza and Silverman, *Learning Assistance*.
31. J. M. Ignash, "Who Should Provide Postsecondary Remedial/Developmental Education?" in J. M. Ignash (ed.), *Implementing Effective Policies for Remedial and Developmental Education*, New Directions for Community Colleges, no. 100 (San Francisco: Jossey-Bass, 1997).
32. NCES, "Remedial Education."
33. Casazza and Silverman, *Learning Assistance*, 13.
34. Brubacher and Rudy, *Higher Education*, 243.
35. Arendale, *History of Developmental Education*. 1–23.
36. Jeynes, *American Educational History*. 1–469.
37. Ibid., 184.
38. W. J. Urban and J. L. Wagoner, *American Education: A History*, 4th ed. (New York: Routledge, 2009).
39. Robert F. Butts and Lawrence A. Cremin, a *History of Education in American Culture* (New York: Holt, Rinehart and Winston, 1953), quoted in Casazza and Silverman, *Learning Assistance*, 14.
40. Alliance for Excellent Education, *Paying Double: Inadequate High Schools and Community College Remediation* (Washington, DC: Author, 2008).
41. Brubacher and Rudy, *Higher Education*, 75.
42. Boylan and White, "Educating the Nation's People"; Brubacher and Rudy, *Higher Education*, 74–75.
43. Casazza and Silverman, *Learning Assistance*, 20.
44. Frank W. Parr, "The Extent of Remedial Reading Work in State Universities in the United States." *School and Society* 31, no. 799 (1930): 547–48, quoted in Casazza and Silverman, *Learning Assistance*.
45. Ruth E. Eckert and Edward S. Jones, "Longtime Effects of Training College Students How to Study," *School and Society* 42 (1935): 685–88, quoted in Casazza and Silverman, *Learning Assistance*.
46. Brubacher and Rudy, *Higher Education*, 253.
47. Casazza and Silverman, *Learning Assistance*, 17.
48. Cohen, *Shaping American Higher Education*, 10.
49. Brubacher and Rudy, *Higher Education*, 254.
50. Casazza and Silverman, *Learning Assistance*, 17.
51. Cohen, *Shaping American Higher Education*, 112.
52. Martha Maxwell, "Improving Student Learning Skills: A Comprehensive Guide to Successful Practices and Programs for Increasing the Performance of Underprepared Students" (San Francisco: Jossey-Bass, 1979), quoted in Clowes, *Remediation in Higher Education*.

53. Maxwell, "Improving Student Learning," quoted in Casazza and Silverman, *Learning Assistance*.
54. E. Brier, "Bridging the Academic Preparation Gap: An Historical View," *Journal of Developmental Education* 8, no. 1 (1984): 1–53.
55. Rudolph, *The American College*, 63.
56. Brier, *Bridging the Gap*, 3.
57. Casazza and Silverman, *Learning Assistance*, 11.
58. Rudolph, *The American College*, 134.
59. Jeynes, *American Educational History*.
60. Cohen, *Shaping American Higher Education*, 65.
61. Brubacher and Rudy, *Higher Education*, 247.
62. Casazza and Silverman, *Learning Assistance*, 20.
63. Brubacher and Rudy, *Higher Education*, 254.
64. D. McGrath and M. B. Spear, *The Academic Crisis of the Community College* (New York: State University of New York Press, 1991).
65. Dorothy M. Knoell and Leland L. Medsker, "From Junior to Senior College: A National Study of the Transfer Student" (1965), in McGrath and Spear, *The Academic Crisis*.
66. Ibid., 38.
67. A. M. Cohen and F. B. Brawer, *The American Community College*, 4th ed. (San Francisco: Jossey-Bass, 2003).
68. Ibid., 28–29.
69. Brubacher and Rudy, *Higher Education*, 260.
70. J. E. Roueche, *Salvage, Redirection, or Custody? Remedial Education in the Community Junior College* (Washington, DC: American Association of Community and Junior Colleges, 1968); J. E. Roueche and W. R. Kirk, *Catching Up: Remedial Education* (San Francisco: Jossey-Bass, 1973).
71. Roueche, *Salvage Redirection or Custody*; see Richard Bossone, "Remedial English Instruction in California Public Junior Colleges: An Analysis and Evaluation of Current Practices" (Sacramento, CA: California State Department of Education, 1966).
72. Center for Student Success, *Basic Skills as a Foundation for Success in California Community Colleges*, (USA Funds, 2007), 9.
73. Alliance for Excellent Education, *Paying Double*, 3.
74. Strong American Schools, *Diploma to Nowhere* (Washington, DC: Author, 2008).
75. R. Phipps, *College Remediation: What It Is, What It Costs, What's at Stake* (Washington, DC: Institute for Higher Education Policy, 1998); Merisotis and Phipps, "Remedial Education."
76. See, e.g., Eric P. Bettinger and Bridget T. Long. "Addressing the Needs of Underprepared Students in Higher Education Does College Remediation Work?" *Journal of Human Resources* 44, no. 3 (2009): 736–71, and M. Callahan and Donalda Chumney, "'Write Like College': How Remedial Writing Courses at a Community College and a Research University Position 'At-Risk' Students in the Field of Higher Education," *Teachers*

College Record 111, no. 7 (2009): 1619–64; C. A. Kozeracki, "ERIC Review: Issues in Developmental Education," *Community College Review* 29, no. 4 (2002): 95.
77. M. Soliday, *The Politics of Remediation: Institutional and Student Needs in Higher Education* (Pittsburgh, PA: University of Pittsburgh Press, 2002), 23.
78. Ibid.
79. McGrath and Spear, *The Academic Crisis*, 45.
80. Soliday, *The Politics of Remediation*, 21.
81. Brubacher and Rudy, *Learning Assistance*, 248.

3 Developmental Education as a Strategy Toward State and Institutional Goals

1. D. Yanow, "Making Sense of Policy Practices: Interpretation and Meaning," 2012, http://www.academia.edu/1878750/Making_sense_of_policy_practices _Interpretation_and_meaning
2. An additional level would be the national policy environment to include federal policies such as affirmative action, financial aid, and others.
3. Education Commission of the States, *Rebuilding the Remedial Education Bridge to College Success* (Denver, CO: ECS, 2010).
4. Ibid.
5. Elinor Ostrom, "Institutional Rational Choice: An Assessment of the Institutional Analysis and Development Framework," in P. A. Sabatier (ed.), *Theories of the Policy Process* (Boulder, CO: Westview Press, 1999), 35–71.
6. Richard Richardson Jr. and Mario Martinez, *Policy and Performance in American Higher Education: An Examination of Cases across State Systems* (Baltimore, MD: Johns Hopkins University Press, 2009).
7. Elinor Ostrom, "Zooming in and Linking Action Situations," *Understanding Institutional Diversity* (Princeton, NJ: Princeton University Press, 2005), 32–68, 38.
8. Elinor Ostrom, "The Elements of an Action Situation." Unpublished manuscript (Bloomington, IN: Indiana University, 1983), 1–2.
9. www.gettingpastgo.socrata.com.
10. See, e.g., Thomas Bailey, Dong Wook Jeong, and Sung-Woo Cho, "Referral, Enrollment, and Completion in Developmental Education Sequences in Community Colleges," *Economics of Education Review* 29, no. 2 (2010), 255–70; Thomas Bailey, "Rethinking Developmental Education in Community College: CCRC Brief No. 40," Community College Research Center (Columbia University, 2009); Michael Collins, "Setting Up Success in Developmental Education: How State Policy Can Help Community Colleges Improve Student Outcomes (2009), 1–26, published by Jobs For the Future in Boston; Deborah Boroch, Jim Fillpot, Laura Hope, Robert Johnstone, Pamela Mery, Andreea Serban, Bruce Smith, and Robert S. Gabriner, "Basic Skills as a Foundation for Student Success in California Community Colleges." Research and Planning Group for California Community Colleges (RP Group, 2007);

Mary Perry, Peter R. Bahr, Matthew Rosin, and Kathryn M. Woodward, *Course-Taking Patterns, Policies, and Practices in Developmental Education in the California Community Colleges. A Report to the California Community Colleges Chancellor's Office* (Mountain View, CA: EdSource, 2010); Wendy Schwartz and Davis Jenkins, "Promising Practices for Community College Developmental Education: A Discussion Resource for the Connecticut Community College System." Community College Research Center (Columbia University, 2007); Elizabeth M. Zachry and Emily Schneider, "Building Foundations for Student Readiness: A Review of Rigorous Research and Promising Trends in Developmental Education. An NCPR Working Paper." Paper prepared for the National Center for Postsecondary Research Developmental Education Conference (New York, September 23–24, 2010).
11. Richardson and Martinez, *Policy and Performance in American Higher Education*, 2.

4 South Carolina

1. Paul Mackum and Steven Wilson, "Population Distribution and Change: 2001–2010," United States Census Bureau, March 2011, http://www.census.gov/prod/cen2010/briefs/c2010br-01.pdf
2. United States Department of Labor, Bureau of Labor Statistics, "Regional and State Unemployment Annual News Release," Bureau of Labor Statistics, February 29, 2012, http://www.bls.gov/news.release/archives/srgune_02292012.htm
3. United States Census Bureau, "2008–2012 American Community Survey," United States Census Bureau, http://factfinder2.census.gov/faces/tableservices/jsf/pages/productview.xhtml?pid=ACS_12_5YR_S1501
4. United States Department of Education, Institute of Education Science, "Fall 2008 through Spring 2011, Graduation Rates Component," National Center for Education Statistics, Integrated Postsecondary Education Data (IPEDS), http://nces.ed.gov/ipeds/datacenter/InstitutionByName.aspx
5. United States Department of Education, Institute of Education Science, "Fall 2005 through Spring 2011, Graduation Rates Component," National Center for Education Statistics, Integrated Postsecondary Education Data (IPEDS), http://nces.ed.gov/ipeds/datacenter/InstitutionByName.aspx
6. *The Corridor of Shame: The Neglect of South Carolina's Rural Schools*, dir. Bud Ferillo, Ferillo & Associates, 2006, DVD.
7. See http://www.corridorofshame.com/case.php and http://www.judicial.state.sc.us/whatsnew/displaywhatsnew.cfm?indexID=393 for further details about *Abbeville County School District et al. v. The State of South Carolina et al.*
8. United States Department of Education, Institute of Education Science, "Average Undergraduate Tuition and Fees and Room and Board Rates Charged for Full-Time Students in Degree-Granting Postsecondary Institutions, by Control and Level of Institution and State or Jurisdiction: 2011-12 and 2012-13 (NCES Digest Table 330.20)," National Center for

Education Statistics, Digest of Education Statistics, http://nces.ed.gov/programs/digest/d13/tables/dt13_330.20.asp

9. Higher Education Study Commission, "Leveraging Higher Education for a Stronger South Carolina," March 2009, I, http://www.che.sc.gov/CHE_Docs/InfoCntr/HESC_Files/che_2169_Leverage_Report_web.pdf.
10. South Carolina Commission on Higher Education, "Annual Accountability Report: Fiscal Year 2008–2009," September 2009, http://www.statelibrary.sc.gov/scedocs/H5373/001569.pdf
11. Ibid., 48.
12. Ibid., 57.
13. Higher Education Study Commission, "Leveraging Higher Education for a Stronger South Carolina," March 2009, 10, http://www.che.sc.gov/CHE_Docs/InfoCntr/HESC_Files/che_2169_Leverage_Report_web.pdf
14. Ibid.
15. See http://www.scstatehouse.gov/code/t59c104.php
16. See http://www.scstatehouse.gov/query.php?search=DOC&searchtext=remedial%20education&category=LEGISLATION&session=111&conid=7483953&result_pos=0&keyval=1110019&numrows=10
17. See http://www.scstatehouse.gov/code/t59c101.php
18. See South Carolina Commission on Higher Education, "A Closer look at Public Higher Education in South Carolina: Institutional Effectiveness, Accountability, and Performance" or the "Higher Education Statistical Abstracts from 1996–2012," http://dc.statelibrary.sc.gov/handle/10827/5395; http://dc.statelibrary.sc.gov/handle/10827/5396; and http://www.che.sc.gov/CHE_Docs/finance/abstract/Abstract-2012-webaa.pdf
19. South Carolina Commission on Higher Education, "A Closer Look at Public Higher Education in South Carolina: Institutional Effectiveness, Accountability, and Performance," January 2007, 59, http://www.cpec.ca.gov/CompleteReports/ExternalDocuments/SCarolina_A_Closer_Look_January2007-Final2.pdf

5 Oklahoma

1. US Census Bureau, "State Population—Rank, Percent Change, and Population Density: 1980 to 2010," Statistical Abstract of the United States, 2012. Accessed April 23, 2014, https://www.census.gov/compendia/statab/2012/tables/12s0014.pdf; Paul Mackum and Steven Wilson, "Population Distribution and Change: 2001–2010," United States Census Bureau, March 2011, http://www.census.gov/prod/cen2010/briefs/c2010br-01.pdf
2. US Census Bureau, "State and County QuickFacts: Oklahoma," United States Census Bureau, http://quickfacts.census.gov/qfd/states/40000.html
3. Ibid.
4. United States Department of Labor Bureau of Labor Statistics, "Regional and State Unemployment (Annual) News Release," Bureau of Labor Statistics, http://www.bls.gov/news.release/archives/srgune_02292012.htm

5. United States Department of Labor Bureau of Labor Statistics, "Occupational and Employment Statistics," Bureau of Labor Statistics, http://www.bls.gov/oes/2011/may/oes_ok.htm#00-0000
6. Oklahoma Department of Commerce, "Northwest Oklahoma Regional Ecosystem Report," http://okcommerce.gov/assets/files/data-and-research/workforce-data/ecosystem-briefings/Oklahoma_Regional_Ecosystem_Briefing-Northwest.pdf
7. Citizens Commission on the Future of Oklahoma Higher Education, "Final Report and Recommendations," ii, http://www.okhighered.org/studies-reports/citizens-comm/planningcommission.pdf
8. Ibid., viii.
9. Ibid., 22.
10. Ibid.
11. Kathleen McKean, "Educational Reform in Oklahoma: A Review of Major Legislation and Educational Performance Since 1980," *Oklahoma Policy Institute,* March 2013, http://okpolicy.org/wp-content/uploads/2013/03/EdReform_OTAC_fullbrief.pdf
12. McKeen, "Educational Reform"; Oklahoma State Department of Education, "ACE College Preparatory Curriculum Opt Out List, 2011-2012," http://www.ok.gov/sde/sites/ok.gov.sde/files/documents/files/OptOutByDIST_0.pdf
13. Oklahoma State System of Higher Education, "2010 Annual Report: Degrees of Progress," http://www.okhighered.org/studies-reports/annual-report2010.pdf
14. Oklahoma State Regents for Higher Education, "Ten-Year Comparison of Annual Unduplicated Headcount Enrollment 2003-04 to 2012-13," http://www.okhighered.org/oeis/enrollment/Trends/2012-13TenYearComparison.html
15. Oklahoma State Regents for Higher Education, "First-Time Freshman Enrollments at Public and Private Institutions 2008-09 to 2012-2013," http://www.okhighered.org/oeis/enrollment/FTFreshmen/Table_8_2012-13_FTFreshmen.html
16. Oklahoma State Regents for Higher Education, "First-Time Freshman Freshmen Enrollments in Developmental Education Courses 2003-04 to 2012-2013," http://www.okhighered.org/oeis/preparation/remediation%20report/1213FirstTimeFreshmenTable3.html
17. Oklahoma State Regents for Higher Education, "Annual Student Assessment Report," June 23, 2011, 49, http://www.okhighered.org/studies-reports/assessment/2011-student-assess.pdf
18. Oklahoma State Regents for Higher Education, "Educational and General Budgets, Summary and Analysis, Fiscal Year 2010," http://www.okhighered.org/studies-reports/fy10-eg-summary-analysis.pdf
19. David Blatt, "State Question 744: The Wrong Solution." *Oklahoma Policy Institute* 3, no. 2 (July 2010), http://okpolicy.org/files/SQ744_brief.pdf

20. Oklahoma State Regents of Higher Education, "FY 2010–11 Tuition Impact Analysis Report," December 2010, https://www.okhighered.org/studies-reports/tuition-impact-analysis-10-11.pdf
21. Oklahoma State Regents for Higher Education, "Oklahoma's Promise: 2010–2011 Year End Report," http://www.okhighered.org/okpromise/okp-report-10-11.pdf
22. Oklahoma State Regents for Higher Education, "Annual Student Remediation Report," February 2009, http://www.okhighered.org/studies-reports/remediation/remediation-report-2-09.pdf
23. Northeastern State University, "Tuition and Fees," http://offices.nsuok.edu/admissions/TuitionFees.aspx
24. Oklahoma State University, "Cost of Attendance," http://www.osuokc.edu/future/costs.aspx
25. Oklahoma City Community College, "Tuition/Fees/Refunds," http://www.occc.edu/bursar/tuition-fees.html
26. Oklahoma State Regents for Higher Education, "Annual Student Remediation Report."
27. Oklahoma State Regents for Higher Education, "Policy Statement on the Assessment of Students for Purposes of Instructional Improvement and State Accountability," http://tulsagrad.ou.edu/assessmentT/osrhe.htm
28. Oklahoma State Regents for Higher Education, "Annual Student Assessment Report," June 23, 2011, http://www.okhighered.org/studies-reports/assessment/2011-student-assess.pdf
29. Ibid., 1.
30. Ibid.
31. Ibid., 3.
32. Oklahoma State Regents for Higher Education, "Policies and Procedures Manual," http://www.okhighered.org/state-system/policy-procedures/part3.shtml; Oklahoma State Regents for Higher Education, "Academic Affairs Procedures Handbook," http://www.okhighered.org/state-system/policy-procedures/2014/AA%20Procedures%20Handbook%20February%202014.pdf
33. Oklahoma State Regents for Higher Education, "Policies," 184.
34. Oklahoma State Department of Education, "ACE Opt Out List," http://www.ok.gov/sde/documents/2012-01-10/ace-college-preparatory-curriculum-opt-out-list
35. Oklahoma State Regents for Higher Education, "Brain Gain 2010: Building Oklahoma through Intellectual Power," January 1999, http://www.okhighered.org/studies-reports/brain-gain/braingainreport.pdf

6 Colorado

1. US Census Bureau, "State Population—Rank, Percent Change, and Population Density: 1980 to 2010," Statistical Abstract of the United States: 2012, Accessed April 23, 2014, https://www.census.gov/compendia/statab/2012/

tables/12s0014.pdf; Paul Mackum and Steven Wilson, "Population Distribution and Change: 2001–2010," United States Census Bureau, March 2011, http://www.census.gov/prod/cen2010/briefs/c2010br-01.pdf
2. US Census Bureau, "State and County QuickFacts: Colorado," United States Census Bureau, http://quickfacts.census.gov/qfd/states/08000.html
3. Ibid.
4. US Department of Labor Bureau of Labor Statistics, "Regional and State Unemployment (Annual) News Release," Bureau of Labor Statistics, http://www.bls.gov/news.release/archives/srgune_02292012.htm
5. US Department of Labor Bureau of Labor Statistics, "Occupational and Employment Statistics," Bureau of Labor Statistics, http://www.bls.gov/oes/2013/may/oes_co.htm#00-0000
6. Anthony P. Carnevale, Nicole Smith, and Jeff Strohl, "Recovery: Projections of Jobs and Education Requirements through 2020," (Washington, DC: Center on Education and the Workforce, Georgetown University, 2013), https://georgetown.app.box.com/s/kg8r28e48gsaw8ypplxp
7. US Census Bureau, Current Population Survey, Educational Attainment in the United States, 2012 (American Community Survey, 3 year estimates), http://factfinder2.census.gov/faces/tableservices/jsf/pages/productview.xhtml?pid=ACS_12_3YR_S0201&prodType=table
8. Ibid.
9. Ibid., 7.
10. Ibid., 9.
11. US Census Bureau, "American Community Survey," 2008–10, http://factfinder2.census.gov/faces/tableservices/jsf/pages/productview.xhtml?pid=ACS_12_5YR_S1501
12. Colorado Department of Higher Education, "2013 Legislative Report on the Postsecondary Progress and Success of High School Graduates," April 2013, http://highered.colorado.gov/Publications/Reports/Legislative/PostSecondary/2013_Postsecondary_Progress_rel20130416_rev.pdf
13. Colorado Department of Higher Education, "2014 Legislative Report on the Postsecondary Progress and Success of High School Graduates," May 2014, http://highered.colorado.gov/Publications/Reports/Legislative/PostSecondary/2014_Postsecondary_Progress_rel20140505.pdf
14. Colorado Department of Higher Education, 2014 Legislative Report, 8.
15. Colorado Revised Statute, "Title 23, Article 1: Colorado Commission of Higher Education," 2013, http://www.lexisnexis.com/hottopics/colorado/?source=COLO;CODE&tocpath=1W80K9IS5WNSSO2EK,2RM0WSI4QCHMEHP0G,389XJOAWQET4NK2FJ;1KFCTJK08UXKL4J21,2JKGCK59SGWZ9EJWC,3RQ3QG033EOW0EGDO;18H9HOBPHSJS91BT6,2XHLAOOUSKEYSQ2T8,3MQVJCG04NRA3S3YJ&shortheader=no
16. See http://highered.colorado.gov/CCHE/history.html
17. Colorado Revised Statute, "Higher Education Accountability," Article 13, 1985, http://www.colorado.edu/pba/outcomes/ovview/hb1187.htm

18. Colorado State Legislature, "Senate Bill 08:018," 2008, http://www.leg.state.co.us/clics/clics2008a/csl.nsf/billcontainers/DC4745338CA663BB8725737F004D4557/$FILE/018_enr.pdf
19. Ibid., 2.
20. Ibid., 9.
21. Heather Clapp Padgette, "High School Reform in Colorado: A History of Efforts and Lessons for the Future," February 2009, http://www.coloradokids.org/file_download/25c98bb2-9dea-4cdc-a724-a2870c0f5e04
22. Dianne L. Lefly, Cheryll D. Lovell, Jo McF O'Brien, "Shining a Light on College Remediation in Colorado: The Predictive Utility of the ACT for Colorado and the Colorado Student Assessment Program" (CSAP), March 2011, http://www.cde.state.co.us/sites/default/files/documents/research/download/pdf/shiningalightonremediation.pdf
23. Padgett, "High School Reform," 9.
24. See http://www.cde.state.co.us/sites/default/files/documents/cdedepcom/download/pdf/sb212completelegislation.pdf
25. State Board of Education, "Colorado High School Graduation Guidelines," May 2013, 3, http://www.cde.state.co.us/sites/default/files/adoptedgraduationguidelines2013.pdf
26. State of Colorado, "Colorado's Postsecondary and Workforce Readiness (PWR) High School Diploma Endorsement Criteria," April 2013, 3, http://www.cde.state.co.us/sites/default/files/documents/secondaryinitiatives/downloads/pwrendorseddiplomacriteria.pdf
27. State Board of Education, "Graduation Guidelines," 2.
28. Colorado Department of Higher Education, "Degree Dividend: Building Our Economy and Preserving Our Way of Life: Colorado Must Decide," November 2010, http://highered.colorado.gov/Publications/General/StrategicPlanning/Meetings/Resources/strategicplan_final_nov0410.pdf
29. Ibid., 6.
30. Colorado Commission on Higher Education, "Colorado Competes: A Completion Agenda for Higher Education," October 2012, http://highered.colorado.gov/Publications/General/StrategicPlanning/MasterPlan2012/Master_Plan_Final.pdf
31. Colorado Department of Higher Education, "Statewide Remedial Education Policy," November 2004, http://highered.colorado.gov/Publications/Policies/Archive/i-parte11-04.pdf
32. Ibid., I-E-6.
33. Independence Institute, "The Funding Crisis in Colorado's Higher Education System," December 2010, http://tax.i2i.org/files/2010/12/IB_2010_D_a.pdf
34. Padgette, "High School Reform."
35. Lefly et al., "Shining a Light."
36. To maintain the confidentiality of study participants' identities, pseudonyms are used for the college programs.
37. Colorado Commission on Higher Education, "Colorado Competes," 13.

7 North Carolina

1. Center on Budget and Policy Priorities, "States Are Still Funding Higher Education below Pre-Recession Levels," http://www.cbpp.org/files/5-1-14sfp.pdf
2. Six-year graduation rates based on an average of three cohorts who entered college between 2004 and 2006.
3. National Governors Association, "Complete to Compete: North Carolina Higher Education Data Dashboard," 2011, http://www.nga.org/files/live/sites/NGA/files/pdf/C2C-NC-Dashboard.pdf
4. The University of North Carolina Remedial/Developmental Activities Report, The University of North Carolina General Administration, February 12, 2009.
5. UNC, "Remedial/Developmental Education Report 2011-12," University of North Carolina General Administration, February 2013, https://www.northcarolina.edu/sites/default/files/documents/remedial-developmental_ed_2011-12_0.pdf
6. SUCCESSNC NC Community Colleges Final Report 2013, http://www.successnc.org/sites/default/files/SuccessNC%20Report.pdf
7. Ibid., 3.
8. Testing Policies for the North Carolina Diagnostic and Placement Test, State Board of Community College, 2006, http://www.nccommunitycolleges.edu/sites/default/files/state-board/program/prog_3_4.pdf
9. SUCCESSNC Developmental Education Initiative Actvity Report, February 2013.
10. North Carolina General Statutues 115D.

8 Kentucky

1. US Census Bureau, "State Population—Rank, Percent Change, and Population Density: 1980 to 2010," Statistical Abstract of the United States: 2012, Accessed April 23, 2014, https://www.census.gov/compendia/statab/2012/tables/12s0014.pdf
2. US Census Bureau, "State and County QuickFacts: Kentucky," United States Census Bureau, http://quickfacts.census.gov/qfd/states/21000.html
3. US Department of Labor, Bureau of Labor Statistics, "Regional and State Unemployment Annual News Release," *Bureau of Labor Statistics*, February 29, 2012, http://www.bls.gov/news.release/archives/srgune_02292012.htm
4. The National Center for Higher Education Management System Information Center, "State and Local Support for Higher Education Operating Expenses Per Capita, 2011," Accessed April 3, 2014, http://www.higheredinfo.org/dbrowser/index.php?measure=48

5. US, "Educational Attainment, 2008–2012 American Community Survey," Accessed April 3, 2014, http://factfinder2.census.gov/faces/tableservices/jsf/pages/productview.xhtml?pid=ACS_12_5YR_S1501
6. Kentucky Council of Postsecondary Education, "Students Entering College with Developmental Needs," April 1, 2009, http://cpe.ky.gov/NR/rdonlyres/70AD5017-7CE5-4CFB-AAA3-0DD82CECB32B/0/Graph_student_entering_dev_need_20090401.pdf
7. Kentucky Council on Postsecondary Education, "Developmental Education Needs in the 2006 Entering Cohort," August 26, 2008, http://cpe.ky.gov/NR/rdonlyres/B42243CB-D19A-4EC4-AD34-ECF2900D51B1/0/Dev_needs_2006_20090605.pdf
8. Kentucky Council on Postsecondary Education, "Number of Developmental Courses by Subject and Institution," December 30, 2009, http://cpe.ky.gov/NR/rdonlyres/9E26D448-EF95-4910-B3CA-4774C2FF363C/0/Dev_Courses_by_Sector_20091230.pdf
9. Steven L. Beshear, Commonwealth of Kentucky "College and Career Readiness Month Proclamation," September 1, 2010, http://cpe.ky.gov/NR/rdonlyres/0A525B83-84A9-449B-A91D-B097BF7EBA06/0/2010PROC212683.pdf
10. Kentucky Legislative Research Commission, "13 KAR 2:020 Guidelines for Admission to the State-Supported Postsecondary Education Institutions in Kentucky," http://www.lrc.state.ky.us/kar/013/002/020.htm
11. See http://www.lrc.ky.gov/record/09RS/SB1.htm for full text and legislative history of Senate Bill One.
12. Kentucky Developmental Education Task Force, "Securing Kentucky's Future: A Plan for Improving College Readiness and Success," February 2007, http://cpe.ky.gov/NR/rdonlyres/CBAA5350-E515-42E2-8D8B-B5E61286135C/0/DevEdTaskForce_FullReport_FINALFORWEB.pdf
13. Kentucky's College and University Presidents. "The Commonwealth Commitment," September 1, 2010, http://cpe.ky.gov/NR/rdonlyres/8B5B858B-37C1-416E-ABED-63CFC040F817/0/proclamationcampus.pdfCommonwealth Commitment
14. Steven L. Beshear, "Proclamation by Steven L. Beshear," September 1, 2010, http://cpe.ky.gov/NR/rdonlyres/0A525B83-84A9-449B-A91D-B097BF7EBA06/0/2010PROC212683.pdf
15. See http://cpe.ky.gov/news/mediaroom/releases/nr_090110.htm
16. Kentucky Department of Education "News Release No. 14-076," August 20, 2014, http://education.ky.gov/comm/news/Documents/R%2014-076%20 2014%20grads%20ACT2.pdf

9 Rethinking Developmental Education Policy and Practice

1. Kathleen M. Shaw, "Remedial Education as Ideological Battleground: Emerging Remedial Education Policies in the Community College." *Educational Evaluation and Policy Analysis* 19, no. 3 (1997): 284–96.

2. P. Attewell, D. Lavin, T. Domina, and T. Levey, "New Evidence on College Remediation." *Journal of Higher Education* 77, no. 5 (2006): 886–924.; E. P. Bettinger and B. T. Long, "Addressing the Needs of Under-Prepared Students in Higher Education: Does College Remediation Work?" NBER Working Paper No. 11325 (Cambridge, MA: National Bureau of Economic Research [NBER], 2005).
3. J. S. Brubacher and W. Rudy, *Higher Education in Transition* (3rd ed.) (New York: Harper & Row).
4. B. T. Long, "The Remediation Debate: Are We Serving the Needs of Underprepared College Students?" *National Crosstalk* 13, no. 4 (2005), http:www.highereducation.org/crosstalk/ct0405/voices0405-long.shtml.
5. Kentucky Department of Education "News Release No. 14–076," August 20, 2014, http://education.ky.gov/comm/news/Documents/R%2014-076%20 2014%20grads%20ACT2.pdf
6. Davis Jenkins and Sung-Woo Cho, "Get with the Program: Accelerating Community College Students' Entry into and Completion of Programs of Study." CCRC Working Paper No. 32, 2012.
7. Complete College America, *Remediation: Higher Education's Bridge to Nowhere* (Washington, DC: Author, 2012).
8. Speech by President Obama, University of Texas, Austin, 2010.

Bibliography

"13 KAR 2:020 Guidelines for Admission to the State-Supported Postsecondary Education Institutions in Kentucky." Kentucky Legislative Research Commission. Accessed April 23, 2014. http://www.lrc.state.ky.us/kar/013/002/020.htm

"2010 Annual Report: Degrees of Progress." Oklahoma State System of Higher Education. http://www.okhighered.org/studies-reports/annual-report2010.pdf

"2013 Legislative Report on the Postsecondary Progress and Success of High School Graduates." Colorado Department of Higher Education. April 2013. http://highered.colorado.gov/Publications/Reports/Legislative/PostSecondary/2013_Postsecondary_Progress_rel20130416_rev.pdf

"2014 Legislative Report on the Postsecondary Progress and Success of High School Graduates." Colorado Department of Higher Education. May 2014. http://highered.colorado.gov/Publications/Reports/Legislative/PostSecondary/2014_Postsecondary_Progress_rel20140505.pdf

"2014 Legislative Report on the Skills for Jobs Act." Colorado Department of Higher Education. January 2014. http://highered.colorado.gov/Publications/Reports/Legislative/Workforce/2014_SkillsforJob.pdf

"Academic Affairs Procedures Handbook." Oklahoma State Regents for Higher Education, 2014. http://www.okhighered.org/state-system/policy-procedures/2014/AA%20Procedures%20Handbook%20February%202014.pdf

"ACE College Preparatory Curriculum Opt Out List, 2011–2012)." Oklahoma State Department of Education. http://www.ok.gov/sde/sites/ok.gov.sde/files/documents/files/OptOutByDIST_0.pdf

Adelman, Clifford. "Answers in the Tool Box: Academic Intensity, Attendance Patterns, and Bachelor's Degree Attainment." Washington, DC: US Department of Education, 1999.

Adelman, Clifford. "The Toolbox Revisited: Paths to Degree Completion from High School through College." Washington, DC: US Department of Education, 2006.

Alfonso, Mariana. "The Impact of Community College Attendance on Baccalaureate Attainment." *Research in Higher Education* 47, no. 8 (2006): 873–903.

Alliance for Excellent Education. *Paying Double: Inadequate High Schools and Community College Remediation*. Washington, DC: Author, 2008.

"American Community Survey (ACS)." United States Census Bureau. 2012. http://factfinder2.census.gov/faces/tableservices/jsf/pages/productview.xhtml?pid=ACS_12_5YR_S1501

"American Community Survey." United States Census Bureau, 2008. http://www.census.gov/acs/www/data_documentation/2008_release/

"Annual Accountability Report: Fiscal Year 2008–2009." South Carolina Commission on Higher Education. September 2009. http://www.statelibrary.sc.gov/scedocs/H5373/001569.pdf

"Annual Student Assessment Report." Oklahoma State Regents for Higher Education. June 23, 2011. http://www.okhighered.org/studies-reports/assessment/2011-student-assess.pdf

"Annual Student Remediation Report." Oklahoma State Regents for Higher Education. February 2009. http://www.okhighered.org/studies-reports/remediation/remediation-report-2-09.pdf

Arendale, David R. "A Glossary of Developmental Education and Learning Assistance Terms." *Journal of College Reading and Learning* 38, no. 1 (2007): 10–34.

Arendale, David R. "Special Issue: Access at the Crossroads—Learning Assistance in Higher Education." *ASHE Higher Education Report* 35, no. 6 (2010): 1–145.

Astin, Alexander W. "Rethinking Academic Excellence." *Liberal Education* 85, no. 2 (1999): 8–18.

Attewell, Paul, David Lavin, Thurston Domina, and Tania Levey. "New Evidence on College Remediation." *Journal of Higher Education* 77, no. 5 (2006): 886–924.

"Average Undergraduate Tuition and Fees and Room and Board Rates Charged for Full-Time Students in Degree-Granting Postsecondary Institutions, by Control and Level of Institution and State or Jurisdiction: 2011–12 and 2012–13 (NCES Digest Table 330.20)." United States Department of Education, Institute of Education Science, National Center for Education Statistics, Digest of Education Statistics, 2013. Accessed April 23, 2014. http://nces.ed.gov/programs/digest/d13/tables/dt13_330.20.asp

Bailey, Thomas. "Challenge and Opportunity: Rethinking the Role and Function of Developmental Education in Community College." *New Directions for Community Colleges* 2009, no. 145 (2009): 11–30.

Bailey, Thomas, Dong Wook Jeong, and Sung-Woo Cho, "Referral, Enrollment, and Completion in Developmental Education Sequences in Community Colleges." *Economics of Education Review* 29, no. 2 (2010): 255–70.

Bernstein, Alison R. and J. S. Eaton. "The Transfer Function: Building Curricular Roadways across and Among Higher Education Institutions." In M. J. Justiz, R. Wilson, and L. G. Bjork (eds.), *Minorities in Higher Education*. Phoenix: American Council on Education, 215–60.

Beshear, Steven L. "Proclamation by Steven L. Beshear." Accessed January 4, 2012. http://cpe.ky.gov/NR/rdonlyres/0A525B83-84A9-449B-A91D-B097BF7EBA06/0/2010PROC212683.pdf

Bettinger, Eric. P. and Bridget Terry Long. "Addressing the Needs of Under-Prepared Students in Higher Education: Does College Remediation Work?" NBER Working Paper No. 11325. Cambridge, MA: National Bureau of Economic Research, 2005.

Bettinger Eric P. and Bridget Terry Long. "Remediation at the Community College: Student Participation and Outcomes." *New Directions for Community Colleges*, 2005, no. 129 (2005): 17–26.

Blatt, David. "New Ok Policy Issue Brief Finds State Question 744 to Be the Wrong Solution' for Oklahoma." *Oklahoma Policy Institute*, 2010. http://okpolicy.org/new-ok-policy-issue-brief-finds-state-question-744-to-be-the-wrong-solution-for-oklahoma

Boroch, Deborah, Jim Fillpot, Laura Hope, Robert Johnstone, Pamela Mery, Andreea Serban, Bruce Smith, and Robert S. Gabriner. "Basic Skills as a Foundation for Student Success in California Community Colleges." Research and Planning Group for California Community Colleges (RP Group), 2007.

Boylan, Hunter. R. and William G. White, Jr. "Educating All the Nation's People: The Historical Roots of Developmental Education, Part 1." *Research in Developmental Education* 4, no. 4 (1987): 1–4.

Boyer, Ernest L. *College: The Undergraduate Experience in America*. New York: Harper & Row, 1987.

"Brain Gain 2010: Building Oklahoma through Intellectual Power." Oklahoma State Regents for Higher Education. January 1999. http://www.okhighered.org/studies-reports/brain-gain/braingainreport.pdf

Breneman, David W. and William N. Haarlow. "Remediation in Higher Education. A Symposium Featuring 'Remedial Education: Costs and Consequences.'" *Fordham Report* 2, no. 9 (1998): n. 9.

"Briefs Population Distribution and Change: 2001–2010. 2010 Census Briefs." United States Census Bureau. http://www.census.gov/prod/cen2010/briefs/c2010br-01.pdf

Brier, E. "Bridging the Academic Preparation Gap: An Historical View." *Journal of Developmental Education*, 8, no. 1 (1984): 1–5.

Brubacher, John Seiler and Willis Rudy. *Higher Education in Transition*, 3rd edition. New York: Harper & Row, 1976.

Bureau of Labor Statistics. "Local Area Unemployment Statistics," 2011. http://www.bls.gov/lau/

Bureau of Labor Statistics."Regional and State Unemployment (Annual) News Release." February 29, 2012. Accessed May 4, 2014. http://www.bls.gov/news.release/archives/srgune_02292012.htm

Callahan, M. and Donalda Chumney. "'Write Like College': How Remedial Writing Courses at a Community College and a Research University Position 'At-Risk' Students in the Field of Higher Education." *Teacher's College Record*, 11, no. 7 (2009): 1619–64.

Carnevale, Anthony P., Nicole Smith, and Jeff Strohl. "Recovery: Projections of Jobs and Education Requirements through 2020." Washington, DC: Center on Education and the Workforce, Georgetown University, 2013. https://georgetown.app.box.com/s/kg8r28e48gsaw8ypplxp

Casazza, Martha E. and Sharon L. Silverman. *Learning Assistance and Developmental Education*. San Francisco: Jossey-Bass, 1996.
Casazza, Martha E. "Who Are We and Where Did We Come from?" *Journal of Developmental Education* 23, no.1 (1999): 2–7.
Center for Student Success. *Basic Skills as a Foundation for Success in California Community Colleges*. USA Funds, 2007.
Clark, Burton R. "The 'Cooling-Out' Function in Higher Education." *American Journal of Sociology*, 65, no. 6 (1960): 569–76.
Clowes, D. A. "Remediation in American Higher Education." In *Higher Education: Handbook of Theory and Research*, Vol. 8, ed. J. Smart, 460–493. New York: Agathon Press, 1980.
Clowes, D. A. "More Than a Definitional Problem: Remedial, Compensatory, and Developmental Education." *Journal of Developmental and Remedial Education*, 4, no. 1 (1992): 8–10.
Cohen, Arthur M. *The Shaping of American Higher Education: Emergence and Growth of the Contemporary System*. San Francisco: Jossey-Bass, 1998.
Cohen, Arthur M. and Florence B. Brawer. *The American Community College*, 4th edition. San Francisco: Jossey-Bass, 2003.
"Colorado Competes: A Completion Agenda for Higher Education." Colorado Commission on Higher Education. October 2012. http://highered.colorado.gov/Publications/General/StrategicPlanning/MasterPlan2012/Master_Plan_Final.pdf
"Colorado High School Graduation Guidelines." Colorado State Board of Education. May 2013. http://www.cde.state.co.us/sites/default/files/adoptedgraduationguidelines2013.pdf
"Colorado's Postsecondary and Workforce Readiness (PWR) High School Diploma Endorsement Criteria." State of Colorado. April 2013. http://www.cde.state.co.us/sites/default/files/documents/secondaryinitiatives/downloads/pwrendorseddiplomacriteria.pdf
Complete College America. *Time Is the Enemy*. Washington, DC: Author, 2011.
Complete College America. *Remediation: Higher Education's Bridge to Nowhere*. Washington, DC: Author, 2012.
"Cost of Attendance." Oklahoma State University. http://www.osuokc.edu/future/costs.aspx
"Degree Dividend: Building Our Economy and Preserving Our Way of Life: Colorado Must Decide." Colorado Department of Higher Education. November 2010. http://highered.colorado.gov/Publications/General/StrategicPlanning/Meetings/Resources/strategicplan_final_nov0410.pdf
"Developmental Education Needs in the 2006 Entering Cohort." Kentucky Council on Postsecondary Education. Accessed April 23, 2014. http://cpe.ky.gov/NR/rdonlyres/B42243CB-D19A-4EC4-AD34-ECF2900D51B1/0/Dev_needs_2006_20090605.pdf
Dougherty, Kevin J. "Community Colleges and Baccalaureate Attainment." *Journal of Higher Education*, 63, no. 2 (1992): 188–214.

Dowd, Alicia C. and Laura M. Ventimiglia. "A Cost Estimate of Standards-Based Remediation in a Community College Developmental Education Program." Unpublished manuscript, 2008.
"Educational and General Budgets, Summary and Analysis, Fiscal Year 2010." Oklahoma State Regents for Higher Education. http://www.okhighered.org/studies-reports/fy10-eg-summary-analysis.pdf
"Educational Attainment, 2008–2012 American Community Survey." United States Census Bureau. Accessed April 3, 2014. http://factfinder2.census.gov/faces/tableservices/jsf/pages/productview.xhtml?pid=ACS_12_5YR_S1501
"Fall 2005 through Spring 2011, Graduation Rates Component." National Center for Education Statistics, Integrated Postsecondary Education Data (IPEDS) Center. United States Department of Education, Institute of Education Science, Accessed April 23, 2014. http://nces.ed.gov/ipeds/datacenter/Default.aspx
"Fall 2008 through Spring 2011, Graduation Rates Component." Institute of Education Science. National Center for Education Statistics, Integrated Postsecondary Education Data (IPEDS). Accessed April 23, 2014. http://nces.ed.gov/ipeds/datacenter/Default.aspx
"Final Report and Recommendations." Citizens Commission on the Future of Oklahoma Higher Education. http://www.okhighered.org/studies-reports/citizens-comm/planningcommission.pdf
"First-Time Freshman Enrollments at Public and Private Institutions 2008–09 to 2012–2013." Oklahoma State Regents for Higher Education. http://www.okhighered.org/oeis/enrollment/FTFreshmen/Table_8_2012-13_FTFreshmen.html
"First-Time Freshman Freshmen Enrollments in Developmental Education Courses 2003–04 to 2012–2013." Oklahoma State Regents for Higher Education. http://www.okhighered.org/oeis/preparation/remediation%20report/1213FirstTimeFreshmenTable3.html
"Fiscal Survey of the States." National Governor's Association and the National Association of State Budget Officers. Accessed April 28, 2012. http://www.nga.org/files/live/sites/NGA/files/pdf/FSS1012.PDF
"FY 2010–11 Tuition Impact Analysis Report." Oklahoma State Regents of Higher Education. December 2010. https://www.okhighered.org/studies-reports/tuition-impact-analysis-10-11.pdf
"Graduation Rates of 2003 Entering Students by College Readiness." Kentucky Council on Postsecondary Education. Accessed April 23, 2014. http://cpe.ky.gov/info/retention/
Greene, Jay P. "The Cost of Remedial Education: How Much Michigan Pays When Students Fail To Learn Basic Skills. Estimates of the Annual Economic Cost to Businesses, Colleges, and Universities To Counteract Employees' and Students' Lack of Basic Reading, Writing, and Arithmetic Skills. A Mackinac Center Report." Mackinac Center for Public Policy, 2000.
"Higher Education Accountability." Article 13. Colorado Revised Statute. 1985. http://www.colorado.edu/pba/outcomes/ovview/hb1187.htm

Higher Education Study Commission. "Leveraging Higher Education for a Stronger South Carolina." Accessed April 23, 2014. http://www.che.sc.gov/CHE_Docs/InfoCntr/HESC_Files/che_2169_Leverage_Report_web.pdf

Ignash, Jan M. "Who Should Provide Postsecondary Remedial/Developmental Education?" *New Directions for Community Colleges*, 1997, no. 100 (1997): 5–20.

Immerwahr, John. "Public Attitudes on Higher Education: A Trend Analysis 1993 to 2003." National Center for Public Policy and Higher Education, 2004.

Jenkins, Paul Davis and Sung-Woo Cho. "Get with the Program: Accelerating Community College Students' Entry into and Completion of Programs of Study." CCRC Working Paper no. 32, (2012).

Jeynes, William. *American Educational History: School, Society and the Common Good*. Thousand Oaks, CA: Sage, 2007.

Kozeracki, Car A. "ERIC Review: Issues in Developmental Education." *Community College Review*, 29, no. 4 (2002): 83–100.

Lefly, Dianne L., Cheryll D. Lovell, and Jo M^cF. O'Brien. "Shining a Light on College Remediation in Colorado: The Predictive Utility of the ACT for Colorado and the Colorado Student Assessment Program (CSAP)." March 2011. http://www.cde.state.co.us/sites/default/files/documents/research/download/pdf/shiningalightonremediation.pdf

Long, Bridget Terry. "The Remediation Debate: Are We Serving the Needs of Underprepared College Students?" *National Crosstalk*, 13 (2005). http:www.highereducation.org/crosstalk/ct0405/voices0405-long.shtml

Mackum, Paul and Steven Wilson. "Population Distribution and Change: 2001–2010," United States Census Bureau. Accessed April 23, 2014. http://www.census.gov/prod/cen2010/briefs/c2010br-01.pdf

Mazzeo, Christopher. "Stakes for Students: Agenda-Setting and Remedial Education." *Review of Higher Education*, 26 (2002): 19–39.

McCormick, A., Paula R. Knepper, and Laura Horn. *A Descriptive Summary of 1992–93 Bachelor's Degree Recipients 1 Year Later: With an Essay on Time to Degree*. Darby, PA: Diane, 1996.

McGrath, Dennis. and Martin B. Spear. *The Academic Crisis of the Community College*. New York: State University of New York Press, 1991.

McKean, Kathleen. "Educational Reform in Oklahoma: A Review of Major Legislation and Educational Performance since 1980," Oklahoma Policy Institute. 2013. http://okpolicy.org/wp-content/uploads/2013/03/EdReform_OTAC_fullbrief.pdf

Melguizo, Tatiana, Linda Serra Hagedorn, and Scott Cypers. "Remedial/Developmental Education and the Cost of Community College Transfer: A Los Angeles County Sample." *Review of Higher Education* 31, no. 4 (2008): 401–31.

Merisotis, Jamie P. and Ronald A. Phipps. "Remedial Education in Colleges and Universities: What's Really Going On?" *Review of Higher Education*, 24, no. 1 (2000): 67–85.

Mitchell, Michael, Vincent Palacios, and Michael Leachman. "States are Still Funding Higher Education Below Pre-Recession Levels." Center on Budget and Policy Priorities. 2014. http://www.cbpp.org/files/5-1-14sfp.pdf

"Northwest Oklahoma Regional Ecosystem Report." Oklahoma Department of Commerce. http://okcommerce.gov/assets/files/data-and-research/workforce-data/ecosystem-briefings/Oklahoma_Regional_Ecosystem_Briefing-Northwest.pdf

"Number of Developmental Courses by Subject and Institution." Kentucky Council on Postsecondary Education. Accessed April 23, 2014. http://cpe.ky.gov/NR/rdonlyres/9E26D448-EF95-4910-B3CA-4774C2FF363C/0/Dev_Courses_by_Sector_20091230.pdf

"Occupational and Employment Statistics." United States Department of Labor Bureau of Labor Statistics. http://www.bls.gov/oes/2013/may/oes_co.htm#00-0000

"Oklahoma's Promise: 2010–2011 Year End Report." Oklahoma State Regents for Higher Education. http://www.okhighered.org/okpromise/okp-report-10-11.pdf

Ostrom, Elinor. "The Elements of an Action Situation." Unpublished manuscript. Bloomington, Indiana, 1983.

Ostrom, Elinor. "Institutional Rational Choice: An Assessment of the Institutional Analysis and Development Framework." In *Theories of the Policy Process*, ed. P. A. Sabatier, 35–71. Boulder, CO: Westview Press, 1999.

Ostrom, Elinor. "Zooming in and Linking Action Situations." In *Understanding Institutional Diversity*, 32–68. Princeton, NJ: Princeton University Press, 2005.

Padgette, Heather Clapp. "High School Reform in Colorado: A History of Efforts and Lessons for the Future." February 2009. http://www.coloradokids.org/file_download/25c98bb2-9dea-4cdc-a724-a2870c0f5e04

Parker, Tara L. "The Role of Minority-Serving Institutions in Redefining and Improving Developmental Education." *Southern Education Foundation* (2012).

Patton, Michael Quinn. *Qualitative Research and Evaluation Methods*, 3rd edition. Thousand Oaks, CA: Sage, 2002.

Perry, Mary, Peter Riley Bahr, Matthew Rosin, and Kathryn Morgan Woodward. *Course-Taking Patterns, Policies, and Practices in Developmental Education in the California Community Colleges*. Mountain View, CA: EdSource, 2010.

Phipps, Ronald. *College Remediation: What It Is, What It Costs, What's at Stake*. Washington, DC: Institute for Higher Education Policy, 1998.

"Policies and Procedures Manual." Oklahoma State Regents for Higher Education. http://www.okhighered.org/state-system/policy-procedures/part3.shtml

"Policy Statement on the Assessment of Students for Purposes of Instructional Improvement and State Accountability." Oklahoma State Regents for Higher Education. http://tulsagrad.ou.edu/assessmentT/osrhe.htm

Ravenel, Daniel, J. Boone Aiken, Claude Eichelberger, Jerry Govan, Doris Helms, Scott Ludlow, Marlowe, Layton McCurdy. and John Montgomery.

"Leveraging Higher Education for a Stronger South Carolina." South Carolina Commission on Higher Education, 2009. http://www.che.sc.gov/CHE_Docs/InfoCntr/HESC_Files/che_2169_Leverage_Report_web.pdf

"Regional and State Unemployment Annual News Release." United States Department of Labor, Bureau of Labor Statistics. Accessed February 29, 2012. http://www.bls.gov/news.release/archives/srgune_02292012.htm

"Remedial/Developmental Education Activities Report 2011–12." University of North Carolina General Administration. February 2013. https://www.northcarolina.edu/sites/default/files/documents/remedial-developmental_ed_2011-12_0.pdf

Richardson, Richard Jr. and Mario Martinez. *Policy and Performance in American Higher Education: An Examination of Cases across State Systems.* Baltimore, MD: Johns Hopkins University Press, 2009.

Roueche, John E. *Salvage, Redirection, or Custody? Remedial Education in the Community Junior College.* Washington, DC: American Association of Community and Junior Colleges, 1968.

Roueche, John E. and W. R. Kirk. *Catching Up: Remedial Education.* San Francisco: Jossey-Bass, 1973.

Rudolph, Frederick. *The American College and University: A History.* Athens, GA: The University of Georgia Press, 1990.

Russell, Alene. *Enhancing College Student Success through Developmental Education.* Washington, DC: American Association of State Colleges and Universities, 2008.

"SB1 An Act Relating to Student Assessment." Kentucky Legislative Research Commission. Accessed May 4, 2014. http://www.lrc.ky.gov/record/09rs/SB1.htm

Schneider, Anne and Helen Ingram. "Social Construction of Target Populations: Implications for Politics and Policy." *American Political Science Review* 87, no. 2 (1993): 334–47.

Schramm, Wilbur. *Notes on Case Studies of Instructional Media Project.* Washington, DC: Information Center on Instructional Technology, 1971.

Schwartz, Wendy and Paul Davis Jenkins. *Promising Practices for Community College Developmental Education: A Discussion Resource for the Connecticut Community College System.* New York: Community College Research Center, Teachers College, Columbia University, 2007.

"Securing Kentucky's Future: A Plan for Improving College Readiness and Success." Kentucky Developmental Education Task Force. Accessed April 23, 2014. http://cpe.ky.gov/NR/rdonlyres/CBAA5350-E515-42E2-8D8B-B5E61286135C/0/DevEdTaskForce_FullReport_FINALFORWEB.pdf

"Senate Bill 08:018." Colorado State Legislature, 2008. http://www.leg.state.co.us/clics/clics2008a/csl.nsf/billcontainers/DC4745338CA663BB8725737F004D4557/$FILE/018_enr.pdf

Shaw, Kathleen M. "Remedial Education as Ideological Battleground: Emerging Remedial Education Policies in the Community College." *Educational Evaluation and Policy Analysis,* 19, no. 3 (1997): 284–96.

BIBLIOGRAPHY   191

Smith, Matthew. "Choosing Who Delivers: The Impact of Placing Limits on the Delivery of Remedial Education at Four-Year Institutions." Accessed July 2, 2012. http://gettingpastgo.org/wp-content/uploads/2012/06/GPG_Choosing-Who-Delivers.pdf
Soliday, Mary. *The Politics of Remediation: Institutional and Student Needs in Higher Education*. Pittsburgh, PA: University of Pittsburgh Press, 2002.
"South Carolina Code of Laws." 2013. http://www.scstatehouse.gov/code/t59c104.php
"South Carolina Legislature." 1995–96. http://www.scstatehouse.gov/query.php?search=DOC&searchtext=remedial%20education&category=LEGISLATION&session=111&conid=7483953&result_pos=0&keyval=1110019&numrows=10
"State and County QuickFacts: Colorado." United States Census Bureau. Accessed May 30, 2014. http://quickfacts.census.gov/qfd/states/08000.html
"State and County QuickFacts: Kentucky." United States Census Bureau. Accessed April 23, 2014. http://quickfacts.census.gov/qfd/states/21000.html
"State and County QuickFacts: Oklahoma." United States Census Bureau. Accessed June 3, 2014. http://quickfacts.census.gov/qfd/states/40000.html
"State and Local Support for Higher Education Operating Expenses Per Capita." National Center for Higher Education Management Systems. Accessed April 3, 2014. http://www.higheredinfo.org/dbrowser/index.php?submeasure=81&year=2010&level=nation&mode=data&state=0
"State Population—Rank, Percent Change, and Population Density: 1980 to 2010." United States Census Bureau. Statistical Abstract of the United States: 2012. Accessed April 23, 2014. https://www.census.gov/compendia/statab/2012/tables/12s0014.pdf
"Statewide Remedial Education Policy." Colorado Department of Higher Education. November 2004. http://highered.colorado.gov/Publications/Policies/Archive/i-parte11-04.pdf
Strong American Schools. *Diploma to Nowhere*. Washington, DC: Author, 2008.
"Students Entering College with Developmental Needs." Kentucky Council of Postsecondary Education. Accessed April 23, 2014. http://cpe.ky.gov/NR/rdonlyres/70AD5017-7CE5-4CFB-AAA3-0DD82CECB32B/0/Graph_student_entering_dev_need_20090401.pdf
"Ten-Year Comparison of Annual Unduplicated Headcount Enrollment 2003–04 to 2012–13." Oklahoma State Regents for Higher Education. http://www.okhighered.org/oeis/enrollment/Trends/2012-13TenYearComparison.html
"The Funding Crisis in Colorado's Higher Education System." *Independence Institute*. December 2010. http://tax.i2i.org/files/2010/12/IB_2010_D_a.pdf
The Corridor of Shame: The Neglect of South Carolina's Rural Schools. Dir. Bud Ferillo. Ferillo & Associates, 2006. DVD.
"Title 23, Article 1: Colorado Commission of Higher Education." Colorado Revised Statute. 2013. http://www.lexisnexis.com/hottopics/colorado/?source=COLO;CODE&tocpath=1W80K9IS5WNSSO2EK,2RM0WSI4QCHMEHP0G,389XJOAWQET4NK2FJ;1KFCTJK08UXKL4J21,2JKGCK59SGWZ9EJWC,3RQ3QG033EOW0EGDO;18H9HOBPHSJS91BT6,2XHLAOOUSKEYSQ2T8,3MQVJCG04NRA3S3YJ&shortheader=no

"Tuition and Fees." Northeastern State University Admission and Recruitment. http://offices.nsuok.edu/admissions/TuitionFees.aspx.
"Tuition and Fees." Oklahoma City Community College. http://www.occc.edu/bursar/tuition-fees.html.
Urban, Wayne J. and Jennings L. Wagoner, Jr. *American Education: A History*, 4th edition. New York: Routledge, 2009.
United States Census Bureau. 2010. http://www.census.gov/2010census/data/.
United States Department of Education. "Remedial Education at Degree-Granting Postsecondary Institutions in Fall 2000, NCES 2004–010." Washington, DC: National Center for Education Statistics, 2003.
Vandal, Bruce. "Getting Past Go: Rebuilding the Remedial Education Bridge to College Success." Education Commission of the States, 2010.
Yin, Robert K. *Case Study Research: Design and Methods*, 4th edition. Thousand Oaks, CA: Sage Publications, 2009.
Zachry, Elizabeth M. and Emily Schneider. "Building Foundations for Student Readiness: A Review of Rigorous Research and Promising Trends in Development Education." NCPR Working Paper. Presented at the NCPR Developmental Education Conference: "What Policies and Practices Work for Students?," 2010.

Index

academic support, 38, 56–9, 63–4, 78–81, 124–6, 136, 146, 159–61, 163
accountability, 35–7, 47, 53, 60–2, 81–2, 89–91, 94–5, 97, 113, 115–19, 150
  measures, 134, 138–9, 146
  as policy lever, 139
  systems, 41–2, 71–2
Achieving the Dream, 115, 141, 157
ACT, 47, 72, 76–7, 83–5, 90, 93–6, 120, 136–9, 143, 145, 148, 151, 159
admissions
  conditional, 21–3
  guidelines, 136, 154
  index, 105, 110
  standards, 117, 146
African American, 12, 23, 41, 43, 50–1, 65, 87–8, 112, 127, 133–4, 146
alignment of K-12 and higher education. *See* coordination
American Association of State Colleges and Universities (AASCU), 8–9
Asian American and Pacific Islander, 41, 43–4, 65, 87–8, 112, 133, 135
assessment, 34–7, 52, 63, 67, 69, 71–3, 76, 78, 90, 93, 95, 96, 119, 120, 136–9, 143, 145–6, 151, 155, 158–9

Baltimore City Community College, 3
blended college-level courses. *See* instructional delivery
Brown University, 20

California State University, 2
Citizens' Commission (OK), 66
City University of New York (CUNY), 2, 8
collaboration, 60, 65, 80, 84, 94, 96–7, 136, 141–3, 158–9, 162
college access, 3–5, 19–26, 28, 30, 33, 39, 65, 67–8, 85, 90, 91, 97, 105, 108, 112, 118, 119, 124, 130, 137, 153–6, 159, 163
College of New Jersey, 17
college readiness. *See also* preparation (academic), 4, 33, 37, 52, 65, 76, 90, 91, 98, 134–40, 142, 143, 147–8, 151, 159
Colorado, 37, 38, 87, 88, 110, 112, 157, 158, 164
  Achievement Plan for Kids (CAP4K), 90, 91, 97, 108, 164
  Commission of Higher Education, 89, 91, 93
  Department of Higher Education, 89, 91, 96, 109
  General Assembly, 89
  State Assessment Program (CSAP), 90, 94
  Statewide Remedial Education Policy, 92, 93, 108
Columbia University, 21, 28
Common Core, 91
community college, 3, 6–13, 19, 25, 28–9, 33–4, 39–41, 55, 64, 68, 71, 74–5, 78–80, 85, 86, 103, 112–15, 119–22, 124, 131, 133, 134, 146, 147, 151, 154, 157, 159
Complete College America, 3, 67, 160

coordination of K-12 and higher
  education, 96, 109, 155–6, 162
Connecticut, 2
Cornell University, 26

data collection and utilization, 34–8,
  60–2, 109, 117, 138, 150–2, 157
developmental education
  cost of, 5–8
  definition of, 1, 2, 95
  effectiveness of, 10–13
  funding of, 2, 5, 8, 35, 37, 51, 97,
    101–3, 108, 109, 120, 128, 144,
    154, 156, 160–2
  mainstream, 154, 156, 157
  modularization of, 124, 146, 147
  responsibility for, 99, 101

economic development, 19, 47, 62, 135,
  151, 163
educational attainment, 10, 13, 35, 44,
  50, 63, 88, 151
enriched courses. *See* instructional
  delivery

fiscal strategies, 34, 36, 37, 59, 101,
  104, 128, 139, 144
Florida, 2

Getting Past Go, 35, 158

Harvard University, 17, 20, 21, 22, 25,
  27
Historically Black College and
  University (HBCU), 24, 122, 131,
  149

institutional mission, 74, 98, 109, 112,
  114, 131, 155, 156,
instructional delivery, 37, 56–8, 74, 98,
  120–6, 137, 146, 156, 159–60

K-12 education, 22, 45, 46, 60, 62, 67,
  68, 84, 85, 87, 90, 92, 94, 96, 102,
  109, 116, 133, 141, 142, 155, 161

Knowledge in the Public Interest, 35
Kentucky, 3, 38, 123–52, 155–64
  Community and Technical College
    system (KCTCS) 134–36, 140–2,
    144–7, 162
  Council for Postsecondary
    Education (KCPE), 134, 135,
    137–43, 162
  Department of Education (KDE),
    137, 138, 140–3, 147, 148, 159, 162
  General Assembly, 136
  Senate Bill One, 137–47, 150, 151,
    159, 162–4
King's College, 17

Latina/o, 41, 43, 65, 87, 88, 106, 112,
  133, 152, 162
leadership, 44, 96, 109, 139, 140, 162
learning communities, 99, 125, 127,
  150
Lexington Community College, 134
Louisiana, 2

Massachusetts, 21
Minority-serving institution, 106,
  120, 122
Morrill Act, 19, 20, 22–4

Native American, 65, 87, 88
North Carolina, 2, 37, 38, 111–31, 154,
  157, 159, 160
  Community College System
    (NCCCS), 111, 112, 113, 115
  General Assembly, 111–15, 118
  Performance Measures Committee,
    115
Northeastern State University, 70
Northern Oklahoma College, 80

Ohio, 2, 11, 24
The Ohio State University, 24
Oklahoma, 37, 38, 65–86, 158, 161
  City Community College, 71
  State Regents for Higher Education
    (OSRHE), 67, 71, 81, 82

Oklahoma State University, 71, 80

P-20, 91, 97
placement (of students in developmental education), 11, 13, 14, 29, 34–7, 52, 57, 63, 72, 75, 76, 79, 82, 93, 95, 96, 99, 109, 114, 119, 120, 136–8, 143, 145, 151, 154–5, 158–9
PLAN, 136, 139, 143
preparation (academic). *See also* college readiness, 7, 9, 11, 12, 20–2, 25–8, 31, 48, 49, 65, 67, 68, 73, 75–7, 49, 80, 81, 83–7, 90, 97, 98, 107, 116, 123, 127, 144, 154, 162, 199
Pima Community College, 3
President Obama, 3, 5, 8, 163
Princeton University, 21, 28

race, 3, 30, 41, 43, 64, 66, 88, 127, 134, 135, 152, 155, 158, 162, 163
recession, 88, 94, 101, 111, 133, 144
remedial education (definition of). *See* developmental education
Rose State College, 80

SAT, 47, 55, 93, 95, 120, 121
social support, 34, 36, 38, 104, 107, 109, 125, 126, 128, 131, 149, 160
South Carolina, 3, 38, 39, 41–64, 136, 154, 157, 159, 160
  Education and Economic Development Act, 47, 60
  Commission on Higher Education (SCTCS), 41, 42, 46, 51, 52, 53, 60, 61

General Assembly, 45–7, 53
Technical College System (SCTCS), 41, 42, 43, 49, 61, 62, 63
Stanford University, 25
state priorities, 13, 14, 34, 35, 44, 66, 90, 112, 163
summer bridge programs, 24, 38, 99, 103, 127, 129, 130, 146, 149, 151, 159, 160
supplemental instruction, 38, 57, 58, 63, 99, 125, 150, 156

transfer, 7, 9, 11, 13, 28, 54, 55, 78, 80, 113, 121

underpreparation. *See* preparation (academic)
University of Buffalo, 24
University of Central Oklahoma, 80
University of Illinois, 25
University of Kentucky, 134
University of Massachusetts Boston, 35
University of Michigan, 17, 25, 26
University of North Carolina, 111–14, 116–19, 121, 128, 130
  general administration, 113, 116
University of South Carolina, 41, 47
University of Wisconsin, 22
unemployment, 42, 65, 87, 133

Vassar College, 22

workforce development, 3, 19, 23, 24, 44, 66, 91, 112, 133, 164

Yale University, 21, 28

GPSR Compliance
The European Union's (EU) General Product Safety Regulation (GPSR) is a set of rules that requires consumer products to be safe and our obligations to ensure this.

If you have any concerns about our products, you can contact us on

ProductSafety@springernature.com

In case Publisher is established outside the EU, the EU authorized representative is:

Springer Nature Customer Service Center GmbH
Europaplatz 3
69115 Heidelberg, Germany

www.ingramcontent.com/pod-product-compliance
Lightning Source LLC
LaVergne TN
LVHW051912060526
838200LV00004B/104